Vulnerability Management

Vulnerability Management

Second Edition

Park Foreman

CRC Press
Taylor & Francis Group
Boca Raton London New York

CRC Press is an imprint of the
Taylor & Francis Group, an **informa** business
AN AUERBACH BOOK

CRC Press
Taylor & Francis Group
6000 Broken Sound Parkway NW, Suite 300
Boca Raton, FL 33487-2742

International Standard Book Number-13: 978-0-367-23514-7 (Hardback)

Visit the Taylor & Francis Web site at
http://www.taylorandfrancis.com

and the CRC Press Web site at
http://www.crcpress.com

To my wife, Katharina, for her support,
frankness, perspective, and dedication

Contents

Preface

Vulnerability management (VM) has been around for millennia. Cities, tribes, nations, and corporations have all employed its principles. The operational and engineering successes of any organization depend on the ability to identify and remediate a vulnerability that a would-be attacker might seek to exploit. What were once small communities became castles. Cities had fortifications and advanced warning systems. All such measures were the result of a group recognizing their vulnerabilities and addressing them in different ways. Today, we identify vulnerabilities in our software systems, infrastructure, and enterprise strategies. Those vulnerabilities are addressed through various and often creative means.

This book is a guide for the security practitioner, security or network engineer, security officer, or CIO seeking understanding of vulnerability management and its role in the organization. Significant areas of vulnerability management are covered to serve various audiences. Chapters on technology can provide an executive with a high-level perspective of what is involved, provided that the executive does not attempt to go too far into the detail. Other chapters on process and strategy, although serving the executive well, will provide an engineer or security manager with perspective on the role of VM technology and processes in the success of the enterprise.

I recommend that any reader seriously interested in the topic of vulnerability management read completely the chapters most relevant to their area of interest and all other chapters at least cursorily. It is insufficient to participate in any process without a longer view of all its facets. So often, employees worry that their role in a process seems meaningless. Hopefully, the recommended approach to this book will, in some measure, assuage these concerns.

Acknowledgments

To dedicated security professionals everywhere to whom success means keeping the organization out of trouble. Hopefully, this book augments your views on risk or helps to grow the strength of security professionals.

About the Author

Park Foreman is a Security and Compliance Architect at IBM Cloud Brokerage Services where he designs security controls supporting customers in their migration journey to cloud services. He is a recognized expert in vulnerability management, incident management, and cyber security strategy. Park holds a Master of Science degree in information security and assurance and CISSP-ISSAP certification among others. Originally starting his information security experience in college working on operating system kernel security design, he went on to work in application security at Bell Labs and network security in the banking and telecommunications industries.

In addition to the first and second editions of this book, Park has also published articles in the ISSA Journal and presented at security conferences. At IBM, Park continues to work across business units on developing new technologies and methods to secure cloud services and applications.

Chapter 1

Introduction

Vulnerability management (VM) is the cyclical practice of identifying, classifying, remediating, and mitigating vulnerabilities. This is a broad definition that has implications for corporate or government entities, which will be discussed in this book. It is not a new discipline, nor is it a new technology. This vital function has been a normal part of hardening defenses and identifying weaknesses to systems, processes, and strategies in the military and in the private sector. With growing complexity in organizations, it has become necessary to draw out this function as a unique practice complete with supporting tools. This has resulted in an important refinement of the definition of VM as a segment of risk management.

1.1 The Role of Risk Management

Risk management seeks to identify the conditions or events under which a loss may occur and then find the means to address that risk. Addressing risk can take the following forms:

Accept the risk; that is, do nothing and let it happen. This is also known as retention.
Mitigate the risk; that is, prevent it from happening.
Reduce the risk; that is, reduce the consequences by actions such as ensuring against the event.

In VM, we look at risks resulting from flaws in systems, processes, and strategies. Figure 1.1 shows the relationship of VM with a risk management program. The purpose is to discover and address risks that result from vulnerabilities under the control or influence of the organization. Other aspects of risk management

1

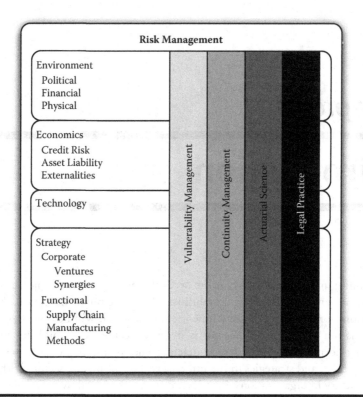

Figure 1.1   Role of vulnerability management in risk management framework.

related to event probability analysis and continuity management are not directly concerned with vulnerabilities.

VM typically focuses attention on technical software and system configuration vulnerabilities. There are also vulnerabilities related to corporate strategy, economics, and the environment whose detection cannot be automated. They require the attention of a risk manager. These vulnerabilities exist in areas such as business processes, strategies, and supply chains. Every action or plan that a business has could be exploited through design flaws or a lack of adaptability. It is the larger role of the risk manager to recognize and address these challenges. In this book, we will discuss primarily the former type of vulnerabilities; however, some attention will also be given to the latter.

1.2 Origins of VM

VM has been around for a long time yet few have paid attention to it until recently. The military has long understood and perfected VM through ritual and practice. Inspections of defenses from the organization and deployment strategy down to the individual soldier and weapons are the equivalent of audits. The recursive training, equipping, and rearrangement of defenses is a form of remediation or hardening. But these activities have not come without an understanding of the enemy.

A student of military history can easily recognize how one opponent vanquished another by exploiting a vulnerability or strategic error. These victors are often hailed as geniuses, rather than the losers being seen as incompetent. Consider, for example, the Battle of Cannae where Hannibal collapsed his center line to envelop the Romans so that he could attack from all sides, thereby defeating them. Hannibal is considered a genius for this now-classic tactic. However, one might also see this as a flawed strategy of Varro, one of the Roman consuls at the battle. Varro believed that the Roman army could drive through the center of Hannibal's front line and drive the entire enemy line to the river at their backs. What he did not consider was the essential discipline for maintaining a uniform front line, which was undeniably a vulnerability.

Yet, in the business world, we tend to view the failure to be prepared for risk as an example of incompetence. This is especially true when the corporation is generally perceived as being strong, wealthy, and able to dedicate the resources to addressing risk.

As an IT discipline, VM has been immature and its users naïve about its application: immature because strong, enterprise-ready technology is only now becoming available, and naïve because the need for a complete, integrated solution with well-defined processes has not been fully recognized. Although military discipline may not seem necessary in a corporate environment, the lack of discipline leads to the one key vulnerability that is not discovered or not remediated and that may eventually lead to catastrophic losses.

1.3 Introducing the Security Industry and Its Flaws

Not so surprisingly, corporations and governments alike have relied on new products to "bolt on" security to their networks. The security industry has focused on selling products and services that require upgrades and maintenance. If there is a security problem that seems to emerge, a vendor has developed a solution. When users started abusing network ports to reach into other host services in a remote network, the industry gave us firewalls. When viruses became a problem, the industry offered us antivirus software and services. When worms like Sasser were found, antivirus vendors put more antivirus functionality in the network. When in-house applications became more of a target, application firewalls were offered.

Unfortunately, very few of these solutions seem to address the central problem. Most security problems result from a failure to code, patch, configure, or design in a secure manner. This is the military equivalent to a lack of training of the troops, lack of oversight by commanders, and failure to provide adequate equipment. Just as technology vendors continue to provide us with productized solutions, you can hand the troops all the weapons that can be bought but these will not be the targets of your enemy. The product purchase scenario is a strategic failure.

It is not my intent to disparage the use of these and other security technologies. They are an important part of an overall security strategy. However, while all of these bad things were happening, few people were focused on identifying and fixing what was exploited, and none of these technologies can fully make up for a failure to use strong passwords or keep shrink-wrapped software patched.

The value of most security products in a network comes from their ability to temporarily mitigate risks for which you do not have a more permanent or reliable solution. The antivirus product is a good idea so long as you get updates quickly and those updates are accurate. When the latest virus comes out, the product should quickly be prepared to stop it until the vendor of the target software supplies a patch. Eventually, the virus will find its way into the organization and around some defenses. The important thing is to get a permanent fix in place before that happens.

1.4 Challenges from Government and Industry

The IT department faces many other challenges from the governments of the world. Varying degrees of legislation from one jurisdiction to another create a minefield of legal and operational challenges. Multinational companies are particularly challenged. In some countries, regulators and labor unions treat intrusion detection with suspicion on the grounds that it may be an invasion of privacy. In other countries, the collection of Internet surfing activity for a particular user is compulsory and must be supplied to the authorities upon request. Vague yet onerous regulations such as the Sarbanes–Oxley (SOX) Act in the United States have resulted in a multitude of security controls that offer little value but considerable expense. This makes active defense of a network in a globally managed package an even bigger challenge because security managers must now differentiate compliance activities from those that bring real security.

Add to all of this the industry standards for security controls and the associated certifications and audits. The alphabet grows constantly: SAS 70, SOX § 404, ISO 17799, ISO 27001, PCI, FIPS, HIPAA, GLB, IEEE P1074, EAL. Standards and certification are important, but they often distract us from our most central problems: vulnerable software, architecture, and strategy. There is no long-term substitute for well-written, tested, and properly configured software deployed thoughtfully with solid practices.

1.5 Sources of Vulnerabilities

Software companies are also a real challenge to software buyers everywhere. Their coding practices can stand a lot of improvement, as can their basic designs. Some want to sell more products, so they continue to introduce more functionality without securing what was built before. A new electronic communications protocol or new application using that protocol is developed. But they never secure the protocol from the beginning. The vendors also do a fairly poor job of notifying users and issuing patches. The problem is motivational because they see patching as a cost greater than the benefit since no one is paying for the additional development work. In some cases, a vendor is entrenched in the market and customers have few alternatives. The cost of changing software makers can be expensive for a company with thousands of units deployed and hundreds of trained support staff.

1.6 Example of Flawed VM

When we do perform the VM function, it is usually halfheartedly. One company attempted to deploy VM agents throughout the enterprise as an act of payment card industry (PCI) compliance. The auditors told them they should do it, and so they did it without regard for the benefit or the effect. As a result, the only tangible requirement was that the technology be deployed. No one considered what would happen after that. Obvious questions such as "on which hosts do we install the agents?" and "what vulnerabilities do we have to fix first?" were ignored. I refer to this as the check box security strategy. Someone to whom a company has delegated authority provides a checklist of what to fix, and then the company complies.

Another obvious problem with this security approach is that a tool that can help address the root cause of so many vulnerabilities would have no official owner. Instead, in my example, the agents and server were installed without anyone to maintain them. No matter how hard you try, maintenance does not happen by itself. Someone has to read the reports, repair or reinstall components or agents, and make sure the reporting server stays healthy. Someone also has to monitor the overall system to make sure that it achieves its objectives. This is the equivalent of deploying a division of troops without a leader. They would be badly coordinated and ineffective.

1.7 Why VM Is Important

For a corporation, resources are quite limited. It can only spend so much on a risk, so an early analysis of risks is certainly important. However, I would argue that there is little excuse for not performing the VM function. It seems difficult to justify spending limited funds on intrusion detection or security event management when VM has not been implemented. Although VM involves more complex processes and systems, the risk profile of a company can look quite different when there are fewer critical vulnerabilities to defend.

In this book, you will find far more than a description of the technology and a few tips on how to get it going. You will gain an in-depth understanding of how

VM works from both technology and process perspectives. Neither one is very useful without the other. Technology tools are facilitators of the process. Much time will be spent understanding this. Experience in the uniqueness of your company's environment will bring you to the realization that only those who are very serious about having a strong, secure infrastructure are needed. Anything else is a waste of money and time.

You will also gain an understanding of the strategic significance of vulnerabilities and their control. Beyond the concern for a single host or network device, vulnerabilities can exist at other levels that can only be addressed by adjustment to the technology strategy. It is risk management at an organization and industry level, and it transcends any technology.

Chapter 2

The Vulnerability Experience

2.1 Introduction

Vulnerability management (VM) is a subject that fits nicely into all of the other management disciplines found in frameworks such as the Information Technology Infrastructure Library (ITIL), and the international standards ISO 17799 and ISO 27001. These disciplines are generally created for the purpose of dealing with the persistent industrial stream of some phenomena that is a direct consequence of business activities. Taking the ITIL framework as an example, incident management, a set of processes supported by people and technology, addresses faults in IT infrastructure. Those faults are not part of the normal operation of the infrastructure and underlying services.

Similarly, VM pertains to managing the vulnerabilities resulting from the poor design, development, configuration, or quality control of an IT component. What is remarkable is that the IT industry seemed quite surprised by the need to manage these vulnerabilities. Since the beginning of software development, it has been obvious that flaws in programming, or bugs, occur when the programmer fails to fully consider how the program could be used; in other words, vulnerabilities result from a failure to fully consider the use cases of a product within the overall system, given possible inputs and outputs, and a failure to identify what would exceed acceptable operational parameters.

2.2 The Vulnerability Creation Process

For the uninitiated, the idea of vulnerability management in all its details is a lot to grasp. But if you remember Computer Science 101, there is input, output, and processing. Every program has this. An e-mail program accepts input—a message sent by someone. Then, the program processes it, breaking the message into parts that can be understood by a person. Finally, the program has outputs: it displays the e-mail message to the user, with all the related formatting.

This all seems quite simple, but we should consider how these programs are developed now:

1. Concept and proposal: A business or government operation has a required function.
2. Requirements gathering: The developer analyzes the requirements and clarifies them with the business.
3. Design: A design is developed against the requirements.
4. Code: Programmers write the code and test it.
5. Test: If we are a thorough development operation, the quality assurance team makes sure that the code meets the requirements.
6. Deployment: The business installs the software on production systems and announces it to the world. Or, the software is shrink-wrapped and shipped to stores everywhere.

If this sounds familiar, it should be; it's the systems development life cycle (SDLC). At each step along the way, there are problems that result in missing something that users ultimately regret. So, let's complete the story:

7. Identification: A hacker, researcher, or end user finds a flaw in the processing of inputs, outputs, or interaction with other system functions. This could also be considered hidden or new functionality.
8. Exploitation: A person then tries to see how many ways this flaw can be manipulated to exceed the original requirements of the software.
9. Compromise: An additional piece of software is developed and deployed to recreate these circumstances and automate the new functionality.

This, too, should sound familiar. It is the world we have lived in for many years. Three factors have made items 7 through 9 more commonplace and more problematic than ever: complexity, communication, and interoperability.

2.2.1 Complexity

The environment and systems upon which these programs operate are enormously complex. Layers upon layers of software components underlie any given application. Even the most fundamental computer software component is absurdly complex, with myriad modules to perform critical functions interacting with more complex and diverse hardware options. Consider, for example, the traditional "hello world" program that all computer science students learn when starting out. The task is simply to write a program that will output a text string. In a graphical environment, this type of program can become quite large. First, there is the interpreter that must run to load the program, read the instructions, and perform the tasks. Additionally, the program must interface with the environment through a library. This is a piece of code that takes the simple programming instructions and applies them to the operating environment. In this case, the library may be a general input/output (I/O) library to create a window on the screen and map the text into it. To support this library, the operating system has several additional functions that must be loaded to communicate with the drivers supporting the graphics card and display. This creates a very complex chain of connections that are all potential attack vectors in the security world.

To demonstrate how this complexity can quickly be exploited through another component in the system, let's create a hypothetical program. The job of this program is simple. It is supposed to accept input from a file and display it on the screen. When the user receives a file in e-mail, he saves the attachment to the local file system and runs the program we have created. Selecting the file as input, the program does exactly what it is supposed to do. This is where things go wrong and the finger-pointing begins.

The file contains a sequence of non-displayable bytes that cannot be processed by the general I/O library used by the program. It causes that library to jump to a memory location whose address is a remnant of the file. The remaining contents of that file are left in the memory space where the library was running. That part of the file is a malicious program that gains control of the computer but acts as though the library completed its task successfully.

In this example, the program that we wrote did what it was supposed to do. But the complexity of the underlying components was not accounted for in our code. The argument begins when you want to decide who should fix this problem. Should you have validated the input data for proper display before processing? Should the library author have done so? This argument, though interesting, is beyond the scope of this chapter. In some cases, however, you will have to think about this when evaluating in-house and vendor-supplied software.

2.2.2 Communication

Internet protocol (IP) is a fundamental protocol that enables our programs to operate over distances. It allows more complex software to work in modules processing information at various levels in a hierarchy. Those levels are often separated by network connections that are filled with IP-based messages.

But IP was originally designed for the U.S. Department of Defense to provide resilient communications in the event of a nuclear attack; the idea being that if one location in the network were destroyed, traffic could be routed around it to continue operation. This functionality was built with the idea that the military would have a closed communications system. Unfortunately for the military and the world, IP has come to be used in open networks where just about anyone can gain access. This is a clear case of the misapplication of a technology. It is being used far beyond its original use case.

The ability of one system to communicate with another and subsequently to manipulate the inputs and internal processes of a peer on a network removes the physical barriers to abuse. Remote access is a key element of enhancing productivity. But like everything we do to improve the work environment, this is a double-edged sword. The problem is further compounded by the fact that networks are complex and tools are put in place to make them simpler.

The domain name system (DNS) is a good example of this. At one point, it became too difficult to remember all those thousands and then millions of IP addresses for applications whose components are spread throughout the world. So, someone invented DNS to allow us the convenience of easy-to-remember names. This system was never designed to be secure, only efficient. It has since been widely abused by hackers. Even the underlying software of DNS servers is under constant attack. This trend is likely to continue unabated.

2.2.3 Interoperability

All manufacturers of hardware and software components today strive for this golden capability. If they don't, they have a smaller market. Imagine an operating system that does not use the common server message block (SMB) file sharing protocol, or a printer that only works with a particular word processor. This would be unacceptable. This problem was recognized early in the computer industry as technologies gained some level of ubiquity in corporate and government operations. Consider, for example, the extended binary coded decimal interchange code (EBCDIC) and the American Standard Code for Information Interchange (ASCII). Both of these data encoding schemes were created for the purpose of making the exchange of information among systems and programs consistent and the processing of such information repeatable with minimal variation.

I am not suggesting that these encoding methods are in any way inherently vulnerable. But it is the compatibility of all the components of a system that make it more vulnerable. A particular program that processes ASCII characters may have a flaw. If that same ASCII processing is used in several programs, then the impact of the vulnerability is all the worse. One part is used to exploit another part. A buffer overflow in one program can give someone access to the entire system. If a standard component used broadly in a computer system by a variety of programs turns out to have a vulnerability, then it is possible that all programs that use the component could be vulnerable.

A more concrete example of how this interoperability has led us to serious, widespread vulnerabilities is the Microsoft Windows Graphics Device Interface (GDI+) buffer overflow.[1] The GDI+ application program interface (API) provides programmers with a set of libraries for displaying and printing information.

In this case, the component that processes Joint Photographic Experts Group (JPEG) images fails to parse the inputs in a safe manner. When the JPEG image is formatted poorly, the program fails and allows that remaining portion of the image to stay in computer memory and possibly be executed as a program. This is obviously a problem.

But the problem is compounded by the fact that the GDI+ product is an API. This means that many programmers all over the world can use a version of the API to perform functions. The installers for these programs, in some cases, want to be sure they have the right version of the GDI+ API available. So, they install their own copy. Thus, some computer systems could end up with several vulnerable versions of the API in different parts of the target's file system. To address this, every vendor would have to identify and patch their products.

2.3 Creating Vulnerabilities: An Example

Now, let's walk through a scenario using all of the previously mentioned items to understand how bad things happen to well-intentioned programs. The e-mail program mentioned at the beginning of this section is a great example. Later, we will walk through all the steps of the SDLC and discover what can go wrong.

1. Concept and proposal: XYZ Company decides that the world would be a better place if they could send e-mails to each other using a special program that presents and manages the e-mails better than any other program on the market. It will use a specially adapted format that puts unique functionality inside the messages. *What could go wrong?* Complexity has been introduced into a system that is relatively simple. Similar to the GDI+ API example, more complexity creates more opportunities for faults. If the new functionality is so critical to the success of a product, the security of the unique parts of the system will have to be stressed from the outset of the project. At a minimum, the reliability and security of the key components should almost be a feature in the concept.

2. Requirements gathering: The detailed requirements for all the functionality are gathered from those who have created the concept. There is tremendous enthusiasm for all the great capabilities that will be included and how they will enhance the business model. This should lead to great things one day. *What could go wrong?* None of the requirements include security or reliability features. These capabilities should be part of any application requirements. Every idea that comes out of the requirements gathering process creates a certain amount of scope creep that can lead to fundamental design flaws. In addition to minimizing growth in cost and schedule, containing scope during the requirements phase can minimize the opportunity for the creation of vulnerabilities.

3. Design: Details of the application, including databases, file systems, and operating system compatibility, are designed on paper. *What could go wrong?* The design, like the requirements, considers only functionality. All of the focus is on getting the application working. Some work should be put into having the application create restrictive areas of dataflow prior to any processing that can validate inputs and outputs to ensure that they stay within the application's functional parameters. Points of data validation and authorization should be established for interprocess communications. One process should be able to verify that the data coming from another process are valid and that the source process is legitimate and operating with authorization. Some threat modeling should begin at this phase. By identifying the areas that are at high risk for exploitation, the team can focus efforts on making sure the most vulnerable components are especially hardened.

4. Code: After the design is complete, the programs are written. *What could go wrong?* This is the most famous part of systems development in the vulnerability world. The programmers fail to agree on best practices for coding to avoid problems like buffer overflows or other such vulnerabilities. Secure coding best practices should be used, such as bounds checking in dynamically sized data structures and input validation.

5. Test: Testing goes at a feverish pace. Bugs are found and quickly fixed. Testers keep verifying that all of those requirements that did not include security components are correctly implemented. *What could go wrong?* Testing of the application has the most time pressure. Managers want to see the product in production and have little tolerance for delay. Testers focus only on functionality and often skip regression tests. This is when developers break things for the sake of getting through this phase. Some kind of penetration testing of the product should be conducted with guidance from the previously mentioned threat model.

6. Deployment: Finally, the product is ready. It is packaged and shipped to unsuspecting customers worldwide. Documentation is included that explains how to install and use the program. *What could go wrong?* The documentation does not include any information about the most appropriate, secure configuration of the system upon which the software will run. It does not say that certain ports should not be open on the network interface to any IP address except the supporting server. Some plans should be made by the development team to respond to vulnerabilities that are discovered. At this point, a much larger group of penetration testers will begin working on the application.

7. Identification: An interested user of the application wonders what would happen if an e-mail is sent with an unusually designed message that matches the processing requirements for a particular module of the e-mail software. But, the user structures the message to be larger than that module's standard data structure calls for. The program crashes, leaving the operating system with fragments of the message in memory.

8. Exploitation: The user now wonders whether he could imbed a program in the previously mentioned message to stay in memory and run. It works. A small "hello world" program runs.
9. Compromise: The now-very-excited user develops a more improved version of the message that creates more messages using the program and sends copies of itself to others in the address book;—an address book that is made more accessible by the powerful functionality built into the e-mail software. The new product's first e-mail worm is born!

(Guidance: Remove the vulnerabilities that could be exploited early and often. Long term, this decreases the workload on IT and Security, and lowers the cost of detection and prevention tools to achieve a similar level of security.)

2.4 Rationale for a VM Program

So, why do we undertake a VM program? There are several good reasons, which are either technical or just make good business sense. Choose what best fits your situation.

2.4.1 Overexposed Network

In the context of IT security, businesses have two kinds of objectives: mission and compulsory. A mission objective is directly related to producing revenue or enhancing profits. Compulsory objectives are those that must be achieved as a matter of prudence or regulation. Insurance is an example of a compulsory objective. Companies purchase liability insurance to reduce their exposure to loss. Many organizations place a high priority on meeting mission objectives and not compulsory ones. Network security is another example of a compulsory business objective. In this scenario, network-based defenses are inadequate to stop a well-designed attack. Naturally, some companies may choose to perform a risk analysis and will subsequently determine how much to spend on network security. Sometimes the size and complexity of the network make cost-effective defenses impractical to meet the risk. In other cases, the company simply chooses to accept the risk.

If your company has strong network defenses, then perhaps there is a lot of focus on detecting and preventing an attack. However, blocking in the network or on the perimeter is not enough. It is unlikely that the defenses are completely reliable and foolproof and that they address all of the potential attacks from every vector. Any security professional knows that the insider threat is as great as the external one. Most defenses are not directed toward insider threats. At present, it is not financially practical to put intrusion protection, antivirus, content filtering, traffic analysis, and application behavior analysis on every single port on a network of 50,000 nodes. Even if one could achieve this in a financially sound way, additional, redundant layers of defense will be needed because some of those network-based defenses will have weaknesses that are exploited and may even be used against the organization. For example, there are several well-known methods for evading intrusion detection systems. Encryption is a simple method for obfuscating an attack. Applications that use encryption are very helpful in concealing attacks.

The only way to address these weaknesses is a basic defense-in-depth strategy that removes single points of failure. Most network security strategies rely on perimeter and/or bolt-on defenses, which, if they fail, will leave a vulnerable host wide open to exploitation. This is overexposure at its worst. There is a perception of security but no real security without adding additional layers, one of which must be a host hardened against attacks by taking away the vulnerability.

2.4.2 No Standard for Secure Systems Configuration

Large companies typically develop one or more standard configurations for systems connected to a network. This includes standards for desktop and server operating systems, network devices, and even printer configurations. These standards often have security practices built in. When these standards are absent, more vulnerabilities are likely to exist than when the standards do not exist. The mere fact that a standard exists suggests that some care and thought is being given to the state of a device.

However, even if there are standards, configurations can age. Once a standard is established, it is difficult to change and bring all hosts into compliance. Even if there is a patch management system in place, those configurations cannot be fully addressed by patches. In most cases, patch management systems will not find everything requiring remediation. It is no substitute for VM.

The negative side of standardization is the ubiquity of vulnerabilities. If a standard configuration is deployed globally and has a vulnerability, then the vulnerability is everywhere. If not detected and remediated quickly, it can lead to serious security problems.

2.4.3 Risk of Major Financial Loss

When the risk of a breach is high, concerns of management naturally turn toward the impact of realizing the risk; that is, with increasing regulation from government and an aggressive tort system, the potential for financial loss greatly increases. These losses can come from litigation and/or civil penalties. Imagine losing a client's confidential data due to failure to remediate a critical, published vulnerability. I can see the tort lawyers circling!

California Civil Code § 1798.84 specifies considerable penalties for companies doing business with California residents when those companies fail to notify the victims of a security breach within a certain period of time. The damage from such disclosure could be large but so could the civil penalties. The legislation is only one example of a growing trend toward punishing companies responsible for data breaches regardless of their physical location because they do business with local residents.

2.4.4 Loss of Revenue

A more direct loss, such as that of revenue or potential revenue, is of major concern in any business. When a client is lost, the business suffers not only the loss of revenue but also the damage to its reputation. It is ten times harder to recover from this than any other kind of loss. Customer confidence must be re-earned to the extent that it overcomes the bad taste of the past. And this applies to future customers as well. It is generally much more difficult and expensive to win new customers against the headwind of a highly publicized security incident.

Oddly, it is beginning to appear that consumers are easier to appease than corporate customers. For some reason, consumers tend to forget or ignore security breaches for a specific company more frequently than do business customers. However, consumers gradually become wearier of conducting transactions with any company that ultimately lead to more expensive government regulation. Businesses can do everyone a favor by being more diligent in managing vulnerabilities.

2.4.5 Lost Productivity

When systems are compromised, they often become unusable for a period of time. If these are critical systems, significant productivity is lost from employees who cannot perform their jobs. Less measurable than employees just sitting around are the cases where employees can continue working but take much longer to complete a task. This work-around environment can sometimes be difficult to start and equally difficult to stop once the affected systems are returned to service. Even if current records are available at the conclusion of an incident, the data must be resynchronized with the now-operational system.

It is also often the case that many time-consuming activities must take place before a system is returned to service. The system must be analyzed for the cause of the failure, rebuilt, patched, additional security considered, and closely monitored for a secondary attack. To add to this, IT employees who must clean up the mess are taken away from other activities that could be more directly focused on producing more income, reducing costs, and enhancing productivity in other areas. The latter point further extends into the opportunity cost of not meeting a market need in a timely manner. After all, there are no IT cleanup guys just sitting around waiting for something to happen. Existing resources must be redirected to put out fires.

2.5 VM Program Failure

Before we continue, it is important to clarify something that continually comes up when discussing VM with someone for the first time. VM is not penetration testing. It is only a component of pen-testing that is used to find the exploitable weaknesses that, in combination, will result in a penetration of the internal computer systems. For example, a vulnerability scanner could be used to discover a flaw in an e-mail server that allows the attacker to get a foothold from which he can then safely access another, more critical target inside the organization. The penetration is the act of exploiting a vulnerability to gain access to other systems and possibly related vulnerabilities to achieve a deeper level of unauthorized access.

VM is a discipline. It requires consistency, dedication, and constant reassessment. Although technology is available to make the process efficient, there is no escaping the fact that systems must be patched and configurations adjusted to meet complex and changing business needs. When a company starts a VM program and is ill-prepared, failure is imminent. It is not sufficient to simply purchase technology, turn it on, and expect the rest to tend to itself. Let's take a look at an example of the Acme Company.

2.5.1 Case Study #1: Getting the Organization Behind You

Acme has 15,000 workstations and 130 servers in eight offices worldwide. The management structure is not overly complex and involves at most three layers beginning with the CEO. Manufacturing facilities are in China, with a few key parts-fabrication facilities in North America. The company has modest growth, with mostly manufacturing and sales personnel being added. Engineering is a closely held group headquartered in North America.

IT operations are highly distributed and managed locally by IT managers who were hired by local office managers. Although the local office managers report to a global operations director, the local IT managers have no direct connection to the global IT operations. The global IT budget is modest but sufficient and usually excludes training as the staff is very capable of learning most technologies and processes themselves. Local IT budgets are set by local office managers with the recommendation of the local IT manager. Global IT has overall responsibility for network infrastructure including wide-area network (WAN) and local area network (LAN) configurations. PCs and servers in each local office are managed by the local IT group but are required to adhere to global standards. This structure puts global IT in the position of providing services for networks and security to the local offices but leaves local IT more responsive to the local business requirements, which consist mostly of sales and billing functions.

Last year, an IT employee who was angry that he received no bonus (although his peers did) decided to take revenge. He knew that most of the machines in the company were not patched. Since his computer was connected to the same network, he figured out that he could modify the Sasser worm payload to attack specific hosts. He targeted the workstations of employees who he did not like and who got bonuses.

Unfortunately for Acme, the worm kept going and left several systems disabled. In fact, the worm jumped to several critical servers. Later, forensic investigations revealed the source of the attack. The machines took weeks to patch and restore to service. The cost to the company in productivity and lost revenue was enormous. The employee was terminated.

Acme instituted a comprehensive network monitoring system. They also purchased and implemented a patch management system. An IT employee volunteered to manage the system in addition to his regular job as an e-mail administrator.

First, let's look at the organization chart for Acme in Figure 2.1. It may seem like an unusual structure, but it has served them well for years. With emerging technologies and greater connection to business partners through the Internet, roles such as technology strategy director and a separate IT operations director make sense. Security has recently become a concern, and a small organization is built to address it. Ward, the security and risk manager, used to manage risk in business ventures and is a technology enthusiast. He sees this as a lateral career move, and he has set up an intrusion protection system (IPS) at HQ and is knee-deep in the technology on a daily basis.

Harold, a long-trusted employee, was asked to head up a VM program to avoid any more problems such as those that happened before. He reports to Ward. Harold has thoroughly researched all of the available VM tools on the market, talked to the desktop and server administrators, and finally selected a tool. Devices were deployed in all eight locations to scan for vulnerabilities. Scanning started on May 3. The following is a diary of the events that took place beginning that day.

2.5.1.1 Events

May 3: Harold conducted the initial vulnerability scans of the San Francisco office. There appear to be more hosts than he thought. There are only 300 employees in that location. The scanner reports 4,094 hosts. A tech support call is placed to the vendor, who reviews the configuration and runs some diagnostics and a test scan of a few hosts. The vendor finds nothing wrong and suggests that Harold check the network configuration. Perhaps the routing is sending the scan to another office.

May 4: Harold suspects that there is something wrong with the San Francisco scanner but is not in a position to argue with the support team. Perhaps the scanners have incorrect default routes. But the configuration matches the others. This problem did not show up during product evaluation.

Harold has been informed by the global messaging manager that he is not to scan any of the e-mail servers until he feels confident that it will not disrupt business. He has a service level agreement (SLA) to maintain. Harold is not

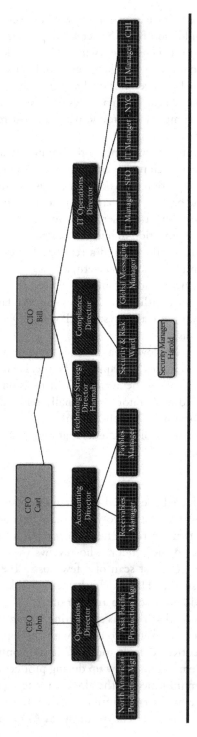

Figure 2.1   ACME organization chart.

happy about this because several critical servers are messaging servers. Some of those servers face the Internet and face higher threat levels. He escalates the situation to his boss, who tells him that he cannot argue the point because he is new in the role and is still trying to build credibility among the rest of the technology managers.

May 7: Scans of all other offices seem normal. The IT managers in those locations have received the initial reports of vulnerabilities.

May 12: After the first week of scanning, the total number of hosts is a little high but can probably be accounted for. Harold is conducting follow-up calls with all the managers.

May 15: San Francisco continues to have scanning problems and still shows 4,094 hosts. Chicago is now showing the same number of hosts. A lengthy review of the scan results shows that hosts are being found on every IP address scanned.

May 16: Overall, host average vulnerability scores have declined dramatically. This seems to be good news except that the top scores remain unchanged. In fact, some of the hosts have gotten worse. Harold e-mails the IT manager in New York to find out the status of remediation.

May 20: Further research shows that the scanners are picking up more hosts at each location, which is what has driven down the average score. Every location company-wide has 4,094 hosts. The scanners have exceeded their licensed host capacity. Furthermore, the New York IT manager has not responded to his e-mail, so Harold gives him a call. The manager explains that he is in the middle of a major deployment, which involves minor design changes, to some of the New York network. He says that once things settle from the deployment, he will have a look.

May 31: Working with technical support, Harold has discovered that something in the network is responding to every IP address and that no host really exists. The work-around for this is to manually enter all of the active host addresses. This is an impractical solution since many of the IP addresses are dynamically allocated. Harold will have to find out what is responding to the device discovery probes.

June 5: None of the vulnerabilities reported have been remediated. Harold consults his manager, Ward, who suggests setting up a conference call with the local IT managers. The earliest he can set up a one-hour call is in a week.

June 12: The conference call has only five of eight required participants. The IT managers say that they have no resources to dedicate to remediation, but they will try handling the highest priority hosts once per week, if workload permits. Addressing Ward on the call, one of the IT managers tells him that he should deploy only one new technology at a time instead of in parallel so they can assess the overall impact before the next deployment. The managers also complain that they were not informed the system would be deployed and are concerned that the scanning is affecting their network performance.

Ward agrees to have scans conducted only at night. The Asia Pacific production manager is also on the call to complain that the scanning may have caused one of his critical servers to fail. Since Asia's daytime is nighttime in the United States, he does not want it scanned until Harold can prove the scan doesn't affect the system.

June 16: Some of the worst hosts in two locations have been remediated. The rest of IT spent the weekend cleaning up a new infection introduced by a user who inserted an infected USB key. Many of the networks are still showing 4,094 hosts even when the scans take place when most of the desktop computers are turned off.

June 23: Harold is buried in tracking down scanning problems and following up on remediation activities. He discovers that the new IPS, which is built into the firewall software, is causing the scans to show a host on every IP address. In an experiment, he turns off the prevention functionality and performs a scan. It works perfectly. Ward, who hears that his recently deployed IPS was turned off in one location, verbally reprimands him for doing this without discussing it with him. He tells Harold to turn it back on and change his scans to focus only on servers for which he can get a static IP and the system owner approves. Harold successfully showed the Asia Pacific production manager that the scans were harmless to his server. The manager allows the host to be scanned and agrees to get critical vulnerabilities remediated in a week.

June 25: The reports coming out of the vulnerability system are not encouraging. For the hosts that are not phantoms created by the IPS system, the scores have improved very little. The trend lines that show the change in vulnerability are upward but no new vulnerabilities have been found. Harold is puzzled by this and contacts the product support line to report a possible bug. They explain that this is normal behavior.

June 30: The new vulnerability scanning system is scanning about 25 active hosts company-wide. The cost per host is about $400, far in excess of the economies of scale he expected. About 17 of the hosts are getting remediated.

July 18: Frustrated, Harold resigns to find work in an organization that "takes security more seriously."

So, what happened to Harold and the Acme Company? Did Acme need more people? Not likely. Did Harold select the wrong product? Probably not. He started out an optimist, with intentions of doing a thorough job, but problems quickly arose creating more work remediating little. The effectiveness of the system and Harold came into question amid waning internal support.

September 5: The *coup de grâce*. In a remote part of the company, an IT employee who is to be terminated decides to go out with a bang. Knowing the state of key server systems based on a flawed standard, he writes a Perl script that employs commonly used administrator passwords to damage dozens of systems. IT managers worldwide are embarrassed and frustrated. They remember that someone was performing the VM function. Too late.

2.5.1.2 Analysis

So, what is required to be successful in a VM program? This example is filled with mistakes from the beginning. Let's look at what went wrong in the previous example:

Process failure: Two problems were related to process. First, there was no formal and complete project plan with support of senior management. What Harold tried to do first was research technology products. Second, Harold failed to focus on process. VM is a process, not a technology solution.

Preparation: The behavior of the technology was certainly a big problem. Several things didn't go well. An IPS was deployed at the same time, but Harold seemed not to know that. Also, the reports coming out of the system were not well understood. Those that were sent to IT managers were apparently ignored. Harold probably thought either they just didn't care or they didn't understand the reports.

Inclusion: The IT managers were clearly not included in many of the planning activities and had little input into the project. If you look at the organization chart (Figure 2.1), you can see that the IT managers report to the IT operations director and are not accountable to the same organization as Harold until you reach the chief information officer (CIO) level. They were understandably defensive about their networks. When confronted with a new technology about which they knew nothing, their reaction was to protect their turf against an invasive tool over which they had no control or input.

Ownership: And what about the conference calls that Harold and Ward set up with the IT managers? Their low attendance rate reflects their level of interest. From Harold's point of view, it may have seemed this way. But, the natural reaction of someone who is busy during the deployment of new technology (in this case, the IPS) and is conducting a major change to the design of a network is to focus on the items for which they are accountable and shun those that generate more work. The IPS was part of the firewall software and therefore considered to be a configuration change to an established technology. Also, the vulnerability scanner spat out reports that demanded administrators do more work. Ignoring the reports would delay accountability and allow risk to remain in the computing environment.

Here is how Harold might have done things differently and achieved a better result:

Ownership: Get direct senior management support for the entire initiative. Make sure that management understands the commitment required to reme-diate and monitor. If you don't lead with this important step, expectations are not set and the required impact on operations is unclear. Harold did not have strong backing to get the attention of local IT managers. Since the IT managers were never included in the planning, design, and selection of the technology, they did not have the opportunity to test and validate the technology in the environment. Also, when remediation wasn't getting done, Harold had nowhere to escalate. Furthermore, senior managers can facili-tate communication with key participants in the program. Ideally, the senior manager communicating the importance of the VM initiative should be a global CIO, CSO, or CISO.

Related to senior management commitment, highlight the requirement that successful remediation is a key job performance indicator. In the previ-ous example, Harold did not have the interest of the local IT managers. They seldom fixed anything because it seemed to them that Harold was whining about how broken their systems were, which created more work for which they would get no recognition. There was simply no incentive. Harold was never received as a key supplier of solutions to crucial IT challenges. On the other hand, if the IT managers were told that they were being measured on their remediation performance, then they would be more likely to comply. In fact, they would quite possibly be proactive. To add a motivational carrot to the stick, a competition for lowest average score might have driven excel-lence into the process. To the individual manager with the lowest average score or perhaps the greatest improvement would go an additional bonus budget.

Preparation: Test! Test! Test! Any system connected to a network with broad-reaching and possibly invasive functionality should be completely tested with all components touched in the environment. Ultimately, a list of criteria for systems that can be scanned should be developed. A list of adverse effects on systems should be well documented and the candidates for not scanning identified.

Process: Change management must be carefully considered prior to any imple-mentation. As it happens, in Harold's company, a new firewall system with a built-in IPS was in the implementation phase. When scans began, San Francisco had already deployed a new firewall. This firewall answered discov-ery scans on every IP address in the range allocated to that location. (More about this phenomenon later in this book.) As Harold continued his scans, the firewalls continued to be rolled out. Eventually, every network was giving him bogus results. Had he participated in the change management process, he would have known that firewalls were being deployed, and he could have tested the effects in advance. Harold could have also correlated the change in behavior of the scans with the sequence of firewall installation.

2.5.2 Case Study #2: Technology Integration Challenge

Abacus Corporation is a global manufacturer and distributor of electronic abacuses that employ LCD technology and a special gesture interface that enables calculations to be performed much faster than with a conventional calculator. By all measures, Abacus resembles a rapidly growing but small electronics company holding a few key patents.

Abacus has manufacturing facilities in Nebraska and Alabama. Syllog, a business partner based in Germany, where most of the exotic devices are purchased, handles distribution. Syllog is a distributor of multiple unique electronic devices mostly to Asian customers and niche retailers in the United States and the United Kingdom. Most of the devices are provided by only three manufacturers with which Syllog maintains close relationships in business and infrastructure. About 40% of Syllog's infrastructure was co-funded by Abacus and serves Abacus directly.

At Abacus, the IT infrastructure is very mature with solid ITIL-based change management and incident management tools. All business partners are required to meet or exceed Abacus's policies and standards. They have implemented a "service desk" model with a few essential modules from the ITIL framework. This service desk is the central point for receiving and managing incidents and escalating changes. Since Abacus is a manufacturing operation with unpredictable order volume, all production is performed on a just-in-time basis. That is to say, they don't design and manufacture their products until they have an order. Furthermore, they are committed to delivering the products within 10 calendar days of order receipt. So, there is little tolerance for downtime.

Sales-related IT operations at Abacus are managed locally with market-specific applications. The varying languages, cultures, and unique business relationships in each market require equally varying hardware, software, and applications. Common operating system and underlying utility software is provided and managed by the global operations. However, the applications and non-ubiquitous software are handled locally. To keep this arrangement, specific service levels have been established between global and local operations groups.

Naturally, management has decided that the next step is to implement a full VM initiative throughout the company. There is strong connectivity to all the sites, including business partners who have also agreed to participate. Abacus uses primarily Microsoft software on desktops and Linux® on servers, with certain offices using a few implementations of Solaris™.

In addition to cleaning up vulnerabilities, Abacus wants to verify compliance and patch status in as many parts of the extended enterprise as possible. They have mature internal processes but few systems support resources. The ratio of support engineers and technicians is about 300 to 1. Automation is a key factor for Abacus. For example, there are about 20 standard systems maintenance and data collection shell scripts that run weekly on Linux systems, so scanning for vulnerabilities by an automated system rather than relying purely on internal processes is essential. The head of the systems engineering group, Carl, is given responsibility for implementation.

2.5.2.1 Events

November 2: With full backing of senior management, Carl has assembled a small team representing the systems support team, desktop engineering, and the director of networks to select a tool and modify existing processes. A budget of $350,000 is approved for the project.

November 23: On time and within budget, the team has selected a combination of two tools that appear to work well with all systems, including network devices for vulnerability scanning of desktops and agents on servers. The original idea was to have the agents run on all systems but the impact on local operations was too great to install and maintain yet another agent on an already crowded desktop. Since the agents seemed to have a low impact on server operations and the reporting provided unique features such as integrated patching, the thinking is that automated patching will help with workload. The compliance reports are exactly what are needed to keep managers focused on achieving the desired results. Total cost: $330,000 installed.

November 30: Acquisition is completed, the software is installed on a server, and hardware devices are deployed throughout the offices as needed. With the consent of the management of the business partners, certain locations that could have experienced problems scanning over the WAN connections have also installed scanners but have complained about the high cost for only a few hosts. To adapt, some of the server agents have been tasked with scanning local desktops without agents.

December 6: A freeze on all noncritical change control items has gone into effect due to the holiday period when many key employees will be on vacation. This lasts for 30 days. Not all of the network scanners have been installed.

January 15: Everyone is back from vacation and Carl has put together a communication plan to keep all key managers in the loop on vulnerability scanning. He has created the initial user names with passwords and privileges representing the six IT directors in key offices. They will be the primary users of the system. One of the agreed-upon process changes is that the IT directors will log in to the system to see the status of vulnerabilities in their area of the company. Access to the vulnerability information for each of these areas is defined by IP address range.

February 2: Initial scans have been completed, and IT directors are automatically informed of the results. They are very satisfied with the quality, content, and accuracy of the reports. It appears to be another technology and process triumph at Abacus. Carl has turned over the system to the production systems support group, which also had members on the VM system development team. Some of the IT managers have complained that they have to go into two separate systems to see all of their hosts. The system that operates the agents is giving them server vulnerability information, and the network scanning system provides desktop information. Carl begins a discussion with vendors on the best approach.

February 10: The IT director in Nebraska asks that all nine members of his desktop support group be given access to the system so they can pull reports and perform the remediation. The system administrator provides a list of information items required to be completed in a form for setting up the users. The form completion, return, data entry, and password verification/reset takes about two days to complete for both VM systems.

February 12: The business partner, Syllog, complains about getting strange scan results. It appears that the names of the desktops on Syllog's network are incorrect and instead are showing hosts on Abacus's server farm. Checking with the IT manager at HQ, it appears that the Syllog manager is in fact getting scan results from both networks. The cause turns out to be the fact that they use the same IP addresses. The vulnerability scanner is reporting correctly to the server, but there is overlap with the IPs.

February 14: The IT manager in another office requests similar access for all of this desktop support team, a total of six people. They must have access to perform their remediation as well. With more users, detailed procedures have to be developed for the two systems operating in combination and separately.

February 18: A technical solution is developed to rely on computer name, not IP address, to identify the host on a report. All of the network definitions and privileges have to be updated to reflect the change. Separately, an initiative is started to integrate the two vulnerability systems into a single reporting infrastructure. This is done by a single systems engineer with extensive experience in Perl programming.

February 23: The remaining IT directors in other locations—six locations in all—also request that their support people be permitted to have access to the VM system. Two of the directors want to divide the responsibility for their systems between two different support groups: servers and desktops. This is because of the specialized skill required in remediation. This makes for the addition of a total of 32 users to the systems.

February 25: After three days of work for one person, the changes to the network definitions and permissions are complete. There are now 47 users of the systems. Some server managers complain that the patches that are installed are not thoroughly tested and need to be scheduled more carefully to not affect production operations.

March 1: The VM team is informed that a user in Nebraska resigned two weeks earlier. Following the user-termination process, the user's access is revoked. A replacement user has not been found. Therefore, only the IT director in Nebraska can run those reports.

March 4: Initial reports show a significant lag between the time when vulnerabilities are reported and the time they are finally fixed. After about a day of calls, the VM administrators determine that the delay is caused by the time between finding the vulnerabilities on the report and entering them into the incident and change management systems. The process that was defined in the beginning works fine but requires up to three weeks to enact remediation. Carl has a meeting with the compliance director and the information security director to discuss the current performance of the new system and the slow remediation issue. The compliance director points out that the maximum allowed time for remediating a critical vulnerability is seven calendar days. According to the reports in the system, this is taking two to three weeks.

March 5: The Microsoft-based systems are configured with credentials using Active Directory® to perform in-depth scans. In effect, these credentials allow the scanner to log on to the system to check critical patches and configuration items. Management reports have been consolidated from the two systems into a single report that is run on demand through a Web interface. The systems engineer begins work on detailed remediation reports. However, many of the data elements from the two systems do not directly match. One uses Common Vulnerabilities and Exposures (CVE) codes to identify vulnerabilities, and the other uses Bugtraq identifiers.

March 10: Carl has spent the last week trying to perfect the current process for reporting and remediation and has only gained about one day of time on average. The central problem seems to be that those entering the information into the incident and change management systems have other responsibilities, including performing the actual fixes. Issuing patches through the patch management system can fix some items. These changes happen quickly with little problem and can be addressed within a day or two. However, about 30% of the vulnerabilities require manual intervention. Furthermore, the agent-based VM system seems to be designed to use its own internal change management system with no ability to automatically export changes and import change release status.

March 11: The UNIX®-based systems are not yet being scanned. Each one of them has to be set up manually with the appropriate credentials for in-depth inspection by the new system. This is a time-consuming process that requires numerous change management events to be created. To save time and work, some changes are bunched together in the system. But they can only combine those events for systems that have the same configuration, that is, virtually identical systems such as in a load-balanced configuration.

March 12: After careful consideration and discussion with his boss, Carl decides that the best course of action is to bring in a special developer to interface the patch, change, and incident management systems with the new agent-based VM system. However, the systems engineer who has been coding Perl reports has no time to work on the system further given a hectic change schedule. The engineer turns over all the code to Carl.

March 20: An initial assessment with the developer and the vendor's support team results in an estimate totaling $152,000. There are three primary reasons for this: First, the system is designed to generate only Simple Network Management Protocol (SNMP) traps when a vulnerability is found. None of the change or incident management systems are compatible with this protocol. A custom interface will either have to be written into the VM system or into the internal systems. Second, the workflow from incident management to change management allows for automatic generation of change events only when an incident is entered manually. An automated interface will have to be developed to put entries into both systems and link them together using information from the incident management database. Furthermore, the process is different for vulnerabilities than for other incidents because there must be a verification scan before the change can be closed out. Finally, the VM system uses CVE and Bugtraq numbers to identify what patch needs to be applied to a system. The patch management system uses a proprietary set of codes that is more specific about which patch is required. Additional data would have to be developed to properly match these codes and identify where they do not properly align.

March 23: Total estimated costs of the system in a fully functional state are now $482,000 (initial $330K + $152K). Senior management senses that this might turn out to be a money pit and limits total expenditure to what was initially requested ($350,000). For the money that is left ($20,000), the developer can send the required XML-formatted messages to the incident management system to save some data entry time. After that, Carl's budget is depleted.

Epilogue: For the remaining year, VM system users are pleased and yet confused about the incomplete process involved in remediation. Considerable ongoing effort is put into remediating and closing out incidents. Users still have to create change requests, run verification scans manually, and then close out changes. Carl continues to believe that senior management is penny-wise but pound-foolish. Some wonder why the company didn't just go with a single system and avoid all the confusion.

2.5.2.2 Analysis

Events seemed to unfold rather smoothly at the start. This was clearly a very mature IT operation with strong process management and supporting systems. Project management seemed very structured. There was good executive support for the initiative and a budget was set and agreed upon. Carl, the project manager, involved all the right parties to get mutual ownership. This last factor is what allowed the systems to stay in operation even after shortcomings became apparent.

First, let's address the issue of process, so that it is clearly understood how it works at the Abacus Corporation. Although they are very disciplined and efficient, IT seems to suffer from this process.

An incident, in the ITIL framework definition, is some event that disrupts the agreed-upon service level and underlying business activity. Service levels are set for vulnerabilities and remediation time frames, and a newly discovered vulnerability will result in a potential failure to meet SLAs if not corrected in a timely fashion. When a vulnerability is discovered by Abacus's new VM system, an incident must be generated in the incident management system to track the resolution. Since Abacus runs a lean IT shop, the service desk functions are performed by a variety of IT staff, depending on the type of event to be handled. So, the service desk is a very dynamic entity with the support of software-based routing to the appropriate parties. See Figure 2.2 to follow this process.

Vulnerability information is assessed by the appropriate individuals depending on the network and host type affected. If a vulnerability is critical, an incident is created to track the vulnerability to resolution. Noncritical vulnerabilities are put into a scheduled change process for nonurgent changes.

When a resolution involves a change that is complex, and it is determined that to implement the change may impact other functions, a change is initiated in the change management system and a change ticket is generated. This allows affected parties to be included in the change process with appropriate notification of potential impacts. It also informs the manager of the change of the technical configuration elements of the target.

Once a patch is applied or a configuration updated to remediate the vulnerability, a change ticket is conditionally closed. The change ticket is closed with the caveat that the same vulnerability must not appear in the next vulnerability scan.

A vulnerability scan is run again, either as a part of the regular schedule or manually upon request. The scan performed on request typically is faster and only targets the systems affected by the change.

The incident ticket will be closed after the change ticket closes. This takes place automatically between the change and incident management systems, but only if the incident management system automatically produced the change ticket.

To the uninitiated, this may seem like a cumbersome process, but the staff at Abacus is very disciplined and well-trained. The process works exceptionally well at providing the critical production systems, typically uninterrupted and predictable service. So, in this case, the process seems to be well-managed. However, there are several deficiencies in the systems integration process.

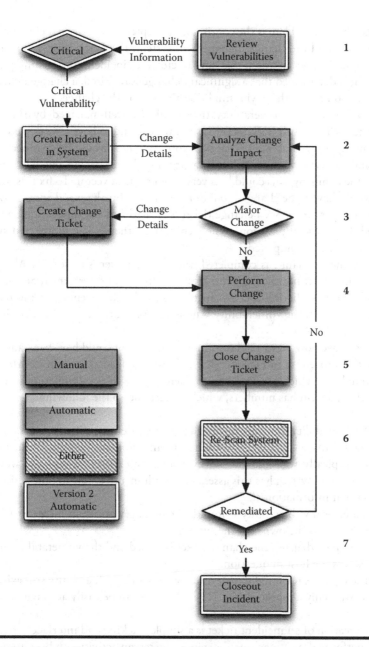

Figure 2.2   Abacus Corporation vulnerability service desk process.

One obvious problem is the continuous interplay between the incident management system and the change management system. For every critical vulnerability, IT personnel in a service desk role have to create an incident for tracking purposes. Then, if it is determined that a significant change is required, a change ticket has to be created to notify others who might be affected by the change.

An example of a vulnerability that would be well-managed by this process would be if a Microsoft SQL server system were found to have a weak password on a commonly utilized user ID. That password weakness would be a vulnerability. If that database server were accessible by a large number of people, possibly even from outside the company, this could be a very serious attack vector. To fix this, the password would have to be changed, but doing so might break several applications that rely on that password. So, a change ticket is created and the application owners are notified. Once the application owners coordinate the change to affected systems, the change can be completed.

Now, once a change is completed, the change ticket is closed. At Abacus, the ticket is closed but not the incident. First, a scan must be performed on the system to verify the remediation success. In this example, the strength of the password would be tested. If the vulnerability is no longer present, then the incident is manually closed.

So, we have now performed four manual tasks that could have been automated. Follow this procedure in Figure 2.2. The boxes are shaded to indicate which steps are manual and which are automated. There is little to no automation in this diagram. The diagram has numbers, which correspond to the following:

1. A vulnerability manager reviews a report to identify critical vulnerabilities in hosts. This activity is ideally suited to an automated system. Vulnerabilities are typically well-known and evaluated by experts around the world. An automated system has this assessment built in and is able to take action based on that information.

2, 3. If a critical vulnerability is found, the manager opens an incident ticket and assigns it to the owner of the system.

4, 5. After remediating, the change ticket is closed and the vulnerability manager rescans the host in question.

6, 7. The report is reviewed to determine whether the vulnerability still exists. This is essentially a repeat of step 1, which again can be easily automated.

The creation of an incident ticket is a simple tracking and interface activity that can be performed by a machine. In step 3, the rescan activity can be automated by interfacing the change management system with the VM system to allow for notification that a change was complete, thereby initiating a follow-up scan. Alternatively, the action may take place manually, depending on the process used. If the process called for waiting until the next scheduled scan, then step 4 is not required. If a manual scan is called for in the process, then a rescan may be necessary. One refinement of the rescan process is a limitation or parameter applied to the target. For example, a particular host or network of hosts may have a constraint that only allows them to be scanned at night in case service is affected. This would prevent any potential outage during business hours. Therefore, once the change is complete, the rescan will only take place later that night and not immediately.

Now, let's look at the process from an automated perspective. Refer to Figure 2.2 again. The following process closely resembles the earlier process. However, in the diagram, I have indicated some steps with double boxes to indicate where automation can be performed (Version 2 Automatic). In each automated step, the process is greatly accelerated to require only seconds to complete. The following numbers are also indicated in the diagram:

1. Critical vulnerabilities cause the VM system to automatically create an incident ticket and assign it to the individual specified for the network where the host resides. In this case, this individual is known as the incident manager. The incident ID is captured by the VM system.
2. The incident manager reviews the required change and determines whether it requires significant work or can affect other systems.
3. The incident manager goes into the incident management system to flag the incident as a required change, which is instantiated in the change management system using the existing interface between the two systems.
4. The change is performed as planned by an engineer, possibly the incident manager.
5. The change activity is closed out via the incident management system user interface by the engineer who performed the work. There is no way to automate this action, but it requires little effort. In fact, some change management systems have the ability to listen for e-mail message replies to update status. This update automatically triggers notification to the incident management system to tentatively close the incident.
6. The incident management system then sends a confirmation message to the VM system using the incident ID. Indexed using the incident ID, another scan on the single host is initiated, checking for the specific vulnerability and any others.
7. If the vulnerability is not present on the follow-up scan, a confirmation is sent to the incident management system to close the incident. If the vulnerability is still present, the incident confirmation is rejected, causing another notification to the incident manager. Steps 3 through 6 are repeated.

Another problem with the implementation is the selection of two separate products that were never designed to work together. Although some products on the market can perform both agent-based and network-based vulnerability assessments, the previous scenario is a common one. This is often the case when two seemingly ideal products lack the key compatibility to "hit a home run" in the VM game.

As a result, users were initially forced to work with two different systems. At first, the agent-based system scanned only servers and the host-based system scanned only desktops. This logical separation fit the company management model of local versus global separation of responsibilities. But, when the agent-based system was used to scan desktops where a network-based scanner was not financially feasible, the division of responsibilities and system usability broke down.

An enthusiastic attempt to rescue the effort was made by a knowledgeable systems engineer. However, the low-hanging fruits were the management reports. Since no system interaction was necessary, data gathering and normalization were simpler. There were still issues with data structures and standard values across systems. These are all the same problems that would be found in any other application. Later, we will see where the industry is making strides toward avoiding these problems.

In addition to the automation surrounding identification, remediation, and unified reporting, other systems can be integrated to great advantage.

On February 10, nine user IDs are requested for addition to the system. At this point, the system administrator should perhaps be wishing that this was an easier task. It has been time-consuming to collect the data and enter them into the system. Since Abacus is a Microsoft shop, why not integrate the user identification and authentication with Active Directory? Or even use the almost-ubiquitous Remote Authentication Dial-In User Service (RADIUS) protocol. This piece of system integration is essential for most enterprises today that employ some standard type of authentication mechanism. We also see that several other users had to be added to the system as well on February 13, 14, and 25. There were eventually almost 50 users to set up. When one user left the company, Carl's team only found out two weeks later that they could remove the user's access. It is more likely that the user assigned to an Active Directory group had already been removed or disabled.

An example of how a directory structure might align with a VM system is shown in Figure 2.3. There are objects and actions in the VM system. A group or user can be a member or a role, which includes various combinations of object and actions. For example, an individual with the administrator role would be responsible for maintaining all areas of the system. Therefore, he would be given access to all objects and all actions. However, the previously mentioned engineer would only have access to reporting capabilities in a particular office. So, that group's permitted action would be "Report" and the permitted objects would be those "Networks" that are in the local office.

Each of the groups or users could be assigned to one or more roles and networks to give them the capabilities required as shown in Figure 2.4. The power of this arrangement comes from the fact that when a user changes to another group, the user will assume the roles of that group and not the one from which he came. For example, if an engineer moved from the IT department in California to the Desktops group in Nebraska, that engineer would then be able to have access to vulnerability information only for his new position. Vulnerability managers would

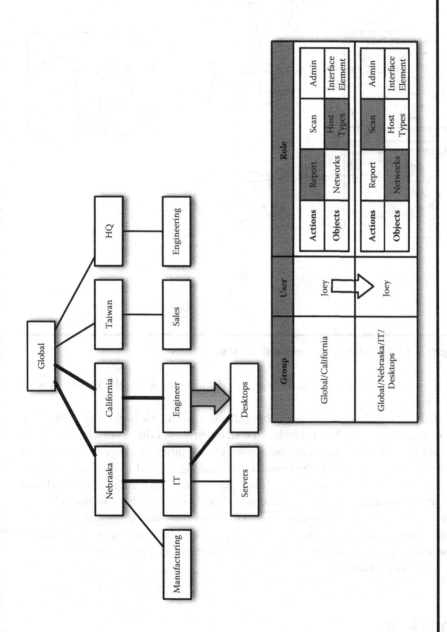

Figure 2.3 Vulnerability system roles aligned with directory structures.

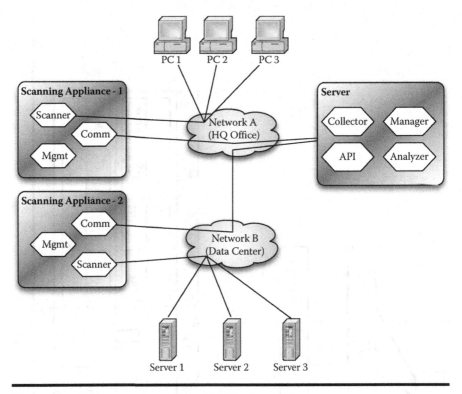

Figure 2.4   Directory structure and VM system roles.

similarly only be able to perform scans on the assigned networks associated with their group.

This kind of integration seems obvious now, but at the beginning, this many users might have been inconceivable to Carl or the rest of the team. This also sends us back to our earlier discussion about how vulnerabilities get created. This scenario is similar to one in which the original system designers fail to take into account all the ways a system may be used. It is a requirements gathering activity with too many assumptions. Carl's design and selection team should have worked out precisely who would use the system, how many users there would be, and what types of activities were likely to take place with those users. There would be terminations, new hires, analysts reviewing reports, and perhaps others who change the scanning parameters or schedules.

End Note

1. *Source:* MITRE Corporation, CVE-2004-0200. GDI = Graphics Device Interface.

Chapter 3

Program and Organization

3.1 Introduction: Program Structure

The structure and composition of an IT or compliance organization can have a significant impact on the effectiveness of vulnerability management (VM). It is important to understand the relationship between the business stakeholders and the managers of underlying IT assets. It is this relationship that should reflect the adage that IT exists to support the business. If you can get the support of the business, then IT will be driven to support a VM program and comply with supporting policy. To put it more simply, VM must be a business priority. Otherwise, it is not worth doing.

Support of the business is the essence of the VM program. It encompasses all activities, technology, and personnel to specify, design, deploy, and operate the VM function. This program is supported at the outset by a charter. All activities, policies, procedures, and plans should be in furtherance of that charter, which functions like a constitution for the program. It lays down the principles under which activities are conducted. When questions arise about policy, procedures, or organization, the charter can be consulted to determine whether decisions are being made in alignment with the business.

The charter is not a lengthy document with a lot of detail but rather a few carefully crafted sentences reflecting ethics, goals, and priorities of the company as they should be reflected in the VM function. For example, if the company is intensely focused on availability of computing services because it is the primary generator of revenue, then a statement about not interfering with production computer operations should be included. If the firm is more interested in the loss of confidential information, then a statement about identifying and remediating threats to confidentiality would be first. In the latter example, this would tend to place a higher priority on remediating vulnerabilities that might allow data to be stolen. For example, weak passwords and spyware would be addressed before a denial-of-service weakness in a domain name system (DNS) configuration. That is not to say that the DNS configuration weakness is unimportant; it is simply not as important as the potential theft of client data or intellectual property.

During development of policies, procedures, and organization structure, new information is discovered that provides feedback into the overall program design. That feedback loop may affect the organization structure or policies. Figure 3.1 illustrates the relationship among the program phases during the development cycle:

Concept and proposal: This phase defines the business value that is to be provided to the business, the general concept of VM, and, at a high level, how one plans to achieve the results. This activity is primarily the responsibility of the program manager.

Charter development: This phase is the construction of a charter. These are the guiding principles and goals of the program. This will be discussed in depth in this chapter. The charter is authored by the program manager and/or the executive sponsor.

Figure 3.1 Program phases during development cycle.

Policy: These are the policies that support underlying business objectives, including any code of ethics that might exist.

Organization structure: An organization or combination of several organizations will fit together in a loosely coupled fashion to support the VM program.

Procedures: These are the detailed procedures that must be followed to support the VM program on a daily basis.

A capable program manager will be able to control the quality of each component and mediate the flow of feedback to keep the overall program on track. Note that it is unlikely that the program charter will change based on feedback from other phases. The charter would only be modified for clarification should a lack of clarity be discovered for the purposes of making key decisions. It may also be modified if the company business model changes or ethical standards change through acquisition.

From our illustration, we can see a clear hierarchy of development. But no single phase comes to an absolute close because there is ongoing maintenance of those phases. The major components can be complete, although some of the content may require minor but important adjustments. It is this dynamic that makes for a successful program. The flexibility of the phases is ameliorated by feedback from later phases. An example of how feedback would change activities in a particular phase of a VM program is the discovery that a complex and difficult change management procedure could not accommodate a particular policy. That policy could be modified to still achieve the purposes of the VM program charter but allow for a very different procedure that is more compatible with existing change management procedures.

3.2 The VM Program and Technology Development

There is also a major technology development component to the program. This development process can also inform the previously mentioned phases. So, if we add to our diagram the technology development process, as in Figure 3.2, we can see a parallel set of activities.

When the development of technology takes place in parallel with the organizational and procedural phases of the program, feedback must also inform upwardly, adjacently, and downwardly. Adjacently, policy development may inform engineers on how to design a system. Or, innovative design of the system may provide the ability to simplify procedures. We saw this in the previous chapter where a systems integration effort could have a major impact in simplifying incident and change management processes. Downwardly, a subtle policy change may make coding of the system much simpler by removing an unnecessarily onerous internal audit capability. A good example of this would be if the audit function required that every scan track each action taken by the system to detect vulnerabilities. This would be

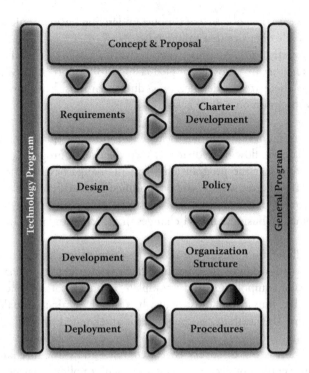

Figure 3.2 Vulnerability management and parallel development process.

an ill-informed policy because such recording activity would overwhelm any scanning software, hardware, or supporting network with audit information that would equal or exceed the actual vulnerability information discovered. It would be more effective to consider the vulnerability result data as audit information itself.

Often overlooked, upward feedback across disciplines is quite important. For example, the development of the VM program can cause a contradiction in policy to surface. Evidence of that contradiction can be fed back into the earlier policy development phase. For example, during VM program development, it may be discovered that a particular vulnerability is simply not found in the types of systems being scanned. So, a policy that requires all systems to be scanned for UNIX® shell vulnerabilities would not apply to the part of the business that relies solely on Microsoft applications. The policy would have to be modified with words such as "where appropriate."

The feedback from the technology development program will inform the parallel organizational program. For example, the discovery of a feature in the VM system technology may affect the intrusion prevention capability in a positive manner. So, an enhancement of the intrusion prevention policy, technology, and related procedures may be necessary. Performing this function during the earlier planning phase will naturally integrate VM into other parts of the organization as well as identify where technical planning is required to integrate with the intrusion prevention system (IPS). However, not all good ideas occur before development. It is the job of the technology project manager to work with the team to determine whether such discoveries merit additional development effort.

In Figure 3.2, you can see how the technology development track of the program might work in conjunction with the overall program. Try moving in all directions and consider the scenarios under which one phase may inform another.

3.3 Who Gets Involved?

I have already discussed how the support of senior management is important to drive a VM program from the top down. But, there are other participants whose roles should not be overlooked. A clear definition of these roles can prevent considerable political strife, streamline the development of process, facilitate the deployment of technology, and encourage the assignment of individuals and groups to the VM effort.

VM program participants fall into two basic categories. One is a contributing role that helps the program get started and operate. These participants are not directly involved in performing vulnerability assessments, but the process cannot proceed without their help. Then, there is the operational role. These participants are direct actors in the day-to-day operation of the VM technology. They perform the scans, assess the vulnerabilities, and make sure that the priorities are raised to the right constituencies. They also ensure that the VM technology continues to function optimally in a dynamic environment.

Some of the key groups involved in the VM process are asset owners, Security, Human Resources, IT, vulnerability managers, incident managers, change management, and compliance management. Each of these roles is either directly involved in the VM process or is at least affected significantly by it.

3.3.1 Operational Roles

Other roles to be filled in the ongoing operation of a VM program have both direct and indirect participation and contribute greatly to the program's effectiveness. The roles are defined early in process development with more concrete modifications when hardware and software are procured. This is because the selection of technology will impact how people work, their involvement in the communications among other groups, and the nature of their interdependencies. If an automated process fulfills a key activity in a role, then the requirement for the role may be diminished altogether.

For example, at the outset, it may be planned to have a role of an administrator to take discovered critical vulnerabilities and distribute the remediation requests to the appropriate system owners or administrators. However, it may subsequently be determined that the selected technology can automate this process; and therefore, the role is minimized to one of monitoring.

3.3.1.1 Vulnerability Manager

This role is responsible for ensuring the correct configuration and operation of the technology, as well as creating, monitoring, and distributing reports as needed. It is by no means a simple administrator role. The individual must be able to interpret technical reports produced by the system and to explain the cause and remediation for a vulnerability. Knowledge of operating systems, networks, and security practices is required. This individual will interact with system administrators and network managers to ensure that the vulnerability identification and remediation processes meet goals.

3.3.1.2 Incident Manager

When vulnerabilities require attention, one person must take responsibility for remediation. It is often the owner or administrator of the vulnerable target. This individual should have insight into the configuration and operation of the target and be able to assess the impact of a change to that system. This person, known as an incident manager, will work with the vulnerability manager to complete the required remediation tasks. It is the responsibility of the incident manager to follow up on the assigned remediation tasks until they are complete. In some cases, this role is combined with the role of change manager. For example, smaller organizations may have one person to field all work for engineers and administrators. This person could be responsible for receiving incidents, coordinating changes, and distributing remediation work.

3.3.1.3 Change Manager

In a more complex remediation scenario where multiple systems or business functions may be affected by a complex change, the change manager will act as a project manager to oversee the full extent of the change. This manager will inform the affected parties, coordinate activities, perform testing or ensure that proper testing is completed, and work with the vulnerability manager to verify compliance.

3.3.1.4 Compliance Manager

This role is primarily one of a recipient and end user of the VM system and also one of the principal beneficiaries. In a normal compliance function, the compliance manager is tasked with ensuring that the systems in use by the company adhere to policies and standards. This manager is generally a recipient or consumer of reports from the VM system. More importantly, in a dynamic environment, the compliance manager will review trend reports to determine whether there is a continuous or repeating activity that results in a system being out of compliance. This allows the compliance manager to discover processes in the organization that may be flawed in a way that leads to repeat policy deviations.

In an environment where service level agreements (SLAs) are used to establish service levels, the VM program manager may create an SLA for the compliance manager to ensure that audits take place at the required frequency and the appropriate checks are run on each target. Metrics for this are simple and easily derived from the vulnerability scan results.

3.3.2 Contributing Roles

The groups most commonly having a contributing role in the VM process are asset owners, Human Resources, IT, and Security. The last group, Security, may be surprising to you in that one would expect a direct operational role rather than a contributing one. Although it may be the case that Security is the principal operator of the system, we discuss it at a higher, abstract level as a customer that contributes requirements.

3.3.2.1 Asset Owners

Asset owners are those who ultimately pay for things and derive the most benefit. They control the purse strings and therefore have considerable say over what gets done. In many organizations, the asset owner is the line of business. This either happens through a chargeback mechanism or direct purchase. This becomes most apparent at the middle and upper levels of management.

It is natural for typical IT workers to consider the systems they administer as their own. This sense of ownership is not founded in reality but only from an emotional attachment. Working through their managers will ultimately yield better cooperation in a large organization when making plans to assess the security posture of an asset. Maintaining emotional separation from the asset will enhance objectivity when making key decisions about the asset's security posture. Two very important contributions of an asset owner are the asset classification and valuation functions, which cannot and should not be performed by the administrator of a system. There will be more on this topic when we discuss planning and execution of the VM program.

3.3.2.2 Security

Security departments are often the groups dealing directly with VM. However, organizations with a strong focus on service management, as described in the

Information Technology Infrastructure Library (ITIL) service management framework, may consider this a subset of the existing framework. In either case, a close and cooperative relationship between the security function and IT should exist. A partnership will make VM implementation easier, and you will likely receive better internal support.

Since security is the ultimate goal of a VM system, it is natural that Security is a key participant and possibly full owner and operator of the VM program. Depending on the type of business, however, it is possible that other groups such as Compliance will take on this role. For example, companies that depend heavily on payment card industry (PCI) standards compliance may wish to have the compliance organization take ownership of the process while partnering closely with Security as a customer and key constituent.

3.3.2.3 HR

Human Resources is one of the most overlooked groups. VM systems often find critical compliance problems, which can expand into evidence of security incidents perpetrated by an employee. HR is an instrumental part of the reporting process as well as the "stick" part of security policy. Ultimately, HR is there to help manage the risk to the company from things that employees do. Any reporting process that is developed should probably consider the relationship with HR should action other than patching and configuration management be required.

HR is also involved in the creation and maintenance of performance management programs. With careful planning, it is possible to tie vulnerability remediation performance to employee performance objectives. To achieve this, it may be necessary to give HR a clear understanding of how the VM program and support systems work. HR can then work with the VM program manager to determine what their role will be in mediating any potential conflicts that may arise with managing an employee.

3.3.2.4 IT

Information technology is obviously heavily involved in technology and process. If you are working as a separate security or compliance group, I recommend partnering with an IT project manager to get the technology deployed. A senior IT manager would also be very helpful in getting systems and networks remediated. The VM program manager should work with senior IT managers to develop the process and identify the key individuals who will oversee the work. In all likelihood, you will have to get some initial guidance from managers and then propose a process. Be sure to furnish a diagram. IT people work well with drawings and seem to commonly prefer analyzing existing design.

3.4 Policy and Information Flow

Any compliance or security initiative must be supported by policy. This is not a discussion of the merits of policy or the process of its creation but rather definition. We will focus specifically on the types of policy required to complete the documentation chain from the intent of the business to the effective remediation of vulnerabilities.

3.4.1 Existing Policy

Existing security policy should have sufficient coverage for the presence of unauthorized software and acceptable use. The VM system will likely find more than one occurrence of these kinds of violations. Some amendments to these policies may be necessary if they specify the means that must be used to detect violations. Similar to the examples in the previous section on the VM program and organization, operational experience will inform policy in an adaptive, cyclic process. If acceptable use is a priority, you will have to be sure to have a supporting process to tackle new discoveries.

Also, the VM system itself may be considered a violation of policy. Be sure that the use of the system is included in any list of authorized IT or security systems. Consider, for example, the scenario where an employee has been discovered by the VM system to be an egregious violator of company policy. If the employee is being terminated and his attorney discovers that the system itself is a violation of corporate policy, serious liability could result in some jurisdictions.

3.4.2 New Policy

VM compliance policy is sometimes necessary for enforcement of remediation activities. Depending on your organization, a policy that directs IT managers to make remediation a priority is helpful. The policy should provide for the following:

Prioritization of vulnerabilities: The vulnerabilities found will be prioritized. In many cases, more vulnerabilities are found than can possibly be fixed in a reasonable amount of time. You will have to specify what gets done first. It is even possible that you may want a policy statement of the circumstances under which systems administrators should drop everything they are doing and remediate or shut down the system in question.

Valuation of assets: Every system is a company asset. It has to be given a value, which can be used in the prioritization process. We will discuss this more in Chapter 6.

Time limits: Depending on the severity and type of vulnerability, time limits for remediation must be set. This is, in effect, a service level agreement (SLA) for the organization. You will have to consider the risk or threat to the organization based on several criteria. Those criteria, however, would be left to a supporting standard.

3.4.2.1 Usage Policy

Another important type of policy pertains to the usage of the VM system itself. This policy would highlight key operational constraints. Among the types of constraints necessary are the following:

Types of systems exempt from scanning: This can include other security devices or critical network devices that are known to be adversely affected by scanning.

Operational requirements for scanning approval: One must have consent of a system owner and/or administrator.

SLA parameters: This requirement specifies what parameters must be included in any scan specification for a given network or group of targets. This might include time of day, bandwidth limitations, operational impact assessment, and scan termination request response time. These parameters in particular are important to maintaining a healthy relationship with system owners. If scans interfere with the systems and their operating environment, system owners are not likely to grant ongoing permission to continue scanning.

3.4.2.2 Ownership and Responsibilities

Once a system proves itself to be a powerful tool in managing a critical part of the enterprise, questions such as "who is responsible for the scanning schedule?" and "who decides what gets scanned and when?" are likely to arise. These questions are reasonable given the insecurity that comes with what is perceived as an invasive activity. The best thing to do is avoid contention over these issues by getting it all decided in advance. Be forewarned that ambiguity is the enemy of process.

The first step in establishing clear ownership is to build it into the policy. The roles for key functions in the process should be clearly specified in the title. At a minimum, these roles must include the following:

Scan parameters definition: The business and technical parameters used for scanning must be defined and carefully controlled. Although others may participate in the process of scanning, careless changes to parameters can cripple a host or an entire network.

Scan scheduling: The schedule for a scan has a lot of thought built into it. These considerations should not be trifled with. A change in a schedule can have as big an impact on business operations as a change in parameters.

Report distribution: Vulnerability reports are confidential data. In the wrong hands, these reports can be very damaging. For a hacker or a motivated, disgruntled employee, a vulnerability report is a road map to trouble.

Local host remediation: When a host cannot be patched or fixed through an enterprise host management tool, it has to be remediated by a local administrator or other individual appropriate to your organization.

Global remediation: Conversely to local host activities, global tools also remediate hosts over a network. One or more organizations are responsible for this remediation. For example, the desktop team may be responsible for general host patching and the security group may have to keep antivirus and encryption programs updated. All such organizations should be identified in advance and made active participants and contributors to VM process development.

3.4.3 Compliance and Governance

Eventually, the progress in remediation has to be monitored by someone to maintain good governance. In an organization of less than 10,000 hosts, it is often sufficient for this individual to be the person responsible for scanning. However, in larger organizations, it is preferable to have a compliance group perform this function. Additionally, Compliance would monitor the configuration and operation of the system on a regular basis.

Figure 3.3 shows how the compliance organization uses the current operations documentation, process documentation, and scan results to verify compliance.

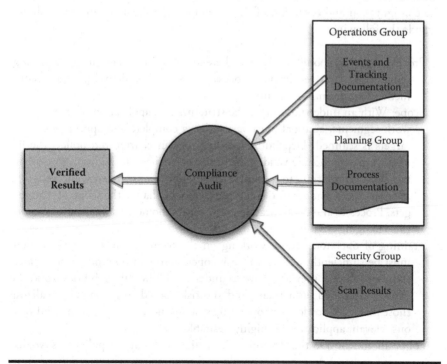

Figure 3.3   Compliance data flow.

These three pieces of data have an important relationship. Operations documentation tells the compliance group what activities were undertaken by the VM group. Compliance should verify that VM activities are conducted in accordance with policy.

Process documentation defines in unambiguous detail the steps to perform the VM function. It is against this documentation that the compliance function will verify the operations activities and supporting output documents. The process documentation itself should be checked against policy to ensure conformity. In some cases, this step is not necessary in the compliance monitoring function because compliance may be a part of the creation of the VM process. In that case, an external audit is occasionally warranted.

Finally, the scan results data are detailed in reports from the vulnerability scans. These reports should reflect the level of compliance achieved by each IT group responsible for remediation. Later, we will discuss in some detail the content of these reports and their relevance in a mature, successful VM program.

3.4.3.1 System Audit

Another critical step in the governance of VM is auditing. During an annual audit of security mechanisms, it is advantageous to have an external party review the configuration and operation of the system. The elements of any audit should include the following:

Process: Auditors should verify that there are no critical flaws in the scanning, remediation, and verification processes. The auditor should provide recommendations on improvements.

Scope: With an understanding of the structure and application of existing network segments, auditors must verify that a complete and appropriate set of targets is scanned. Depending on the program charter and policy, the list of targets may include vendors or business partners. In addition to existing targets, it is important to recognize that organizations, systems, and networks are dynamic. Changes to the environment will change the scope of scan targets. Processes and configurations of scanners should be sufficient to adapt to this changing environment.

Training of operators: Those working on the technical details of the system must be sufficiently well-versed in its operation. Not only must they understand operations, they also have to understand how vulnerabilities work, the threats associated with them, and the risks posed to a company realizing those threats. Knowledge of operating systems, networks, protocols, and various relevant applications is highly desirable.

Policy alignment: Do the VM operations align with current policy? As we discussed earlier, VM processes are derived from policy, which is derived from program charter or business objectives. Over time, policy can drift and no longer meet the program requirements. This is not through negligence but a natural tendency of individuals to adapt to a changing environment without the perspective of overall impact to the program charter.

As circumstances gradually change in networks and systems to respond to the changing business environment, the business needs will no longer be reflected in the policy. For example, the business typically may sell its products through personal sales contacts. Therefore, there are no policies regarding proper use of encryption or handling of customer financial data. Then, they discover untapped markets that are accessible online. The current policy may state that electronic payment data must be exchanged through bank transfers and not through company systems. However, in the newly adopted online sales model, customers provide payment information, which is handled by company computer systems. Now, numerous vulnerability and compliance issues in encryption, network design, and system configuration arise. Since the policy has never been amended, it is difficult to discover and remediate compliance problems in these systems. Furthermore, the systems in question may be out of scope for VM altogether.

3.5 Summary

The VM program can face many challenges in a large and complex organization. Politics, fear, and the natural tendency of people to resist change must be overcome. The basic tools for success are inclusiveness, executive support, structure, policy, and process. This chapter has outlined many of the basic challenges and how the organizational structure and process can address them. Putting all of these elements together requires considerable planning and support from the top down and the bottom up. The task is 75% science and planning and 25% the art of persuasion and motivation. Listening to the concerns of others will feed all of these tasks without major resistance. It is strength of organization covered with the softness of planned integration.

Chapter 4

Technology

4.1 Introduction

Vulnerability assessment technology comes in multiple flavors designed for various deployment strategies. These strategies are largely the result of restrictions imposed by the business-operating model. Factors such as the distribution of facilities and organization of infrastructure have a major influence on the technology choices made. Cost and efficiency are also ever-present factors in any decision. The selection criteria will be discussed in the next chapter. In this chapter, we will discuss the variety of technologies and the unique features and issues of each.

Notice to the reader: This chapter assumes that the reader has a strong familiarity with network protocols such as TCP/IP, virtual private networks (VPNs) and the Open Systems Interconnect (OSI) model.

There are five common, industry-accepted approaches to vulnerability management (VM) technology:

- Active scanning
- Passive assessment
- Agents
- Hybrid
- Inference

There are subtle variations on these approaches to provide flexibility to different business structures. Before we get into a discussion of these architectures, we should review some basic terminology. Some of these terms have already been used in this book because their meanings may seem obvious. But I will be more precise and complete here:

Vulnerability: A weakness in the software or hardware that allows use of a product beyond its design intent with an adverse effect on the software, system,

49

or data. This is a loaded statement but accurate. If you refer back to our discussion on the systems development life cycle in Chapter 2, you will see that design, one of the earlier stages, can be a significant source of vulnerabilities. Small errors in design decisions can lead to major failures in production. In many instances, the design of an application reflects a naïve view of how the application might be used.

Exposure: The revelation of information about a system that can be used to assist an attacker in exploiting one or more vulnerabilities. Version number of an application is an example of data that may reveal potential vulnerabilities. Knowledge of a vulnerability or potential vulnerability can be considered an exposure. It is information that generally is not necessary for the user population to have since it is not the intended function of the owner of the system.

Target: A host, application, virtual host, or group of hosts that is in range of a scanning device and is designated for vulnerability assessment. When performing a scan, the scanner is directed at a target by its Internet protocol (IP) address, group of IPs, or name. A target is simply the subject of a scan. It may be specified or discovered automatically.

Discovery: A phase in the scanning process that finds targets connected to the network segment in a specified range.

Scan configuration: The set of parameters used to create a planned scanning event. This may include IP address range, ports, dates and times, bandwidth limits, credentials, or special checks to perform.

Vulnerability check: Exactly what it sounds like; a particular set of items to check on a target that may reveal the presence of a vulnerability.

Compliance check: Similar to a vulnerability check, this does not necessarily discover a vulnerability but a failure to comply with established company policy. For example, if passwords are required to be at least 10 characters long, the compliance check will generate an event to record instances where the password is outside of the requirement, in this case shorter than 10 characters.

Security posture: The net resulting security state of a host, network, or organization based on the factors affecting that state.

Attack vector: Akin to a vulnerability, an attack vector is the basic strategy used by a miscreant to compromise a system. This includes the exploitation of one or more vulnerabilities or design deficiencies.

Common Vulnerabilities and Exposures (CVE): A list of common names provided by MITRE Corporation (cve.mitre.org) for vulnerabilities that are publicly known. This is a popular list of vulnerabilities used as a reference when analyzing and remediating vulnerabilities. It is not the only source available nor should it be considered complete. But, it does bring a degree of standardization to the identity of vulnerabilities.

Scanner: A vulnerability scanner in the form of software or hardware that performs vendor and user-designated checks. Scan configurations are sometimes used to specify which scanner will perform the checks.

Audit: The scanning of one or more targets to determine the vulnerabilities present.

Vulnerability assessment: Synonym for audit; commonly referred to as an assessment.

It is expected that you will already have a good knowledge of networks and popular operating systems. Also, throughout most of our discussions, we will assume that the target environment predominantly uses IPv4. Although IPv6 is an emerging standard, its use is still not sufficiently widespread to justify a lengthy discussion. Furthermore, none of the VM tools on the market today appear to support IPv6 host discovery or scanning.

4.2 General Architecture

Here, we will discuss in depth the components and their interaction in three types of architectures: stand-alone hardware, agent, and passive network analysis. We will not discuss the software architecture because it is so similar to stand-alone hardware. The primary difference is that the vendor is not supplying and maintaining hardware.

4.2.1 Hardware: The Appliance Model

The hardware appliance model is exactly that: hardware with built-in software to perform the desired vulnerability scans. The devices typically are placed throughout a network and report back to a central server. The scanning appliances usually are complete but simple computer systems. A typical design has an operating system (OS), supporting software modules, and the specialized code written by the developers to perform scans and communicate results. Some vendors use open-source tools, and others will use a commercial OS and components.

One major advantage of a hardware-based system is that the vendor will have in-depth knowledge about the configuration of the host. The vendor takes responsibility for the maintenance and stability of that configuration. Any failure of the software to perform as advertised should be addressed in the client–vendor relationship.

In deployment, the hardware approach has the disadvantage of having to be shipped to the location and installed by someone who may not be qualified to do so. In most cases, however, deployment is not so complex. If the local technologist can configure a typical host computer, he or she can configure a vulnerability scanner. If you are uncertain about the capabilities of local personnel, then you may be well-advised to preconfigure the device and provide simple installation instructions.

In most designs, each scanner will report back to a central server. The vulnerability and compliance information collected will be transmitted back to the server for analysis and reporting. Devices will also receive assessment instructions over the network. Those instructions may be delivered by polling, on-demand connection, or through reverse polling. The impact of these strategies will be minimal but important, depending on your network security architecture.

Polling is the process of taking a poll of the vulnerability scanners associated with a central server. Each scanner typically is contacted through a transmission control protocol (TCP) port with special authentication methods that keep the entire conversation encrypted. The devices that are polled may be only those for which the server has a job prepared or in progress. The server checks the status to see if any data are available or if the unit is ready to accept a job. This approach can be cumbersome but has the advantage of only requiring a connection originating from the server. In some cases, not all scanners are polled unless there is scheduled work that can result in not knowing the status of a scanner until that time. Most vendors that poll will poll all scanners. Figure 4.1 illustrates the simple polling approach.

Reverse polling is the process whereby each scanner contacts the server on a regular basis. Should there be a job scheduled for the scanner, it would then be

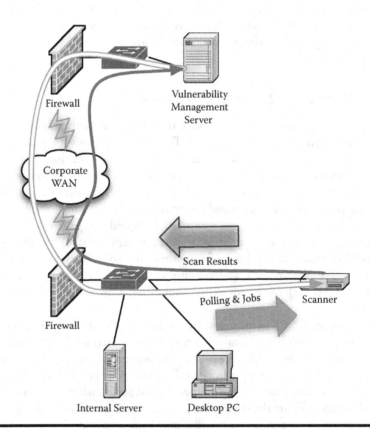

Figure 4.1 The simple polling approach.

provided. The same strong authentication and encryption methods apply. The scanner will send the results of the scan back to the central server either during the scan or at the conclusion, depending on the software designer's choice. This approach has the added advantage of allowing the scanner to complete a local job even if the connection with the server is lost. The scan results may simply be cached until a connection can be re-established.

Reverse polling also has an advantage when deployed in a secure zone where inbound communications to the scanner may be undesirable in order to limit possible external connections. This is also a disadvantage should the scanner be deployed outside the organization's boundaries because accommodations must be made in the security infrastructure for connections from the scanner.

4.2.2 User-Supplied Hardware and Virtualization

This is similar to the appliance approach; the distinction is that you provide your own hardware to support the vulnerability tool. This is obviously very common with open-source products such as Nessus®. Most vendors prefer not to offer software-only solutions because they are difficult to support on a large user base with large variations in the hardware. A well-controlled hardware platform will provide more consistent performance and predictable behavior, enabling vendors to squeeze out all the necessary performance for the product and meet customer expectations. This will become more apparent later when we discuss the operating details of a vulnerability assessment tool.

A solution more palatable to vendors is a virtual machine version of their products. The hardware environment is more predictable and manageable in a virtual machine because it is abstracted and controlled by the underlying hypervisor. Precise specifications can be made for the amount of memory, CPU, network connections, and other hardware elements to be made available to the product. Also, the OS version and configuration are controlled by the vendor, which eliminates errors in configuration and provides more predictable, supportable behavior.

Some major advantages of the virtual machine approach are easy deployment in a virtual environment, power savings, no shipping costs to remote facilities, and more efficient use of existing hardware.

4.3 Agents

Agent technology has come a long way since its inception using the rudimentary technology of the 1990s. For several years, "agent" was a bad word to systems engineers because they were blamed for lack of stability and impact on system reliability. Once operating systems improved memory and process-handling capabilities, agents developed to enhance the functionality of systems and people without requiring their direct involvement. The key distinction between an agent and a utility is that an agent can accept a set of instructions or parameters and then continuously and autonomously pursue the results. An agent is more than a tool. It is an assistant. The capabilities of vulnerability agents are relatively simple in comparison to what has been envisioned by systems designers.

4.3.1 Agent Architecture

Agents typically execute one or more services in the background of a system with system privileges sufficient to carry out their purposes. These services normally consume very little CPU resources except when requested to perform a major task. Usually, at least two services are running at any given time with other active services, depending on the architecture of the product. Vulnerability assessment agents are inextricably linked to the audit of the target, whereas appliances can be used for more than one audit method.

As shown in Figure 4.2, one service listens on the network for configuration and assessment instructions from a controlling server. This same service or an additional

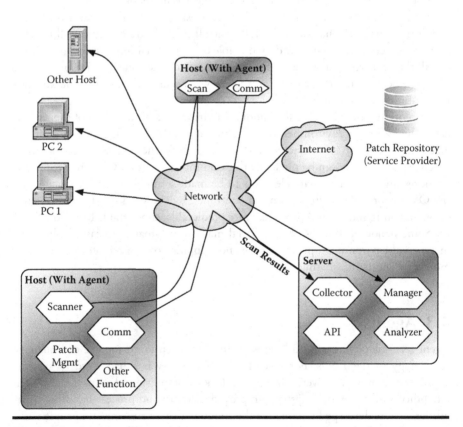

Figure 4.2   Agent architecture.

service may be used to communicate assessment results back to the server. The second service is one that performs the actual vulnerability assessment of the local host and, in some cases, adjacent hosts on the network.

The basic kinds of agents include the following:

Autonomous: They do not require constant input and operation by another system or individual.

Adaptive: They respond to changes in their environment according to some specified rules. Depending on the level of sophistication, some agents are more adaptive than others.

Distributed: Agents are not confined to a single system or even a network.

Self-updating: Some consider this point not to be unique to agents. For VM, this is an important capability. Agents must be able to collect and apply the latest vulnerabilities and auditing capabilities.

A VM agent is a software system, tightly linked to the inner workings of a host, which recognizes and responds to changes in the environment that may constitute a vulnerability. VM agents function in two basic roles. First, they monitor the state of system software and configuration vulnerability. The second function is to perform vulnerability assessments of nearby systems on behalf of a controller. By definition, agents act in a semiautonomous fashion. They are given a set of parameters to apply to their behavior, and they carry out those actions without further instruction. An agent does not need to be told every time it is to assess the state of the current machine. It may not even be necessary to instruct the agent to audit adjacent systems.

Unlike agents, network-based vulnerability scanners typically are provided detailed instructions about when and how to conduct an audit. The specifics of each audit are communicated every time one is initiated. By design, agents are loosely coupled to the overall VM system so they can minimize the load and dependency on a single server.

The method of implementation involves one or more system services along with a few on-demand programs for functions not required on a continuous basis. For example, the agent requires a continuous supervisory and communication capability on the host. This enables it to receive instructions, deliver results, and execute audits as needed. Such capabilities take very little memory and few processor cycles.

Specialized programs are invoked as needed to perform more CPU-intensive activities such as local or remote network audits. These programs in effect perform most of the functions found in a network vulnerability scanner. Once completed, the information gathered is passed onto the supervisory service to be passed back to the central reporting and management server.

The detection of local host vulnerabilities is sometimes carried out by performing an audit of all configuration items on the target host in a single, defined process during a specific time window. An alternative approach is to monitor the configuration state of the current machine continuously. When a change is made, the intervening vulnerability assessment software evaluates the change for vulnerabilities and immediately reports the change to the management server. This capability is intertwined today in the growing endpoint security market. The detection of configuration changes and added capability of applying security policy blurs the relationships among endpoint protection, configuration compliance, and vulnerability audit. This combination will ultimately lead to tighter, more responsive security.

4.3.2 Advantages and Disadvantages

A significant advantage of this agent approach is the scalability gained from its distributed nature. Since the number of agents deployed is only limited by the number of compatible hosts and licensing costs, it is theoretically possible to perform an audit of every machine without generating any network activity except to configure the agent and report results. Although the audit is not performed over the network, the communication between the agent and the server is not always minimal. Depending on the complexity of the host and vulnerabilities, considerable reporting traffic can be generated. Nevertheless, the scan does not take place over a network link.

Some obvious advantages are that there need be little concern for deploying additional hardware, and there is less concern that sufficient bandwidth and scanner resources are available.

Agents are encumbered, however, by a few basic problems:

- They may conflict with other applications running on the target. This is a common problem for all software running on complex computer systems today. Testing is the only solution.
- They may not have sufficient privileges in local security policy to audit every configuration item.
- They may have errors that cause them to terminate, and notification of failure may not come to the management server for some time, during which an audit window could be missed.
- Agents may not be available for the OS maker and version in use. Almost everyone makes an agent for Microsoft Windows® but far fewer will support Linux®, FreeBSD®, or Solaris™.
- Imbedded systems such as cash registers and other point-of-sale devices are tightly built and leave no accommodation for agents. Yet, payment card industry (PCI) security standards require file integrity monitoring on these systems.
- Given the limited size, space, and performance of an agent, it will not likely have the ability to cover the thousands of possible vulnerabilities.
- On virtual machines, there can be many agents running simultaneously, which can adversely impact the performance of the underlying hardware and host OS.

■ The agent itself can become a target of an attacker as a result of a vulnerability. Since agents typically listen on the network for instructions from a server, an opening is available for exploitation.

The vulnerability audit agent has many advantages over other methods:

■ It sees all vulnerabilities, some of which are not available over the network unless the scan is authenticated.
■ The agent can run even when the system is not connected to a network.
■ It does not actively engage with the software installed on the system to find a vulnerability, thus minimizing the chance of disrupting operations.
■ Since it does not operate over the network, it will not draw the attention of a network intrusion prevention system (IPS), nor will it create excessive network traffic. In fact, the total traffic load is likely far less than typical Web surfing activity.
■ As locally running software, it can extend functionality into more active endpoint security functions.

4.3.3 Detection Methods

Agents have a far more integrated view into the inner workings of a host. They are placed in a position to be aware of any changes to the system as soon as they occur. Although implementation does not always take this approach, doing so brings it much closer to sharing capabilities with endpoint security agents.

File checksums, the contents of registry entries, and configuration files are analyzed for vulnerabilities. Since the type of host is well-known to the agent, the specific set of necessary vulnerability checks are known in advance. Since the agent typically runs as a system process, it has access to all of the files and even memory space necessary to make an accurate assessment the instant a change takes place. Only updates need be sent to the agent from a central server to continue accurate detection. Network scanning methods may require more time to detect the changes since they typically do not scan a single host constantly.

Some agents also possess the ability to perform some network-based active scanning checks against other targets in the network. Most configuration plans allow only for scanning of adjacent systems on the same physical network.

4.4 Passive Network Analysis

Passive network analysis involves installing a piece of equipment on a network switch to listen to a copy of the traffic and analyze it for vulnerabilities. This is similar in functional design to an intrusion detection system (IDS) or a sniffer. A piece of hardware with a network port is connected to the network switch carrying the

Table 4.1 Active and Passive Scanner Comparison

Type of Network Traffic	Active Scanner	Passive Analyzer
ARP	From single VLANs	From multiple VLANs, including remote ones
TCP.IP of target	From actively scanned target	From multiple targets, any talking on monitored VLANs
VLAN tags	From connected VLANs	From multiple VLANs
Protocols observed	Only those in the parameters specified for the scan	Any and all protocols used by the host
Applications discovered	Those that the scanner knows to find, including non-network applications	Any applications that use the network connection

Note: ARP = address resolution protocol. VLAN = virtual local area network. TCP.IP = transmission control protocol/Internet protocol.

traffic to be examined. A command on the network switch sends a copy of much of the switch traffic to that physical port where the analyzer can read it. Alternatively, a network tap can be used to inspect traffic in a single physical network connection. That connection may carry large amounts of consolidated traffic from multiple networks.

The analyzer looks for several things that can reveal vulnerabilities. The IP addresses, network, application protocols, and general communication patterns are all checked for anomalies or attributes that reveal an exploitable flaw. Table 4.1 shows what the passive vulnerability scanner might get to see when a network tap or port mirror feature is applied compared to what is seen by a vulnerability scanner. Notice that the active scanner has access to information that is not found on the network, whereas the passive scanner possibly has access to information for which the active scanner does not scan.

Port mirroring, also called a switched port analyzer (SPAN) by Cisco, is a very commonly available technology in modern network switches. Figure 4.3 explains how SPAN works. This is a basic SPAN configuration where the contents of a pair of virtual local area networks (VLANs) are copied to a physical port on the switch. The network administrator has the option of specifying ingress traffic only, egress traffic only, or both ingress and egress traffic; typically, both are desirable so that the analyzer can see each side of the conversation. There are complications and limitations to the SPAN function that will vary by model, brand, and features installed on the switch. Some simple switches can only copy traffic that is coming

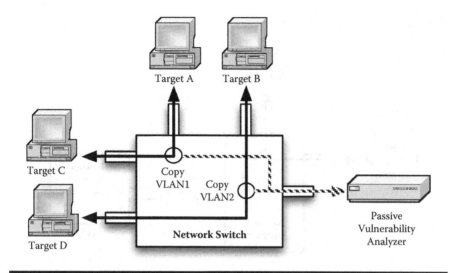

Figure 4.3   A basic SPAN configuration where the contents of a pair of VLANS are copied to a physical port on the switch.

in via a physical port and not off the backplane of the switch. Some can see traffic on a single VLAN, and others can look at trunked VLANs.

One interesting aspect of SPANs that you might notice is that it seems that the analyzer must be connected to the physical switch carrying the traffic to be analyzed. But, there is a modification of SPANs that addresses this issue to limited extent. Remote SPAN (RSPAN) is available on some switch models that allow SPAN results from remote switches to be forwarded to another switch to which the analyzer can be connected. Some of the capabilities for SPANs can become quite exotic at this point. Your network administrator will have to evaluate the requirements carefully and determine the most efficient way to provide the appropriate information to the analyzer. Figure 4.4 shows an RSPAN implementation where targets A and B are monitored on a remote switch (#1). The copy of the traffic is sent to the local switch (#2), where the passive analyzer is connected.

Generally, the traffic that is copied is referred to as being "flooded" onto a special VLAN shared between two or more switches. On Cisco products, this approach requires the creation of an RSPAN VLAN. This is a special VLAN that the switch understands is designed for remote monitoring. With this technique, it is possible to assess vulnerabilities using multiple devices in multiple locations.

It is also possible to include this RSPAN VLAN connection in a wide-area network (WAN) configuration where the remote switch is 100 miles away. This would be an atypical configuration with some bandwidth risks. This leads us to a key disadvantage of the passive approach to vulnerability scanning. You cannot necessarily target remote locations for vulnerability assessment cost-effectively using the

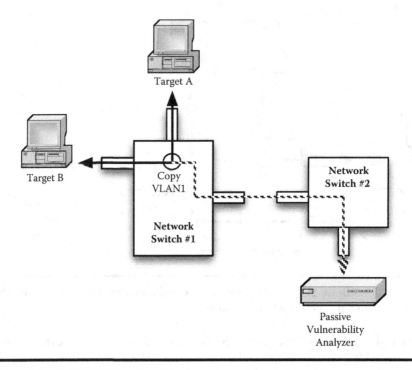

Figure 4.4 An RSPAN implementation where targets A and B are monitored on a remote switch (#1).

SPAN technique. Passive vulnerability analyzers are expensive. Remote locations with 20 to 30 targets talking to each other at 100 Mbps or even 1,000 Mbps are difficult and expensive to monitor since it is necessary to provide sufficient hardware to analyze a large traffic volume. Since it is unlikely to have a WAN link installed at 1 Gbps for monitoring purposes, and purchasing a unit to install locally is impractical, the use of a passive device is not always optimal.

Problems can occur with SPANs and RSPANs that must be assessed by a qualified network administrator. The monitor port, the one to which the analyzer is connected, can become oversubscribed. That is to say, more traffic is going to that port than the port can sustain. Much of that traffic is saved in a buffer that is shared with the networks being monitored. If that buffer becomes full, traffic will slow down for all the ports involved in the SPAN operation. This is easy to see if an analyzer is connected to a 100-Mbps port and is monitoring four other physical network ports with utilization exceeding 40 Mbps each. The total monitored is 160 Mbps. That means there is an additional 60 Mbps that the switch has to save until it can be delivered to the passive analyzer's port. To avoid this scenario, careful analysis of the peak traffic of each target/monitored port must be assessed. If there is an existing IDS/IPS implementation, these SPAN ports can be shared to economize.

An alternative approach to SPAN is a tap, which is precisely what it sounds like: a physical installation into a network connection that allows a passive analyzer to see the traffic. The tap can be electrical in the case of Ethernet or optical in the case of fiber. The Ethernet tap is a little more complex because it requires that power be supplied to the unit. Some taps even have built-in batteries to keep the tap operating should the power supply fail. The optical taps typically do not require any electricity but instead employ a prism known as a beam splitter.

A tap has the disadvantage of managing duplex. Since most networks today are built to send and receive data simultaneously, the analyzer must be able to do the same. In a 100-Mbps Ethernet example, a single cable connected to the analyzer can only listen to either the sending or receiving traffic among the monitored targets. Between two targets, there could be transmission and reception, with each occurring at up to 100 Mbps. So, the total throughput is 200 Mbps, which exceeds the capability of the single analyzer port connection. This problem is addressed by the tap by breaking the conversation up into two separate cables connected to the analyzer. The analyzer then bonds these two sides of the conversations together internally in order to analyze them accurately.

4.4.1 Advantages and Disadvantages

The passive analysis approach has several advantages:

- The analyzer does not interact with the network to discover hosts and their related vulnerabilities. Only the interface through which the user accesses the software to get reports is active.
- Little to no testing is required to be certain there is no negative impact on the network or hosts. Since the technology is completely passive, little verification is required. Even if the device physically fails, it is not placed inline where it would have to handle the bits on the wire.
- Sometimes, the device can be installed in tandem with an existing IDS. This greatly simplifies implementation without any changes to the network switch.
- The discovery process takes place continuously. New hosts are revealed as soon as they are connected to the network and begin communicating. In contrast to the active scanning and agents, vulnerabilities may not be known until the next scan cycle.
- Hidden hosts can be discovered that do not listen for active probing traffic on the network. Instead, these hosts only communicate by initiating conversation on the network and can therefore only be detected passively.
- Since routing protocols and other network information are also visible to the traffic analyzer, it may also be able to map the topology of the network and use this information to create a picture of the attack surface of a more complex network. This type of information can also be obtained by authenticated active scans and by providing configuration data to specialized tools.

There are also some interesting disadvantages to this technology:

- The device typically must be installed on the switch that carries the traffic to be monitored. Remote monitoring of a network often is not practical over a busy WAN connection. This will limit the number of locations that can be scanned. If your organization requires monitoring on a broad geographic scale, this may not be the right technology.
- The mechanism that copies switch traffic to the physical device can cause additional CPU load on the switch. That additional load can lower the performance of routing, access control, or other CPU-intensive operations.
- There is limited visibility into vulnerabilities. Many of the vulnerabilities that can be detected with a host agent or active, authenticated network scan cannot be detected by analyzing network traffic.

Overall, passive analysis may not see as many vulnerabilities on systems but they function 24 hours a day and provide network topology information that would otherwise be unavailable. Changes to the environment on the network and hosts would be detected first using the passive analysis method if those vulnerabilities have a network footprint.

4.4.2 Detection Methods

Detecting vulnerabilities using passive analysis is completely dependent upon being able to dissect and interpret the communication content in all layers of the Open Systems Interconnection (OSI) Model.[1]

4.4.3 Physical Layer

The physical network layer generally is not checked for any vulnerabilities by passive technology. Physical connections are terminated at the network interface adapter on the hardware platform on which the software is deployed. The silicon usually provides minimal information about the physical connection state.

4.4.4 Data Link Layer

This layer is only tested when the vulnerability scanner is connected to the network in a non-promiscuous mode. This means that the scanner will be able to interact with this layer of the network to acquire an IP address in a dynamic environment. The detection capability generally is limited to the switch to which the device is connected. Information can be gathered about other hosts connected to the switch, basic switch configuration items such as speed and duplex, as well as how the switch responds to variations in collision sensing and detection protocols such as carrier-sense multiple access with collision detection (CSMA/CD) in the Institute of Electrical and Electronics Engineers standard, IEEE 802.3 specification. In general, a passive vulnerability analyzer will look for deviations from the IEEE standards.

4.4.5 Network Layer

The network layer is subject to substantial variation. IP addressing, flags, routing information, and option parameters can combine uniquely to identify a host and vulnerabilities. Some of these same combinations will be explored later in Section 4.5, so we will not go into detail here. Suffice it to say at this point that there is an abundance of information to be obtained from the network layer in any network-connected vulnerability assessment technology.

4.4.6 Layers 4 Through 7

The remaining layers can provide large amounts of information about the targets under examination. The passive analyzer will dissect these layers and search for patterns of behavior in the interaction of systems, as well as the specific content of a single packet. It is a complex process with many methods of analysis, and it is more akin to an IDS in design.

4.5 Active Scanning Technology

Active scanning involves using software that can generate packets on the network to actively engage the targets in order to detect their presence and vulnerabilities. It is a more complex but highly scalable approach that is the most popular today. The scanner is connected to the network just as any other host. The position of the scanner relative to the targets is critical in getting the best results. We will talk more about this later.

Active scanning essentially emulates the behavior of hackers to discover targets, with one critical difference. Hackers use tools and techniques designed to conceal their activities, whereas legitimate active scanning tools do not. Scanners also can perform some of the exploits to determine susceptibility. The degree to which these exploits are performed depends on options selected in the scan configuration. Most products avoid using exploits that might have adverse effects on the target without specific selection by the administrator in the scan configuration. Furthermore, it should be understood that most commercial tools are designed to detect vulnerabilities not exploit them. Although they can be used as part of a penetration test, there are other, more appropriate tools to complete such a task.

4.5.1 Advantages and Disadvantages

Some key advantages of active scanning:

- Highly scalable because scanning takes place from a central location or distributed locations of the security architect's choice and does not require software installation on the targets.
- The technology can provide a hacker's view of the network and targets, so the vulnerability manager can have a realistic view of their risks in the production environment.
- Potential to support any networked device, that is, not limited to a compatible platform for an agent.
- Can provide incremental information regardless of platform support (e.g., open ports, identified protocols/applications, banners) even when the VM system has not previously seen the device.

The disadvantages are:

- If the target is not connected to the network, it will not be scanned. Agents can detect a vulnerability when it occurs and report the results the next time the host is connected to the network.
- A potential exists for impact on the network infrastructure since all scanning is so performed. However, some basic planning will prevent such adverse effects.
- Scanning is slower over slow network connections. This is typical in small offices with weak links. Today, we see this frequently in South America, Africa, and some parts of Asia.

4.5.2 Detection Methods

The process of assessing vulnerabilities has three phases: discovery, reconnaissance, and white box testing. The discovery process entails identifying all hosts connected to a particular network or IP range as specified in the scan configuration. Reconnaissance is a process whereby the hosts are profiled for the type, version, and passively detectable vulnerabilities. This is done through creative use of protocols and analysis of application behavior. Once a host is identified, white box testing uses privileged access to gather more information.

4.5.2.1 Discovery

As the name implies, the discovery phase is very active in using key protocols on the network to detect the presence of a target. Not all protocols are reliable, so several can be used. For reasons that will become apparent, sometimes it is necessary to use multiple protocols to verify the presence of the target.

4.5.2.1.1 ICMP

Generally, Internet Control Message Protocol (ICMP) echo requests are used for identification of a host. This is not a perfect solution because, in some cases, network and security devices can interfere or block ICMP types or the protocol altogether. Should the host respond with an echo reply, then the system will note that there is an active host present, and it will be added to the list of targets for the reconnaissance phase. Some tools will use other ICMP types, depending on the environment and approach of the designers.

4.5.2.1.2 Manipulating TCP

Some scanners do not consider ICMP to be reliable since some hosts are configured not to respond to ICMP. So, a TCP synchronization (TCP SYN) packet is sometimes sent using several common ports found on a variety of network devices. Table 4.2 lists some common ports that are scanned to determine whether a host is present.

Other ports may also be scanned, depending on the vendor and how one might configure this phase. Once the SYN packet is sent to the host, a reply of SYN-ACK (synchronization acknowledged) is expected. Should this reply not arrive in time, the scanner will consider the port not responsive and the host not present, that is, unless the host responds on another port. The discovery of these ports is not necessarily a serial process. The scanner may "spray" the TCP SYN packets on many ports and at many hosts simultaneously. This saves time and makes more efficient use of bandwidth. Some performance issues will be discussed later.

Table 4.2 Commonly Scanned Ports

Port	Protocol
20	FTP
21	FTP
22	SSH
23	Telnet
80	HTTP
443	HTTPS
137	NetBIOS Name Service
138	NetBIOS Datagram Service
139	NetBIOS Session Service

Note: FTP = File Transfer Protocol; SSH = Secure Shell; HTTP = Hypertext Transfer Protocol; HTTPS = Hypertext Transfer Protocol/Standard port; NetBIOS = Network Basic Input/Output System.

One potential side effect of the TCP discovery method is the potential for leaving open or half-open sockets. This can have an adverse effect on a system, depending on the application listening and the integrity of the OS protocol stack. Half-open sockets occur when the scanner does not complete the connection setup with an ACK packet. The effects range from memory consumption to denial of service (DoS) for production systems. Normally, this is not a problem since only one active connection is attempted per TCP port. However, a misconfigured scan can change this. A similar phenomenon exists when scanning through a firewall. Many firewalls will function as a proxy for the connection to the host. This imposes a load on the firewall when hundreds or thousands of hosts are scanned at once. Some routers can be impacted as well when they are undersized for their operating environment.

If the connection handshake is completed with an ACK packet, an entry in a connection table is maintained on the host and/or on a firewall. The result is a further consumption of resources until the connection times out or is reset. For that reason, it is important to test the behavior of a scanner and determine whether or not a TCP reset is sent to the host and how that behavior might affect your network on a large scale. If it is possible that a large amount of scanning will be performed through a firewall, then test this scenario. The setup and breakdown of connections on a firewall are two of the more processor-intensive tasks and can degrade performance. This is not absolute, however. Proper scheduling, bandwidth shaping, and connection limits in the scan configuration can help prevent these problems. Figure 4.5 illustrates a scenario where a firewall may be significantly affected by multiple simultaneous scans. As you can see, the total number of connections per second can add up quickly. A scan is far more intense than regular network traffic because it is concentrated into a short time period.

Conversely, a firewall, with all the additional security features that vendors have added, can interfere with a discovery scan. For example, some firewall vendors have

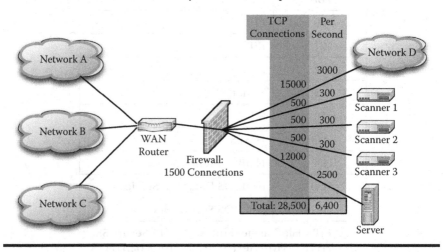

Figure 4.5 A scenario where a firewall may be significantly affected by multiple simultaneous scans.

added intrusion prevention capabilities as well as a SYN proxy. These features can provide false information to a vulnerability scanner, making it seem as though a host exists where there is none. This is because many scanners consider a closed port "response" to indicate the presence of a host. Otherwise, why would there be a response?

These security features can also do the reverse and obfuscate the host and its open ports. Hopefully, the firewall vendor will have the built-in ability to make an exception to the traffic by source IP address. With the correct IP address of the scanner configured in an exception list, the scan should proceed without error.

However, not all firewalls are created equal. For this reason, we will spend a little time discussing packet processing in a firewall as it is related to VM. Figure 4.6

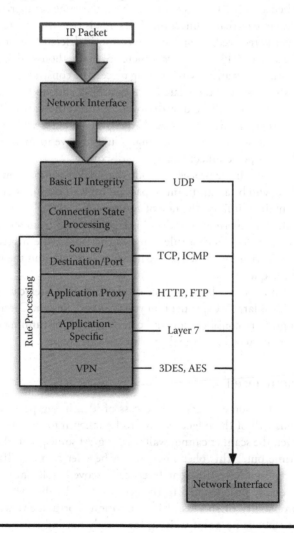

Figure 4.6   The basic structure of how a firewall might handle traffic.

shows the basic structure of how a firewall might handle traffic. Notice the stacked architecture. The reason for this is to qualify traffic for the most fundamental flaws prior to investing more processing cycles. For example, if the TCP flags are an invalid combination, the traffic should be dropped. Much of this processing can be performed in silicon and avoid burdening the firewall CPU further. On the other hand, if traffic is to be processed by some rules, more CPU cycles are required.

The next step in packet processing is to save and monitor the connection state. If a SYN packet is received from a vulnerability scanner, it is compared to entries in a connection table. If the connection already exists, then this is likely a duplicate and the packet is dropped. If the connection does not exist, then an entry is made in the table. When a SYN-ACK packet is received, the same comparison is made to keep track of the state of that connection. The same is true with all related packets. If an RST packet is received, then the connection is deleted from the table. This process can take a lot of CPU resources if there are many thousands of connections per second and other firewall activities taking place. The constraints of this connection table data structure and the related programming code to handle the packets are the parts most crucially affected by discovery scans. If the state table is too small a data structure, then the SYN/SYN-ACK discovery process will rapidly fill this table. If that constraint shows up in testing, you will have to make sure that you limit the number of open connections during discovery.

On the other hand, if the processing code that makes comparisons to this table is inefficient, there will be a significant impact on firewall throughput. In this case, it is vital to maintain a limit on the rate of connections.

Most firewalls process rules in order. A packet is taken from a queue for comparison against the rules. Once a rule matches the traffic, the inspection process stops. The packet is then forwarded to the network interface and the next packet is extracted from the queue.

Another way to avoid a large impact on firewalls is to relocate the scanners around them. This is largely dependent on your network design. Careful placement of scanners is a primary consideration and can be crucial to scanning effectiveness. This topic will be discussed in more detail later in this chapter.

4.5.2.1.3 Performance Issues

We have discussed at some length the process of identifying ports and handling TCP connections. All of these factors have to be taken into consideration during the scan; however, the scanner cannot wait too long. At some point, the transaction attempt will "time out." This phenomenon can be referred to as discovery tolerance. Various vendors have different levels of discovery tolerance. The amount of tolerance is loosely proportional to the accuracy of the discovery with rapidly diminishing probability of successful identification. Fortunately, we know from experience that there is no point waiting for a reply beyond a certain amount of time. Determining that point is the real skill in any fingerprinting activity. The goal is to be complete and accurate, but there is a law of diminishing returns. Two key timers affect the speed of the discovery process: the connection establishment timer and the retransmission timer.

For many TCP implementations, the connection establishment timer (TCP_ KEEPINIT parameter) waits 75 seconds for a response. A simple scan on a single port for 200 hosts would require over four hours to complete if none of the hosts responded. This must be adjusted to wait far less time. One effective approach is to take the maximum round-trip time (RTT) of ICMP echo reply exchanges and add two seconds. This provides ample time for an application to respond on the required port and is likely to be far shorter than the default of 75 seconds.

With TCP connections, a discovery process can also vary the retransmission timer when additional packets are to be exchanged with the target. In normal communications, the timer begins with a value of 1.5 seconds. If no response is received, then the value is doubled to three seconds. If there is still no SYN-ACK, the timer is doubled again and we wait six seconds. This continues repeatedly until we reach a limit of 64 seconds. The process is called exponential backoff (EB). In theory, this should parallel the exponential probability that a response will ultimately be received. However, this is often impractical for host discovery purposes in vulnerability scanning. A typical OS can spend several minutes waiting for a connection to time out.

A more practical approach would be to sequentially increase the retransmission timer by smaller values for a total period of time to be some factor above the average for the target IP range. For example, let's suppose that we are performing a discovery of network A (192.168.10.0/24) with an upper limit of 30 seconds for retransmission. If the first 16 hosts required an average of 10 seconds to respond and the mode was five seconds, we might start our retransmission timer at five seconds and increase the value by five seconds until an upper limit of 20 seconds was reached (2 × average). This is a more sensible approach that will avoid a common IP stack value that can reach several minutes for a single connection. Remember that our goal is discovery of open ports and live hosts not the reliable transmission of data to another host.

There is one other item that can be manipulated, which is not exactly a timer and can speed the discovery process considerably:

> To implement all the timers, TCP only requires that two functions are called periodically: (1) the fast timer is called every 200 ms and (2) the slow timer every 500 ms. TCP uses these two periodic "ticks" to schedule and check all the timers described…as well as measuring round-trip times.[2]

Basically, the OS kernel must check every 200 ms to see if an acknowledgment has been received. In modern networks and operating systems, this is a very long time.

By decreasing this period, the discovery processes can recognize that the probing SYN packets it has sent have been acknowledged in a shorter time and move on to the next probe. If the RTT from SYN to SYN-ACK is 10 ms, then under normal circumstances, the discovery process can wait for up to 190 ms to proceed with the next action. Multiply this number by hundreds of hosts and dozens of ports, and the wasted time can be tremendous.

The one caveat to modifying TCP timers is that some applications are simply slow to respond. This approach works best when probing for open ports but not necessarily for applications. There is a lot of room for creativity in scan performance optimization. This section simply illustrates some of the challenges designers can be confronted with when trying to optimize the scan process and minimize the impact on the network.

4.5.2.2 Black Box Testing

Once the presence of a host has been established and that presence recorded in the memory of the scanner, a series of tests or "checks" are performed to find vulnerabilities. The types of checks are dependent upon the type of host and the configuration of the scanner. Generally, two types of checks are performed. A network-based or surface check is performed, which involves the probing and analysis of what is evident with limited or no access to services on the machine other than what is offered to any other peer on the same network as that which exists between the scanner and the target. This is also known as an unauthenticated check. The other type of check is an authenticated, internal check or white box test. It is performed when the scanner is given special information and credentials to access details of the host, which are generally reserved for trusted entities.

The difference between surface and internal checks is obviously significant not only in the way they obtain information but also in the value and quality of that information. Clearly, more detailed data can be obtained by logging into a host and perusing its configuration. Although the information tells us a lot about the host, it typically does not represent the view of an attacker who performs reconnaissance on an unknown host. Although valuable from an analysis standpoint, some attacks take place by probing the host from the view of an outsider; therefore, information that can be obtained in the same fashion is often more valuable. To summarize, a vulnerability discovered and exploitable from outside a host represents a greater exposure than if the same vulnerability could only be discovered and exploitable from a credentialed or internal check.

There is a common perception that authenticated checks are more accurate than remote checks, but that's often not true. The Windows registry is commonly used for authenticated checks but is often wrong. It's important to consider that not all authenticated checks are created equal and that a remote check is a good method of validating authenticated information.

The black box testing process involves some straightforward testing over the network and possibly some creative use of IP and other protocols. Usually, the simple tests are harmless and efficient. The more exotic manipulation of IP protocols can cause problems on scanned hosts with applications that are ill-prepared to handle many variations. This is a vulnerability in itself. The IP stack of the host usually is capable of handling nearly any variety of traffic, but the overlying applications sometimes are not. It is another area that calls for extensive testing in order to avoid adverse effects on production systems. Most vendors are able to provide a list of known negative application interactions.

Following is a list of some common methods of reconnaissance:

Malformed packets are sent to the host to identify the presence of a vulnerability in the response. This is similar to the discovery process and is sometimes incorporated into the same phase for efficiency. The information sent to the target can be at any one layer or multiple combinations of layers 3 through 7 in the OSI Model.

Normal packets are sent to a known application to obtain results that will reveal vulnerability information. This is very common in the HTTP protocol to obtain information about the Web server, application server, or back-end databases.

Valid information is sent to the target to gather valid header response data that will reveal the version of software answering the service request. This is known as banner checking. Many software applications can obfuscate this information with simple configuration changes, so it is not the most reliable method.

These methods can be summarized conceptually in pseudo code form:

```
Send X to target
Listen for response Y
Match Y to possible response list
If Y is on list, note vulnerability
If Y is not on list, ignore
Get next check; loop
```

4.5.2.2.1 Fingerprinting with TCP/IP

A simple method of fingerprinting is to use the well-understood ICMP. ICMP packets are used to monitor the state of an interface on a host or report the status of access to a connected device. Nine message types are available: four for making queries and five for reporting errors. Each type is defined by a number, as shown in Table 4.3. PING is a very popular program that sends ICMP type 8 messages. Type 8 is an echo request, whereas a type 0 is an echo reply. In addition to an

Table 4.3 ICMP Types

ICMP Code	Type	
0	Echo reply	
1–2	Unassigned	
3	Destination unreachable	
	Code	Meaning
	0	Net unreachable
	1	Host unreachable
	2	Protocol unreachable
	3	Port unreachable
	4	Fragmentation needed and don't fragment was set
	5	Source route failed
	6	Destination network unknown
	7	Destination host unknown
	8	Source host isolated
	9	Communication with destination network is administratively prohibited
	10	Communication with destination host is administratively prohibited
	11	Destination network unreachable for type of service
	12	Destination host unreachable for type of service
	13	Communication administratively prohibited
	14	Host precedence violation
	15	Precedence cutoff in effect
4	Source quench	
5	Redirect	
6	Alternate host address	
7	Unassigned	
8	Echo	
9	Router advertisement	

(Continued)

Table 4.3 *(Continued)* **ICMP Types**

ICMP Code	Type		
10	Router selection		
11	Time exceeded		
	Code	Meaning	
	0	Time to live exceeded in transit	
	16	Fragment reassembly time exceeded	
12	Parameter Problem		
	Code	Meaning	
	0	Pointer indicates the error	
	1	Missing a required option	
	2	Bad length	
13	Timestamp		
14	Timestamp reply		
15	Information request		
16	Information reply		
17	Address mask request		
18	Address mask reply		
19–29	Reserved		
30	Traceroute		
31	Datagram conversion error		
32	Mobile host redirect		
33	IPv6 Where-Are-You		
34	IPv6 I-Am-Here		
35	Mobile registration request		
36	Mobile registration reply		
39	SKIP		
40–254	N/A		

ICMP type, there is a code that is used to report more information about an error. By manipulating these codes into invalid values, the target's response or failure to respond can be captured. This in itself can tell us something about the OS. Some systems do not look at the code field on an echo request. Others do and respond with an error.

Another method of reconnaissance is known as IP fingerprinting. The concept is an elegant form of manipulating inputs into the protocol stack of a target and measuring the results. For a brief review, let's look at the TCP header structure in Table 4.4.

The most useful operational benefit of TCP is the fact that it guarantees delivery by acknowledging the receipt of each packet. That set of flags—SYN, ACK, and RST—are what tell the recipient the purpose of what is transmitted. Our vulnerability scanner is sending SYN packets to the target. But it is the behavior of the rest of the contents of the packet that can reveal something about the target. Sequence number is a good example. So that TCP listeners on hosts do not become confused, every packet includes a sequence number. Since the creation of the protocol, it was found that it is easily possible to "wrap" the sequence numbers because they are of limited size (32 bits). To address the potential for wrapping and having a duplicate sequence number with an old packet being mistaken for a sequence number of a new packet, a time-stamp option was introduced in RFC 1323. This is an optional field and not all operating systems' TCP/IP implementations set the value. When the scanner sees such a value sent when the time-stamp option was never used, the choice in operating systems is narrowed considerably.

Another phenomenon to measure is the incrementing of the time stamp. By first determining the RTT between the scanner and the target, you then know how much time should elapse between TCP segments. The remote OS will increment the time stamp on each segment by a certain value. The way in which the target increments the value can reveal the type of OS.

For example, we know that OS XYZ increments the time stamp by one for every 500 ms of uptime. The average RTT between the target and the scanner is 100 ms, which is 50 ms in each direction, as shown in Figure 4.7. We receive the first segment with a time stamp (TS1) of 100. We acknowledge this segment and start a timer. The second segment with a time stamp of 102 (TS2) arrives and we stop the clock. The elapsed time between segment 1 and segment 2 is 1100 ms. We know that the time in transit for the segments is 100 ms. So the clock value, 1100, minus the RTT, 100, gives us 1000 ms of elapsed time on the host between segments. The difference between TS2 and TS1 is two. This means that, in 1000 ms, the time-stamp value went up by two, which is 500 ms per time-stamp increment. Looking at a table of time-stamp values over time, we know that the target has incremented the time stamp by one for every 500 ms, which is OS XYZ. This technique combined with other fingerprinting methods will ultimately narrow the choice of OSs. This choice is important in determining future steps of vulnerability scanning.

Table 4.4 TCP Segment

0 1 2 3 4 5 6 7 8 9 10 11 12 13 14 15						16 17 18 19 20 21 22 23 24 25 26 27 28 29 30 31
Source Port						Destination Port
Sequence Number						
Acknowledgment Number						
Header Length	Reserved	URG	ACK	PSH	RST	SYN	FIN	Window Size
Checksum						Urgent Pointer
Options (up to 40 bytes)						End of Option
Data						

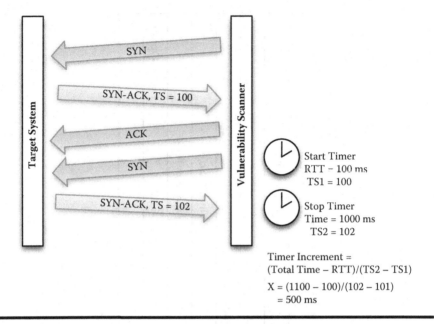

Figure 4.7 **The average round-trip time (RTT) between the target and the scanner is 100 ms, which is 50 ms in each direction.**

Invalid flag combinations are another approach. The normal combinations, SYN, SYN-ACK, and ACK, are expected. But various host OSs react strangely to combinations such as FIN+URG+PSH, which is a combination not seen in a normal handshake. It is referred to as an Xmas or Christmas scan because it lights up the TCP flags like a Christmas tree. Another combination that can possibly fingerprint an OS is SYN+FIN. In addition to host discovery, these types of scans can determine whether a port is open on a host without establishing a TCP connection or half-open connection. That is because IP stacks that adhere to the RFC will respond with an RST packet if the port is open. If closed, there will be no response from the host.

Use of these flags can get more sophisticated as well. If it has already been established that a port is open using a harmless TCP-SYN scan, the same port can be probed with a FIN-ACK combination. It turns out that systems implementing the IP stack from Berkley Standard Distribution (BSD) will not respond according to the RFC with an RST packet. This provides more evidence as to the likely system type of the target.

By combining these and many other types of probes, a decent guess can be made as to the type of system. The work for this has been well-established by the creators of Network Mapper (Nmap; www.nmap.org). They continue to discover new ways to scan and map targets on a network and build those techniques into their opensource tool. A little reading and experimentation with this can be very educational.

However, the topics of OS fingerprinting and IP stack fingerprinting can be tricky, unreliable, and confusing. Some OSs may share the same IP stack code but be different OS versions. For example, a variety of Linux distributions will use the same stack, but this does not necessarily reveal the flavor of the OS. Virtual machine technology can further cloud the issue because the underlying hypervisor OS may respond to network traffic and proxy the connection to the actual host OS. The fingerprinting result can be quite unexpected. Firewall and virtual machines can perform network address translation (NAT) that will conceal the true nature of the target OS.

4.5.2.2.2 Application Fingerprinting: Banners

An important activity in a scan is to determine what applications make themselves known on the network. Similar to OS fingerprinting and IP stack fingerprinting, a vulnerability scanner can attempt to connect to a variety of possible applications on known or unknown ports, a process known as featureprinting. Among the best-known featureprinting methods is banner checking.

Some common applications on systems produce a banner whenever you attempt to connect. The contents of this banner can provide valuable information in determining the version of the OS and the software running on the host. This type of fingerprinting can often be performed by an individual using a simple program available on almost all OS platforms: Netcat.

Let's take the example of a Web server. Figure 4.8 shows a typical Netcat session. When using Netcat, you can specify the TCP port to which you wish to connect. So, in the command line, we type "nc 10.1.1.10 80." This will run the Telnet application and establish a connection to the server listening for connections on port 80.

From here, we are able to issue a command to the remote server. Since this is port 80, it is likely a Web server; so we issue the command: "HEAD/HTTP/1.0" (Figure 4.8a). The server responds with some detailed header information, which tells the type of Web server software and OS. In this case, it is Apache® running on a UNIX® system. This eliminates the possibility of any version of Windows and makes searching for vulnerabilities much easier.

For security reasons, however, server administrators should conceal this header information, particularly the information that is in the "Server" section. But that will not deter a good vulnerability scanner. The scanner may also be able to check for the type of Web server by making an invalid request. By using an invalid version type in the HEAD command, we can see different responses from the various Web server makers. Notice that the Apache Web server comes out with a "400 Bad Request" message (Figure 4.8b). The connection also gets closed; however, on IIS 7.0, the connection is not closed, but the same "400 Bad Request" message is received. But you will also notice that more server information is provided that was not found in the valid request. In earlier versions of IIS,

```
$ nc 10.1.1.10 80
HEAD / HTTP/1.0                          Apache Example

HTTP/1.1 200 OK
Date: Tue, 06 May 2008 23:32:00 GMT
Server: Apache/2.2.8 (Unix)
Last-Modified: Tue, 29 Apr 2008 21:52:29 GMT
ETag: "ea9d61-48f6-44c0a0c71a140"
Accept-Ranges: bytes
Content-Length: 18678
Cache-Control: max-age=86400
Expires: Wed, 07 May 2008 23:32:00 GMT
Vary: Accept-Encoding
Connection: close
Content-Type: text/html
$_
```

(a)

```
$ nc 10.1.1.20 80                        IIS Example
HEAD / HTTP/1.0

HTTP/1.1 302 Found
Cache-Control: private
Content-Length: 142
Content-Type: text/html; charset=utf-8
Location: /en/us/default.aspx
Server: Microsoft-IIS/7.0
X-AspNet-Version: 2.0.50727
P3P: CP="ALL IND DSP COR ADM CONo CUR CUSo IVAo IVDo PSA PSD
TAI TELo OUR SAMo CNT COM INT NAV ONL PHY PRE PUR UNI"
X-Powered-By: ASP.NET
Date: Tue, 06 May 2008 23:58:41 GMT
Connection: keep-alive
$_
```

(b)

Figure 4.8   A typical Netcat session.

you could distinguish it from a reaction of providing a message of "200 OK." Similar methods are used where valid and invalid responses are captured and analyzed. In some cases, these are reported as vulnerabilities or simply information exposures.[3]

4.5.2.2.3 Other Fingerprinting Methods

Other kinds of fingerprinting are performed using protocols such as Simple Network Management Protocol (SNMP), which is a protocol framework that was designed to monitor and manage network devices. This capability is often extended to firewalls, IPSs, and even common hosts. In a bid to participate in

Version	Community	Request ID	Error Status	Error Index	Variables

Figure 4.9 The network manager software sends queries to devices using the SNMP protocol.

simple status-reporting capabilities as well as provide centralized administration of all devices on a network, SNMP has been implemented on just about everything.

Network manager software sends queries to devices using SNMP. These messages have a structure with the format shown in Figure 4.9:

Version specifies the version of the protocol in use. This is necessary so that the target knows how to process the message.

Community is essentially a password used to authenticate the sender of the request. In the example to follow, we will be manipulating this value to search for basic vulnerabilities as well as determine what the device is.

Request ID is a number similar to sequence number used in TCP. This same number would be in the reply to a request so that the requester knows which request the reply applies to. It is only a referential index.

Error status and *error index* are not relevant in this discussion. These values are used by the target when it originates an error message to report to a network management server. These messages are sent using UDP on ports 161 and 162. Although less reliable, UDP is efficient and seldom observed by security professionals because there is so much chatter among network devices using this protocol, it is difficult to observe improper behavior. Because there is no state as in TCP, the protocol is more difficult to abuse. On the other hand, UDP packets are easily spoofed and often pass through network security devices because the network engineers are making life simpler for themselves in order to collect vital network statistics.

Part of the fingerprinting process is to identify devices that have SNMP running. This can be done by issuing a "GetRequest" message using the default community string, "public." This is the same as setting a password to "password" on a conventional host. Some scanners also have the ability to cycle through the default community strings used on a variety of devices. They will also sometimes have the ability to try other community strings specified by the user. You could consider this approach a brute-force attack on the SNMP configuration.

Using a hierarchical structure known as a management information base (MIB), information about the target is requested. All kinds of information can be requested, some of it unique to a vendor. Many installations have SNMP enabled by default and therefore accept requests and expose information. The more common community strings are "public," "private," and "secret." There are also many well-known strings commonly used by specific vendors that go unchanged.

Similar to the approach of SNMP community strings, Telnet and SSH protocols can be fingerprinted. Sometimes, the name of the server or type of OS is presented to the interactive user prior to log-in. The strings that are presented are parsed by the scanner for key words such as "Windows" or "UNIX," etc. No log-in is required to see this information. However, with SSH, if a connection can be established, then we can definitively determine that the service is running and later make an attempt to discover related vulnerabilities.

Several other techniques exist for fingerprinting hosts. One great tool commonly available to illustrate some of these methods is Nmap. It can be found at www.insecure.org. This command-line tool has the ability to sweep through a range of IP addresses with various abuses and uses of the ICMP and TCP protocols. Some of the methods employed were discussed earlier. One should keep in mind that a commercial vulnerability-scanning tool makes great effort not to interfere with other equipment. Scans can still be detected by security equipment as well. It has never been the goal to be stealthy, only healthy.

The fingerprinting process can distinguish a scanner because the output can be used to determine the types of checks and accuracy of overall target vulnerability assessment. A basic understanding of fingerprinting has been provided so you can grasp the complexity of the task. Knowing the correct OS version can help identify which common applications to check for. Alternatively, discovering some applications first can make host identification more accurate as well. The art of coordinating these activities is a subtle but important one for accuracy.

4.5.2.3 White Box Testing

White box testing is a method of discovering vulnerabilities by providing authenticated, privileged, or "open" access to the system configuration so that normally unapparent details can be observed. This type of testing is found in both agent-based technology and active scanning.

4.5.2.3.1 Credentials

To perform this type of testing in an active scanning technology, special credentials are required to authorize remote access by the scanning process to the target. The type of credentials will vary by the target type. Common access methods used are SSH, Windows Management Instrumentation (WMI), Telnet, SNMP, server message block (SMB), and Remote Registry. Windows machines will typically require remote registry or WMI access, whereas *nix machines will use SSH.

One of the common authentication channels is through SNMP. This is a very common protocol used on network devices and printers. It is even found less commonly on general host computers such as desktops and servers. The protocol scheme consists of a management station or stations and several agents, each of which is running on a managed device. SNMP usually is found in three flavors: SNMPv1

(RFC 1157), v2, and v3. Versions 1 and 2 use community strings that function as a single password for execution of commands or gathering information from the managed device. There is no user ID and no way to definitively identify who executed what command. Furthermore, the community string is transmitted in cleartext and generally is considered insecure.

Part of the simplicity of SNMP is the fact that it uses UDP. For those who are unfamiliar with this protocol, it permits unconnected or unguaranteed transmission of packets over the network. This simplicity is also a weakness in SNMP that further allows the protocol to be abused in black box testing. Nevertheless, it is often necessary to use SNMP read-only community strings and commands to gather vulnerability information from targets.

SNMPv3 is enhanced to provide considerably more security. It has security elements to encrypt the content of the messages, authenticate the user making the request, and authenticate the source of the message to avoid spoofing or tampering. In effect, a user ID and password are supplied (secret key). The secret key is used to encrypt the message and include strong tamper resistance.

Telnet, SNMPv3, SMB, WMI, and Remote Registry will apply user ID and password. SSH can employ user ID and password or certificate. Hopefully, none of the targets will require cleartext credentials and Telnet access. This method does appear in many products that are old enough to lack other methods. It is often seen on the control interfaces of uninterruptable power supplies and legacy network equipment. Newer devices are offering SSH as a far superior alternative.

In a commercial VM system, these credentials typically are stored in an encrypted form until they are used. The real challenge is not the application of credentials, as this is well-established. It is the management and deployment of those credentials to the target devices that should be of the greatest concern. This will be discussed in more detail in the chapter on selecting technology, Chapter 5.

Every environment presumably has mostly managed targets. For example, in a large Microsoft Windows environment, Active Directory® is commonly used for authentication, identification, policy management, and basic software deployment. Active Directory can be used to create and deploy a single set of credentials for a given organizational unit or the entire enterprise. These credentials most likely can be installed on 95% of all machines under management. Nonconforming, local instances will likely be found for a few reasons. Some machines may not be a part of the Active Directory domain, which obviously prevents them from being managed. Others may be configured to prevent group policies from being applied. It could be that the application running on the target host may be disrupted by Active Directory activities. However, it may be possible to have the local administrator simply install those credentials manually.

Most of the effort in creating credentials will be and should be focused on getting noncompliant targets into the central management facility or manually installing credentials. These are the hosts that will always be a nuisance if not tackled head on. These hosts tend to linger unconfigured if not addressed up front. Since they are not subject to authenticated scans, their scores may remain misleadingly low and therefore attract little attention from the vulnerability manager.

With established credentials, white box testing can take place easily and quickly. Anything that can be executed from the protocol can be performed. Well, not exactly anything. As a matter of best practice, these credentials should have the minimum privileges necessary to complete the task. This usually means read-only privileges. Scanning in principle should never require the ability to change anything on the target. Anything else should be viewed through a skeptical lens. It may be a case of sloppy coding or software design or perhaps a too-aggressive approach to seeking vulnerabilities. In some rare circumstances, it is possible that the limitation of the target will allow access to critical pieces of information only when the credential is assigned "write" privileges. This usually is caused by oversimplification of privileges by a software developer on the target. Having dedicated credentials for a scan is also important for tracking its usage and ascribing accountability when auditing system access.

4.5.2.3.2 Scanning

When a target is checked for various vulnerabilities, the act generally is referred to as a scan. Think of a scan as a process in which checks are performed. Scanning requires a considerable amount of data collection, organization, and analysis before another check against the same target is performed. This level of complexity demands a hierarchical approach to gathering, storing, and processing of results. One simply does not keep a set of checks for each host type and then run them against the target. This can result in wasted processing, bandwidth, and—worse—corruption of the target. Like a doctor, as the good guys, we are ethically bound to do our best to "do no harm." It would be unacceptable if you visited a physician who never asked about your symptoms or reactions to various conditions but instead simply saw that you are human and performed a battery of tests, some of which may be invasive and irrelevant to your condition.

A more rational approach is to develop a profile of the target and then look for vulnerabilities consistent with that profile. For example, if Microsoft Office is installed on an OS, then there is no point in probing for vulnerabilities associated with WordPerfect®. In addition to running the risk of affecting the machine and consuming network bandwidth, it is also wastes valuable time that can be spent completing the scan of other hosts. It is not unusual to have a particular scanner with a carefully scheduled workload so that all the required scans can get completed in a timely manner to meet a typical reporting schedule.

Another subprocess performed during a scan of a host is a profile that closely resembles a software or configuration inventory. This inventory, once complete, is matched against a list of possible checks to perform for known vulnerabilities. The data structure for such a function resembles Table 4.5. Each process that performs a check searches the "Identifier" column to match the process name, protocol, and

Table 4.5   Vulnerability Database Structure

Identifier	VPointer	CPointer	Category	Description
HKLM/Software/ Mozilla/ CurrentVersion/ 20.0.0.14	9574839	9037593	OS	Mozilla 2.0
HKLM/Software/ Office/MSWord/ CurrentVersion/5	7752955	879	Productivity	MS Word 5.0
SSH: Netoper 14	773845	948346	Utility	Secure Copy (SCP)
TELNET: IOS 11	99175	86849	Network	Cisco IOS
BGP: TCP179 ACK	3980	8756	Protocol	Unfiltered BGP Peer
TCP50: AXFR	122	7112343	DNS	Unauthorized zone transfer permitted

Note: AXFR = Asynchronous Transfer Full Range; BGP = Border Gateway Protocol; DNS = Domain Name System; SCP = Security Certified Program.

result. That match will reveal the presence or absence of a vulnerability, any additional checks to perform, the description, and category. By combining other database tables with configuration parameters and host details, a scan is able to assign a value to the result.

For example, referring to Table 4.5, if a Telnet port generates a reply that contains "Cisco IOS 11*" during the discovery process, then this is compared to the "Identifier" in the table to find "CPointer" 86849. This CPointer directs the scanner to load and execute the checks found with that index. On the other hand, if the discovery or scan phase found "BGP: TCP 179 ACK" in the table, this is automatically known as a vulnerability without further interrogation of the target. Even so, there is still a CPointer indicating that the scanner must perform additional checks because the results of the scan have revealed simultaneously that this is a router running Border Gateway Protocol (BGP) and that there is a vulnerability. So, router checks must be performed in addition to recording the existing vulnerability.

Figure 4.10 shows the basic scanning process in its two constituent parts. The left side of the figure shows the overall scanning process. During this process, the discovery results are read and compared to the vulnerability table. When there is a match, a note of that match is made by creating and adding the list to a target vulnerability object. Once all the vulnerabilities for a particular target have been gathered, the process on the right side is instantiated. I say "instantiated" because more than one of these processes can run simultaneously. Then, the process on the left side repeats.

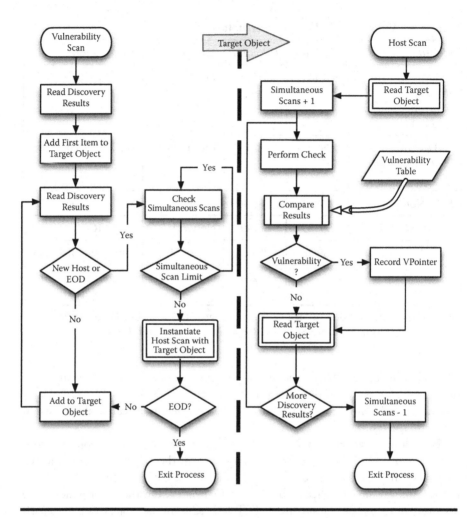

Figure 4.10 The basic scanning process in its two constituent parts.

This target scanning process continues until the process runs out of hosts to scan or the maximum number of simultaneous target scans is reached. When the maximum number of target scans is reached, the process waits until there is room for another instance. When the end of target data (EOD) is reached, the process terminates. Then, subsequent data collection and reporting activities begin. Those future activities will wait until all target scanning processes have completed—reach zero—before reporting all results.

The right side of the process is fairly straightforward. Each item in the list of vulnerabilities to check, CPointer, is read and the corresponding check performed. Once all of the checks are performed, the process exits. Notice that a successful exit of this process decrements the simultaneous scan counter by one, leaving room for the process on the left side to instantiate another. It is critical to take advantage of the multitasking capability of the processor for reasons previously mentioned. Serializing this process will only yield a protracted scan.

As I suggested before, a value will ultimately be assigned to the vulnerability found. This value, however, can be calculated in many ways and will depend on the particular scan software author's strategy. In good security practice and coding practice, this activity should not be performed during the scan. All resources should be dedicated to performing an accurate and timely scan without additional overhead. This also relates to our discussion about good coding practices. There is no benefit to calculating the value of a vulnerability during a scan. It does have value, however, in a later reporting phase. Furthermore, by introducing a value assignment algorithm in the scanning phase, the programmer may also inadvertently introduce a vulnerability or flaw to the code that can be exploited. This is just one more piece of complexity that can be excluded at such a critical stage.

4.5.2.3.3 Performance Matters

During a scan, the goal of the scanner is to get as complete and accurate a scan as possible. However, the performance and behavior of that scan is also important to the vulnerability manager. Ideally, we would like to scan as much as possible during an allotted time window and get complete results. However, we also want to avoid affecting production operations. First, let's look at the potential negative impacts to production and how we might avoid them. Then, we can look at ways to optimize scans.

In most cases, there are four ways in which a scan can adversely affect a production environment:

By consuming bandwidth, preventing other applications from meeting service levels.

By consuming target CPU resources in an already-busy target. Again, this can cause service levels to be missed.

By breaking a target application or OS, causing a DoS and requiring the target to be repaired.

By breaking a component that is facilitating the scan but is not a target. Various network components could be adversely affected by the scan process even though they are not the subject of a scan.

Bandwidth is consumed by network activity. During the scan process, parameters provided by the vulnerability manager are used to size the footprint on the network. Not only is bandwidth a factor, the number of simultaneous connections can affect intermediate devices as well. Since TCP is so commonly used, a connection is established with each target. In some cases, a connection is only attempted, leaving potentially half-open connections. Devices that track the state of connections such as firewalls, IPSs, and possibly routers, can be affected by these connections. The total number of simultaneous connections, and the rate at which these connections are made, may have an effect. Limits on both will go a long way toward maintaining good relations with network management staff.

The most efficient locations in the scanner to impose these limits are the IP protocol stack and interface drivers. Bandwidth limitations are best performed at the interface driver, whereas the connections limits are better applied at the packet-creation phase where the outgoing connections table is maintained. Exceptions must be made to accommodate the critical command and control functions of the scanner. Therefore, the location of the scanner management system should be exempt from such limits.

Bandwidth consumption has the biggest impact on the network when scanning is performed outside of the local segment to which the scanner is connected. In particular, WAN links can be impacted significantly. Using today's most cost-effective technology, most scanners are not able to produce more than 10 Mbps of bandwidth in a typical scan. However, when a T1 is the only connection from a remote office back to the corporate WAN where the scanner resides, it is easy to saturate the link event with a small scan. In most companies, it is often necessary to perform such a scan during work hours when desktop and laptop computers are powered on and connected to the network. So, the impact to business operations is significant.

To determine the appropriate amount of bandwidth to allow for a given target network, I recommend the following strategy:

1. Determine the peak utilization of the WAN link over a two-month period to coincide with the time in the business cycle during which you plan on running the scan. Alternatively, plan to run the scan during a time in the business cycle when bandwidth consumption is relatively low but the targets are still available for scanning.
2. Agree with the local business manager and network operations manager on how much of the remaining bandwidth you will be permitted to use. Set expectations when making this agreement.
3. Perform a test scan of the target network for five or more typical target hosts to gauge how much bandwidth is required. This number will have to be scaled up to derive a more accurate number. One caveat: the accuracy of this estimate will increase when the test scan can more closely reach a maximum number of connections. Sometimes, limiting the number of connections will reduce the maximum bandwidth consumed, and in other cases, it will not. It will all depend on the configuration of each target. Given the highly dynamic nature of a scan, the amount of testing should be commensurate with complexity and variability of the environment and level of criticality of the WAN link to business operations. This is both art and science.

4. Always position the scanning activity as a critical security function that will ultimately provide reports and analysis to the IT and network managers at the site. They should want this as much as you do. In a site with critical hosts, it may be worth purchasing a small amount of additional bandwidth that is dedicated to performing the scans.

Simultaneous connections, on the other hand, are fairly straightforward to manage. As previously mentioned, this parameter may affect bandwidth. The primary goal is not to overwhelm the target or the intervening network and security infrastructure. Even at low bandwidth, small packet sizes and half-open connections can generate a sizable number of simultaneous connections. Since a firewall maintains a state table for each connection, it must perform a little more CPU work for each connection. Large commercial firewalls that typically front a public Web site generally have sufficient resources to handle huge numbers of connections. However, this is not always the case. Firewalls are complex devices running many simultaneous processes. Furthermore, they are mostly single-threaded applications, which limits their performance scalability. Just as DoS attacks are performed on routers by exploiting the reliance of certain features on notoriously limited CPU resources, a scanner can do the same to a firewall. Most of these scenarios can be addressed with the following guidelines:

Test the impact on a firewall under load for a variety of targets. Different targets can generate different connection rates. Monitor the firewall CPU reaction closely. The reaction is not linear. In some cases, packet forwarding latency may result. In other cases, it just takes longer to set up and tear down connections. Manufacturer performance specifications do not apply to traffic generated by vulnerability scanners.

Test scanning against targets where the firewall applies additional distributed DoS and intrusion prevention capabilities. Since firewalls typically interact with the environment at OSI layer 3 and above to provide these services, the firewall may interpret a scan as a threat. It could be blocked or the results of the scan clouded. This is because the firewall features can act like a proxy for a given application. TCP connection attempts will be terminated by the firewall and then reestablished from the firewall to the target only after the handshake is completed with a sanitized upper-OSI-layer result. Any probing performed with a SYN-SYN/ACK-ACK that is not fully completed by the scanner may appear to be an active host where none exists. A solution to this is to configure the firewall to allow the scanner source traffic to bypass all of the firewall inspection filters.

Routers can also be affected. Some routers use their limited processor power to handle invalid TCP flag combinations. This is a common probing or discovery technique used by vulnerability scanners to fingerprint the OS or application. It is also a method for performing a DoS attack against a router. Although it is unlikely that a scanner will generate enough malformed traffic to have a major impact on network devices, you should be mindful of the possibility.

Simulate the typical latency on a WAN circuit in the lab during a scan. This will help gauge scan performance as well as impact to production systems. Some vendors provide tools that can use a packet capture from a network segment and a performance profile, and then recreate the user experience with the scan traffic and any given application injected. For example, an accounting system could be placed on one side of such a device while the scanner is on the other side. The device simulates the traffic conditions at a peak time for a particular office using a previously gathered profile.

Limit the number of TCP and UDP ports that are scanned during discovery and scanning. The tendency is to be as comprehensive as possible because you are not sure what will be found. This may work for an initial scan of a limited number of hosts. But later, you should settle on an acceptable number of ports to minimize the impact on the environment and maximize effectiveness. This is an area with diminishing returns on port numbers scanned at a logarithmic rate. You may also find that reducing the number of ports scanned will substantially lighten the bandwidth load. This is because packets can be large and numerous.

4.5.2.4 Web Application Testing

With so many competitive pressures, it was inevitable that organizations would have to find a way to distinguish themselves in the online world. So, millions of custom applications have been built to deliver customer service and application services that add value beyond original core competencies. It naturally follows that hackers would find common ways to exploit these applications, especially because they are more closely linked to valuable data. What has made these applications even more exploitable is their dependence on standard technologies and infrastructure. This is not intended as a criticism, only an observation. For example, most databases in use today are based on structured query language (SQL). Also, many Web applications use JavaScript™. Both of these technologies are exploitable, depending on their method of implementation. No inherent security controls can be configured to prevent their exploitation at the application level.

An even greater concern is the exploitability of the open-source Hypertext Preprocessor, or PHP, language. It is commonly used to build Web applications and yet has many critical vulnerabilities around which the programmer must code. Since this powerful scripting language is closely integrated with the Web page and user interaction, and since it has so many powerful commands with great flexibility, exploitation is very possible.

Naturally, this Web application phenomenon presents another area of vulnerability testing. These checks have become increasingly important as customer applications have become the primary focus of the serious hacker. There are simple methods to exploit vulnerabilities by merely manipulating the content of the URL in the Web browser. It is also quite easy to manipulate inputs on fields on the screen. So, vulnerability checks must do the same thing in many combinations using many common techniques to replicate possible attack vectors. Following is a list of some of the most common vectors:

Input field manipulation: This involves modifying the input of one or more fields on the screen beyond what is expected by the software in normal operation. Many programmers fail to validate these inputs for size and value boundaries as well as validity. Hackers exploit this by entering characters that will cause the application to process them in a way not originally intended.

SQL injection: This very popular attack vector is used to manipulate the database query language of the back-end database programming to reveal information or even modify the database contents. The process is started by entering the partial SQL string ('or 1=1—) in an input field without the parentheses, which will extend an underlying SQL statement to detect the presence of an unfiltered field and the fact that the SQL language is in use and accessible. This works because the first tick mark (') ends the current input string expected by the SQL code and then adds the logic "or 1=1." The remaining portion tells the SQL server to ignore the remainder of the SQL statement. This is a harmless modification of the SQL query that will determine whether SQL injection is even possible. Vulnerability scanners will perform more in-depth penetration acts to reveal more details about the flaws in handling this input, including what can be discovered about the database configuration.

Cross-site scripting (XSS): This extension of input field manipulation is used to inject JavaScript into a Web site that will appear on other users' browsers and perform actions against other users of the system. These actions include but are not limited to directing user input to another site, capturing user data, and presenting false information. The script information can be combined with an SQL injection attack to store malicious script code in the database of the target system. When this information is retrieved by the Web application for a user, the script is loaded into that user's Web browser and executed to fulfill the purposes of the attacker.

So, Web application checks are available in many VM systems to detect the presence of these vulnerabilities in the code of a Web site. There are other products that analyze the actual programming code, but they are no substitute for the hacker-mimicking process of attacking the application from the outside. By their very nature, these checks are brute force but usually nondestructive. The application checks are run against every field, every hyperlink, and every possible URL of a Web site. The following are more types of checks that can be performed against applications:

Boundary check: This is a test of a range of values that are accepted by an application. It is applied to every field that is found and applies values that can be below, above, and within the range of permitted values as well as trivial values that are outside of the expected data types. For example, an 8-bit ASCII[4] numeric field may have 16-bit Unicode data entered. This is also called stress testing.

Branch test: This program is used to check all of the links and possible paths to be taken in an application. The goal is to achieve as close as possible to 100% branch coverage, meaning that every possible program pathway is exercised. This is partly a discovery process and partly a vulnerability identification process. Some vulnerabilities in this area are the result of branches of code that are so obscure they are seldom accessed. Because of this, it is possible that some code is vulnerable because it was never tested.

Brute force: This type of check typically is used against user ID and password fields. It differs from a boundary check in that there is a large practical range limit for what can be entered. A password field that is eight alphanumeric characters long, for example, has 8**36 possible combinations.

Buffer overflow: This type of check is designed to challenge the target software for scale factors; that is, those inputs whose range affects the allocated memory space. Two types of scale factors can be tested: buffer definition and buffer usage. For example, if a program is designed to accept a certain size of input and store it in a memory buffer, a larger input can cause a buffer overflow. This is an example of a buffer usage scale factor, which occurs when an entered parameter directly or indirectly determines the allocated buffer space. If the parameter causes the creation of a buffer smaller than the input size, then the buffer can overflow on the corresponding input.

Code injection: In many scripting languages, it is possible to accept code as a parameter passed from one process to another. Programmers use this technique to efficiently reuse code or pass advanced parameters from one program to another. Some faults in a program can allow the inadvertent introduction of code by accepting instruction-terminating characters to be entered into a field. This is similar to SQL injection attacks.

Session hijacking: HTTP is a stateless protocol. That means it receives transactions over the network but does not know that the transaction is part of a particular user's session. To keep track of this session or "state," a file called a session cookie is implemented. There are various checks that can be performed to determine whether the session cookie can be manipulated to become a different user and therefore gain access to that user's data.

All of these tests, however, typically are used alone when run automatically. This is a key distinguishing factor between vulnerability testing and penetration testing. A person conducts basic reconnaissance testing using these application-vulnerability scanning tools and then combines the results to form augmented attacks with more revealing results. For example, an SQL injection attack can be used to insert malicious code to obtain another user's session cookie. Then, the session cookie, encrypted or not, can be used to obtain that user's information or change his password to gain his privileges.

4.5.2.4.1 Added Functionality

The VM industry is continuously evolving. The more value that can be demonstrated by the technology, the more competitive the products. VM tools are uniquely positioned to gather information beyond the vulnerability. While the audit process is looking around inside a host, why not check for other things? Configuration items can be enumerated to verify compliance against a standard. This is an excellent opportunity to provide support for configuration management functions and requires little additional effort.

Since the technology is checking for compliance with a standard, why not check against some of the established standards and recommendations provided by the Defense Information Systems Agency (DISA) through the Department of Defense's Information Assurance Certification and Accreditation Process (DIACAP) and the National Institute of Standards and Technology (NIST)? PCI is a common commercial set of security standards. The Center for Internet Security (CIS) provides a set of standard, enumerated configuration items for hardening a system. CIS is exceptional in that the standards are developed through broad consensus. They are an excellent resource to start with in custom policy development.

To summarize, additional functionality is available with VM already positioned in an active scanning role with a presence on nearly every host. Passive scanners are positioned as network sniffers, performance monitors, or general network mappers. The key to these additional functions is driving vendors to provide them, a topic we will discuss in Chapter 5 on selecting technology.

4.6 Hybrid Approach

Combining more than one solution for VM from different vendors can be helpful in responding more quickly and thoroughly to emerging vulnerabilities. However, normalizing the output may be difficult. If you are fortunate enough to deploy more than one type of technology from the same vendor, then perhaps a unified console will eliminate this problem.

Alternative approaches are to allocate the assessment resources by organization or network. For example, it may be beneficial to use passive vulnerability scanners on a public DMZ (demilitarized zone) in order to get 24-hour coverage of the security posture of the hosts. This most current assessment information can be automatically fed to a security event/incident management (SEIM) system. This provides a significant advantage, for newly published vulnerabilities can be taken into account quickly when new events occur to exploit them. Active vulnerability scanners can obtain more in-depth analysis of the back-end systems and worksta-tions where rapid response may not be as critical.

The combination of agents in DMZs and active scanners in the internal net-work is an excellent choice. The agents are positioned on DMZ hosts so that it is unnecessary to actively scan through the network security systems, which would otherwise require a more complex configuration. Additionally, regular audits or penetration tests of the DMZ should be conducted, and agents serve as a substitute for the regular monitoring provided by active scanning.

4.7 Inference Scanning

One final method of scanning that is seldom used exclusively for vulnerability iden-tification is inference scanning. This method involves the analysis of data that have already been obtained for another purpose to detect the presence of a vulnerability. For example, a configuration management system may have collected detailed con-figuration data on targets throughout an organization. The inference scanning pro-cess would use nonintrusive methods that involve reading the configuration details from the asset database and analyzing them for vulnerabilities. Easy examples of this are discreet configuration items such as SNMP community string or vulner-ability application versions.

Since inference scanning is based on factual information provided during the normal course of gathering configuration data, the reliability of an identified vul-nerability is very high. Also, because the vulnerability detection process is not per-formed by actively probing the host on the network, there is no impact to the target. When used strictly by itself, inference scanning is not always reliable or complete because it would not involve verification by other means. It can, however, be used to augment the previously mentioned scanning processes or as an additional feature to a configuration management product. Furthermore, inference techniques can be used architecturally to make vulnerability scanning more efficient. For example, an active vulnerability scanner might collect all of the possible vulnerability informa-tion and record it for analysis; then, the inference engine would be used to analyze that data for vulnerabilities in the host. In a later phase, certain vulnerabilities would be flagged for verification by other means before being given the designation of vulnerable. Overall, inference scanning is a valuable tool but is not sufficient to deliver the most complete, reliable results on its own.

4.8 Common Vulnerabilities and Exposures (CVE)

Once vulnerability information has been collected, it must be categorized and eval-uated. The methods of evaluation and categorization vary by vendor. This is one key area where many products attempt to distinguish themselves. When a vulnerability is identified, the category typically is assigned according to the type of exploit required or the level of access that is granted. For the purposes of this discussion, we will avoid any vendor-specific approaches and use MITRE's CVE methodology. According to MITRE's Web site (https://cve.mitre.org/about/index.html):

> CVE is a list of information security vulnerabilities and exposures that aims to provide common names for publicly known problems. The goal of CVE is to make it easier to share data across separate vulnerability capabilities (tools, repositories, and services) with this common enumeration.

4.8.1 Structure

MITRE is a nonprofit organization that has been making a valuable contributions to VM for years. They have been able to provide an open, standardized platform for the sharing of vulnerability knowledge. When someone discovers a new vulnerability, they frequently (but not always) report this discovery and its details to MITRE, who quickly publishes the information. Unfortunately, standards are still difficult to get adopted in products. There will be more on this in Chapter 5 on selecting technology.

Every CVE is given an identifier. In effect, this identifier allows a variety of tools from different vendors to speak the same language. A CVE provides the same description for all vendors and the same references to additional information sources. For example, "CVE-2001-0010: Buffer overflow in transaction signature (TSIG) handling code in BIND 8 allows remote attackers to gain root privileges." This is the same understanding for everyone. It cannot be confused among various vendors.

The references in the CVE will ultimately lead a vulnerability manager to the National Vulnerability Database (NVD) run by the NIST. CVE-2001-0010, mentioned earlier, has related information in the NVD, as shown in Figure 4.11:

Overview: This is a summary of the vulnerability that resembles the CVE description.

Impact: The impact section attributes a score to the vulnerability should it be exploited. More on this later when we discuss the Common Vulnerability Scoring System (CVSS).

References to advisories, solutions, and tools: These are typically Internet references to obtain more-detailed information about the vulnerability, how to detect it, and how to remediate. In this example, information about patches from various vendors is supplied.

Vulnerable software and versions: A list of the version numbers that are known to possess this vulnerability. This further helps with the detection process.

Technical details: This is information about the exact nature of the vulnerability; for example, how the software will react when exploited and why this is bad. Again, this item usually contains links to the site where the researcher has published information about his discovery.

Vulnerability Summary CVE-2001-0010
Original release date: 2/12/2001
Last revised: 5/2/2005
Source: US-CERT/NIST

Overview

Buffer overflow in transaction signature (TSIG) handling code in BIND 8 allows remote attackers to gain root privileges.

Impact

CVSS Severity (version 2.0 incomplete approximation):
CVSS v2 Base score: 10.0 (High) (AV:N/AC:L/Au:N/C:C/I:C/A:C) (legend)
Impact Subscore: 10.0
Exploitability Subscore: 10.0

Access Vector: Network exploitable
Access Complexity: Low
Authentication: Not required to exploit
Impact Type: Provides administrator access, Allows complete confidentiality, integrity, and availability violation, Allows unauthorized disclosure of information, Allows disruption of service

References to Advisories, Solutions, and Tools

CERT/CC Advisory: CA-2001-02
Name: CA-2001-02
Type: Advisory, Patch Information
Hyperlink: http://www.cert.org/advisories/CA-2001-02.html

External Source: Security Focus (disclaimer)

Name: bid 2302

Type: Advisory, Patch Information
Hyperlink: http://www.securityfocus.com/bid/2302

External Source: PGP Security (disclaimer)

Name: Vulnerabilities in BIND 4 and 8

Type: Advisory, Patch Information
Hyperlink: http://www.pgp.com/research/covert/advisories/047.asp

External Source: REDHAT (disclaimer)

Name: RHSA-2001:007

Hyperlink: http://www.redhat.com/support/errata/RHSA-2001-007.html

External Source: NAI (disclaimer)

Name: 20010129 Vulnerabilities in BIND 4 and 8

Hyperlink: http://www.nai.com/research/covert/advisories/047.asp

External Source: DEBIAN (disclaimer)

Name: DSA-026

Hyperlink: http://www.debian.org/security/2001/dsa-026

Vulnerable software and versions

Configuration 1
– ISC, BIND, 8.2.2 P7
– ISC, BIND, 8.2.2 P6
– ISC, BIND, 8.2.2 P5
– ISC, BIND, 8.2.2 P4
– ISC, BIND, 8.2.2 P3
– ISC, BIND, 8.2.2 P2
– ISC, BIND, 8.2.2 P1
– ISC, BIND, 8.2.2
– ISC, BIND, 8.2.1
– ISC, BIND, 8.2

Technical Details
Vulnerability Type No vulnerability type mapping is available.

CVE Standard Vulnerability Entry:
http://cve.mitre.org/cgi-bin/cvename.cgi?name=CVE-2001-0010

Common Platform Enumeration:
http://nvd.nist.gov/cpe.cfm?cvename=CVE-2001-0010

Figure 4.11 CVE-2001-0010.

Notice that CVEs are identifiers and not actual technical details. The main purpose of a CVE is to provide a cross-platform standard for identification of vulnerabilities. To support the quality of this identification mechanism, each vulnerability is subjected to a review process. At first, candidate status is given. This status means that the information is out there but has not been granted CVE status. A CVE editorial board discusses the merits of the candidate and votes on whether or not the vulnerability should receive full CVE entry status.

There are some caveats to the CVE database. First, it is not a vulnerability database. It is a database of vulnerability references. Second, it does not include all known vulnerabilities. It only contains those that are publicly known. So, it is possible that a vulnerability exists of which a vendor or researcher is aware but it does not appear in the CVE list. In some cases, this is because the researcher has agreed with the maker of the software that he will not reveal the vulnerability until a public patch has been released. Naturally, the researcher will want credit for the discovery.

To continue our CVE discussion, CVE items have one of two statuses: candidate or entry. An editorial board must vet the proposed vulnerability prior to it being granted entry status. Until that time, the vulnerability has candidate status. This status is provided on the CVE list when you view the details. When reading a CVE, check this status and review the reference to form your own opinion about the credibility and accuracy of information provided.

4.8.2 Limitations of CVE

CVE has definite limitations and is by no means an answer to all standards issues related to VM. As previously mentioned, CVE does not have a comprehensive list of all vulnerabilities in existence. Some vendors are able to identify vulnerabilities that CVE does not seem to record. Also, it does not necessarily contain all of the metadata needed to make a vulnerability system perform all of the functions that a technology vendor wishes to perform. Naturally, it shouldn't since it is intended to provide the common-denominator information useful to everyone.

CVE is not always kept up to date. Many vulnerabilities remain in "CAN" or candidate status for years. One wonders if these vulnerabilities will ever be updated when they are known to be accurate. It is possible that some of these are configuration best practices but not necessarily to be considered vulnerabilities. Inversely, CVE does not contain all product best-practice configuration vulnerabilities since they are too numerous to review and include for the many thousands of products in use around the world.

4.9 The Standard for Vulnerability Test Data

Typically, the vulnerability information used by a particular vendor of a VM scanner or analyzer is stored in a database that is designed to work seamlessly with the software. Since standards are usually a few to several years behind industry, none of

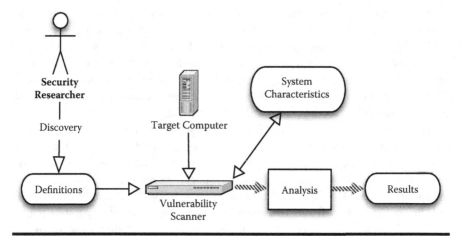

Figure 4.12 The OVAL process.

these databases are alike. The vulnerability data and method of identification vary widely from one product to another—that is, there is no standard.

However, MITRE has driven the idea of a standard for just this type of data structure. It is called the Open Vulnerability and Assessment Language or OVAL®. As the name implies, it is a language that is structured using Extensible Markup Language (XML) to record the details of the state of a machine (target) that has a particular vulnerability. It employs the state machine approach to identifying a vulnerability, which is a highly structured way of indicating the vulnerable state and the non-vulnerable state. So, let's examine the OVAL process in Figure 4.12 to understand its benefits.

We start with the security researcher who discovers a new vulnerability in product X. Having firsthand knowledge of the vulnerability and how it can be identified in a vulnerable target, the researcher encodes the details of that vulnerability in an OVAL-standard-formatted XML document. This document describes exactly how to identify the vulnerability on a target by providing the information of the state of particular items that constitute a vulnerable machine. This method of vulnerability identification is called a test.

4.9.1 Definitions Schema

At a higher level, OVAL consists of three types of documents called schemas. The definitions schema is used to encode the state of various parts of a computer system that must exist in order to be subject to a particular vulnerability. For example, a target system may need to have a Windows 2003 server with Service Pack (SP) 2, Internet Information Services (IIS), and anonymous Web access configured to be vulnerable to vulnerability XYZ. These schemas provide the framework for encoding such conditions.

Other definitions exist to capture other important information to help round out the VM process. Patch definitions record the specific conditions that must be present in order to be eligible for a patch. The idea is to avoid haphazardly applying patches to a system inappropriately. So, the ability is provided to specify, for example, that a vulnerability that is fixed by Windows 2003 SP 2 is only applied when the target system is in fact Windows 2003 and has only SP 1 installed. The patch definition capability can go far beyond this, but this understanding is sufficient for the scope of this book.

An OVAL inventory definition is just what it sounds like: a description of what defines a particular inventory item. If you want to specify that the SNMPv3 service is installed on a router, certain items must be checked to be certain it is present. The inventory definitions provide the XML schema to achieve exactly this. Since vulnerability scanning and automated configuration discovery are so closely related, it makes sense that OVAL should include this capability.

One additional area where the VM industry has very sensibly gone is compliance management. The MITRE team has understood this, and OVAL includes a schema for compliance definitions. Similar to the other schema, compliance specifies the conditions under which a system is compliant with a particular policy. Again, this is a natural extension to VM tools and processes.

4.9.2 System Characteristics Schema

This schema is designed to provide a standard definition of target system characteristics. These system characteristics, once collected, can be analyzed to identify vulnerabilities. When all of the target characteristics are collected, the vulnerability analyzer would compare them to the details in the definitions data to discover vulnerabilities. The design of the system characteristics schema is roughly parallel to that of the definitions schema. Although this schema is vulnerability focused, it also amounts to a list of configuration items in a configuration management database.

4.9.3 Results Schema

This third and final high-level schema is designed to provide a standard structure for recording the results of the vulnerability assessment. The primary benefit is that once a vulnerability is discovered, the details are captured in a format that many other security tools can interpret to properly apply patches, update configurations, initiate change processes, and take other mitigation actions as necessary. The results schema very specifically captures the details of a particular vulnerability on a specific target.

4.9.4 Nuts and Bolts[5]

In the OVAL specification, tests are formatted in the OVAL definitions schema and are defined by a <definitions> tag. Tests are recorded using three key XML elements: <objects>, which is the item being tested; <states>, which are the values of the objects to be tested; and <tests>, which are the tests to be performed against those objects using the previously mentioned <states>. An ID is assigned to each definition, object, state, and test using a notation resembling reverse DNS entries. Let's take a look at a partial example of an OVAL definition, which is a check to see whether Windows XP® is installed. This is an abbreviated version, so we do not spend time on details that are not instructive on this topic:

```
1  <definitions>
2    <definition id="oval:org.mitre.oval:def:105" version="3" class="inventory">
3    <metadata>
4     <title>Microsoft Windows XP is installed< title>
5     <reference source="CPE" ref_id="cpe:/o:microsoft:windows_xp"/>
6     <description> The operating system installed on the system is Microsoft
Windows XP. </description>
7    </metadata>
8    <criteria operator="AND">
9     <criterion comment="the installed operating system is part of the Microsoft
Windows family" test_ref="oval:org.mitre.oval:tst:99"/>
10    <criterion comment="a version of Microsoft Windows XP is installed"
test_ref="oval:org.mitre.oval:tst:3"/>
11   </criteria>
12  </definition>
13 </definitions>
14 <tests>
15  <family_test id="oval:org.mitre.oval:tst:99" version="1" comment="the
installed operating system is part of the Microsoft Windows family"
check_existence="at_least_one_exists" check="only one">
16   <object object_ref="oval:org.mitre.oval:obj:99"/>
17   <state state_ref="oval:org.mitre.oval:ste:99"/>
18  </family_test>
19  <registry_test id="oval:org.mitre.oval:tst:3" version="1" comment="a
version of Microsoft Windows XP is installed"
check_existence="at_least_one_exists" check="at least one">
20   <object object_ref="oval:org.mitre.oval:obj:123"/>
21   <state state_ref="oval:org.mitre.oval:ste:3"/>
22  </registry_test>
23 </tests>
24 <objects>
25  <family_object id="oval:org.mitre.oval:obj:99" version="1" comment="This
is the default family object. Only one family object should exist."/>
26  <registry_object id="oval:org.mitre.oval:obj:123" version="1"
comment="Registry key that hold the current windows os version">
27  <hive>HKEY_LOCAL_MACHINE</hive>
```

```
28   <key>SOFTWARE\Microsoft\Windows NT\Current Version</key>
29   <name>CurrentVersion</name>
30   </registry_object>
31   </objects>
32   <states>
33   <family_state id="oval:org.mitre.oval:ste:99" version="1"
comment="Microsoft Windows family">
34   <family>windows</family>
35   </family_state>
36   <registry_state id="oval:org.mitre.oval:ste:3" version="1" comment="The
registry key value is 5.1">
37   <value>5.1</value>
38   </registry_state>
39   </states>
```

4.9.4.1 <Definitions>

In this example, there are a few basic components to know: definitions, tests, objects, and states. These are the high-level containers for the parts of a vulnerability check. The definitions come in four different classes as previously described: vulnerability, patch, inventory, and compliance. This example indicates in the "class" that it is an inventory definition in line 2. Line 3 is a metadata tag. This begins a descriptive section that can be used by vulnerability assessment software for the end user who may not need to know exactly what happens in this test. The title and description are not the most significant items here. Notice in the metadata there is a reference source in line 5. This refers to a Common Platform Enumeration (CPE) name. This CPE name will be explained later, but for now suffice it to say that this is a specification for a system enumeration.

The ultimate goal in this example is to determine whether Windows XP is installed on a target system. The tests, objects, and states that are compared will evaluate to a true or false answer.

The criteria tag showing the value of "operator" set to "AND" is on line 8. This is a fundamental breakdown of the logic to be applied in the vulnerability check. If X AND Y, then the result is true. In other words, the result of all tests will have a logical AND operation applied. Following that, on lines 9 and 10 are the two criterion type statements to which the operator is applied.

Each criterion or "criteriontype" has a comment and a "test_ref" reference. This reference points to the details of the test that is to be performed. If the criterion is to be negated, then another item is added within the specific criterion statement. This is the "negate = 'true'" statement within the criterion. If this is omitted from the criterion type, the value is assumed to be "false" or not negated.

One other item to know about the criterion as in this example: the first criterion indicates that the test referenced as "oval:org.mitre.oval:tst:99" should be performed. This is a reverse-DNS-style notation showing that the test is from oval. mitre.org and is number 99. All of these references start with the word "oval" followed by org.mitre.oval. Since it is a test, the letters "tst" follow. Finally, a colon and an integer of at least one digit is included. Combined, this pattern forms a unique identifier. It is referred to as a "testIDpattern."

4.9.4.2 <Tests>

After all of the tests are specified in the criteria of a definition, then a new section begins, indicated by the <tests> tag. In this section, the first and very common element is the "family_test" on line 15. Notice that immediately following this element is an 'id="oval:org.mitre.oval:tst:99."' This is the item to which the earlier criterion reference was pointing. What follows are the objects and states to be compared. If the result of the comparison is true, then this is used in the previous definition to evaluate whether the results meet the goal of the definition. Also in the family_test element are "check_existence=" and "check=." These are set to the values "at_least_one_exists" and "only one" respectively. This means that there must be exactly one check but no more. In this case, we will check object 99 against state 99, as indicated on lines 16 and 17.

Then, there is one more test to be performed. In this case, it is a registry test on line 19. Lines 20 and 21 are the object and state to be checked. In this case, it is object number 123 and state number 3.

4.9.4.3 <Objects>

The objects section defines the objects to be tested. In this case, "oval:org.mitre. oval:obj:99" is the reference that is a "family_object" on line 25. This means that the object defines a particular system. It is referenced only by a "family_test" as on line 16. The point is to identify whether the target system is Windows, Mac OS X, UNIX, etc.

The next object is a "registry_object." This type of object applies only to the Microsoft Windows registry key system. That system has three components: <hive>, <key>, and <name>. If you have ever browsed the Windows registry, you will recognize these details. The structure and function of the Windows registry is beyond the scope of this book. It is sufficient to say that the values specified on lines 27, 28, and 29 are the values used to identify the particular item in the Windows registry that we need to test.

4.9.4.4 <States>

Finally, we have the states, which contain the values needed to test the objects. The first item is the "family_state," which defines the state of the family of computer system. In the example on line 33, the "family_state" tag tells us that we are dealing with family state number 99. You may recall that the "family_test" described earlier references to this state on line 17. Back on line 34, the simple value of the "family" is set to "windows."

The one and final state to be defined is the state of the previously mentioned registry key specified in the object on line 26, also known as object 123. To clarify, we are testing that object number 123 (the registry key) has a state number 3 (value 5.1). On line 36, we define the "registry_state" element with a value found on line 37.

The following summarizes, in a more natural language style, what the definitions, objects, states, and tests do in this example:

```
-----------------
Definition: Inventory (line 2)
This is a Windows OS (test 99, line 9)
AND (line 8)
Windows XP is installed (test 3, line 10)
Test 3: Test the Windows family (line 15)
Which has object 99 (line 16) and state 99 (line 17)
Test 99: Test Windows XP
Which has object 123 (line 20) and state 3 (line 21)
Object 99: family_object (line 25)
Object 123: registry_object (line 26)
   Which is "HKEY_LOCAL_MACHINE\SOFTWARE\Microsoft\Windows
NT\CurrentVersion\CurrentVersion" (lines 27, 28, and 29)
State: family_state (line 33)
   Which is Windows (line 34)
State: registry_state (line 36)
   Which has the value 5.1 (line 37)
-----------------
```

Since some tests cannot be performed using a single <state> value, another type of <state> is available in a section called <variables>. This allows the end user to select the value that would constitute compliance.

The folks at MITRE recognized that they could not be everything to everyone, so they made OVAL extensible using a special XML tag in a <metadata> section.

The vulnerability scanner uses a collection of these XML documents to identify a vulnerability in a particular target. Before making the comparison, the scanner assesses the state of the target machine and records this state information in a similarly formatted XML document. Then, an analysis is performed using the vulnerability state information and the target state information. The system state information is collected in a format called the OVAL System Characteristics Schema. This XML document has the configuration data for a target system. Having a standard format helps to standardize communication of this information to other systems. For example, system characteristics could be useful in a configuration management tool or an SEIM.

If a vulnerability scan were to result in the identification of a vulnerability, then that fact and related details are recorded for further processing. It is after this analysis/results step that the real vendor-distinguishing features can be built. But first, the process of identifying the vulnerability is standardized for consistent results. The results are reported consistently by the specification of an XML schema similar to the OVAL definitions schema called, not surprisingly, the OVAL Results Schema.

Note that OVAL only supports authenticated tests that require authorized access to the target. This is a necessary limitation since there may be many innovative ways to perform unauthenticated checks.

4.10 The Standard for Vulnerability Severity Rating

A very important part of evaluating a vulnerability is knowing the impact or risk to the organization. Many vendors have their own evaluation methods. But, there must be some standard with which all software makers and vulnerability researchers can agree on the criteria for rating severity. The Common Vulnerability Scoring System (CVSS) was developed to provide a standard framework for assessing the impact of a vulnerability and its basic characteristics. Although the contents and methodology are not the complete picture, they help to assess risk by doing much of the technical work in advance by the Forum of Incident Response and Security Teams (FIRST). FIRST is a nonprofit group of vendors, researchers, and other volunteers who work to enhance security incident response practices.

CVSS provides relevant vulnerability metrics that the user can look at and quickly determine whether further action is necessary to address risk. These metrics are organized into three groups: base, temporal, and environmental. For each of these groups, a score is calculated. Each group has metrics that are combined to calculate the score for that group. Figure 4.13 shows the relationships among the metric groups, metrics, and equations. You can follow this discussion by referring periodically to the figure. For clarification, items indicated with dashed lines are subequations or subgroups that only provide intermediate values or logical groupings of metrics.

Base metrics are constant. They are fundamental and do not change over time. The metrics of the base group are access vector (AV), access complexity (AC), authentication (AU), confidentiality impact (C), integrity impact (I), and availability impact (A). As any Certified Information Systems Security Professional (CISSP®) should know, confidentiality, integrity, and availability (CIA) form the triangle of security, and so it is no surprise they should be included here.

Each of these metrics of the base metrics group has a value, depending on the severity or impact. For example, AV indicates what kind of access an attacker

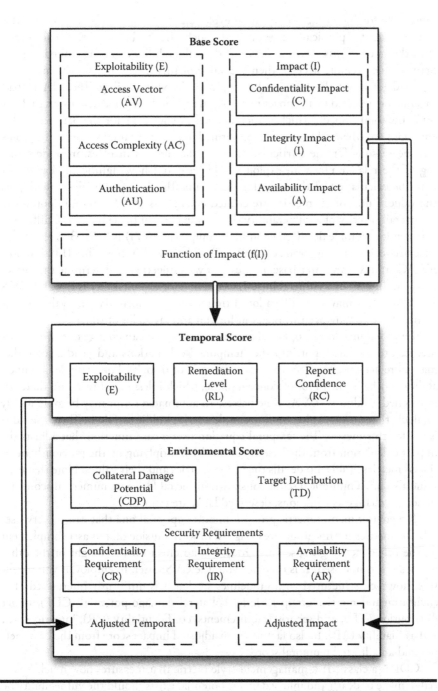

Figure 4.13 Metric relationships in the Common Vulnerability Scoring System (CVSS).

must have for the vulnerability to be exploited. If the vulnerability requires that the attacker be physically present and touch the keyboard (i.e., local access), then the value of this metric is 0.395. If the vulnerability can be exploited over the network (i.e., remote access), then the value of this metric is 1.0. This process is repeated for all of the metrics that apply to the vulnerability. The CIA metrics together are referred to as impact metrics and are combined in calculations to determine the total impact, which is then applied in equations for the base score. The equations are where all the work is performed to produce a total score for the group.

The reasons for the particular value of the metrics involves an understanding of the relative effect an exploit would have and how significant that metric is in the calculation of the score for the group. The greater the effect, the higher the value. But, not all metrics are created equal. AVs may be more important to the overall severity of a vulnerability than complexity of the exploit. The difference between low complexity (0.35) and high complexity (0.71) is 0.36. But, the difference between requiring local access (0.395) and network accessibility (1.0) is 0.605. AV, AC, and AU are three base metrics that work together to determine the overall exploitability (E) of a vulnerability. The equation for exploitability is $E = 20 \times AV \times AC \times AU$. This may seem like a lot of trouble, but the formulas and values of the metrics have already been worked out for you and save a lot of time.

Temporal metrics are optional and have values that can change over time. Base metrics are used as input into the "temporal" calculations and yield a score that may more accurately reflect the risk on a scale of 0 to 10. For example, a vulnerability may be in the proof-of-concept phase, which is less of a threat, and therefore is assigned a value of 0.9. As time passes, an automated script may become widely available that makes exploitation so simple a script kiddie can do it. Then, the value is 1.0 for this metric. The temporal equation uses a case function that adjusts the impact calculation from the base equations by multiplying by the previously mentioned metrics. Table 4.6 details the CVSS metrics and their values. Note that each value also has a numerical score not shown in the table. These numerical scores are subject to change as equations, described later, are refined.

The environmental metric group is another optional one that can be very useful. The metrics in this group are designed to work outside of, but as a complement to, the other metric groups. This group has no effect on the weight of the other metrics if it is not used. It is there for you, the CVSS user, to employ as you see fit. It is, however, structured with guidelines so that it is uniformly interpreted. The environmental metrics group includes collateral damage potential (CDP), target distribution (TD), and security requirements: confidentiality (CR), integrity (IR), and availability (AR). It also factors-in an adjusted impact score from the base metrics and an adjusted temporal score.

CDP is a classic risk-management-style metric that measures how much financial damage or death and injury damage potential exists should the vulnerability be exploited. In risk management terms, it is single loss expectancy (SLE). For those who are not formally trained security professionals, the SLE in risk management

Table 4.6 CVSS Metrics

Metric Type	CVSS Metric	Description	Value
Base	AccessVector	Requires local access	0.395
		Adjacent network accessible	0.646
		Network accessible	1.0
	AccessComplexity	High	0.35
		Medium	0.61
		Low	0.71
	Authentication	Requires multiple instances of authentication	0.45
		Requires single instance of authentication	0.56
		Requires no authentication	0.704
	ConfImpact	None	0.0
		Partial	0.275
		Complete	0.660
	IntegImpact	None	0.0
		Partial	0.275
		Complete	0.660
	AvailImpact	None	0.0
		Partial	0.275
		Complete	0.660
Temporal	Exploitability	Unproven	0.85
		Proof-of-concept	0.9
		Functional	0.95
		High	1.00
		Not defined	1.00

(Continued)

Table 4.6 *(Continued)*   CVSS Metrics

Metric Type	CVSS Metric	Description	Value
	RemediationLevel	Official-fix	0.87
		Temporary-fix	0.90
		Work-around	0.95
		Unavailable	1.00
		Not defined	1.00
	ReportConfidence	Unconfirmed	0.90
		Uncorroborated	0.95
		Confirmed	1.00
		Not defined	1.00
Environmental	CollateralDamagePotential	None	0
		Low	0.1
		Low–Medium	0.3
		Medium–High	0.4
		High	0.5
		Not defined	0.0
	TargetDistribution	None	0
		Low	0.25
		Medium	0.75
		High	1.0
		Not defined	1.0
	ConfReq	Low	0.5
		Medium	1.0
		High	1.51
		Not defined	1.0
	IntegReq	Low	0.5
		Medium	1.0
		High	1.51
		Not defined	1.0
	AvailReq	Low	0.5
		Medium	1.0
		High	1.51
		Not defined	1.0

is how much you expect it to cost should a loss occur one time. Although it is a measure of damage potential, CDP is a scale from 0 to 0.5 and it does not equate to a dollar amount.

TD is the measure of what percentage of the organization is vulnerable. This helps you to assess the scope of the threat in your environment. If 50% of the target hosts have a particular vulnerability, then this metric is considered to have a value of medium. When the TD is calculated in an equation, high = 1.0, medium = 0.75, low = 0.25, none = 0.0, and interestingly, not defined = 1.0. This is interesting because if you don't know the TD, the assumption should be "high," which allows for conservative estimates of damage potential. I recommend that if you know the exact distribution of hosts with a vulnerability in your organization based on the results of a vulnerability assessment, then use this percentage in an exact decimal form. This approach is outside of the CVSS guidelines, but it is more precise than the high/medium/low approach.

The environmental security requirement metrics are unique. These metrics create a weight to the base metrics for CIA. If your particular environment puts a high value on the confidentiality of data, for example, then the value is increased. If the value is medium, the weight of C is neutral. The security requirements are used to reweight the impact (I) metric calculation in the base score. This modifies the base metric group score according to the requirements of your organization. However, if an impact metric from the base group is 0 (i.e., not a factor), then the resulting modified impact score will be unaffected. This is because the equation for modified impact metrics includes a multiplication of the security requirement and the impact value from the base group:

$$
Adjusted\ Impact = \left(10.41 \times \left(1 - \begin{array}{l} ^{min10} \\ (1 - Conf\ Impact \times Conf\ Req) \times \\ (1 - Integ\ Impact \times Integ\ Req) \times \\ (1 - Avail\ Impact \times Avail\ Req) \times \end{array} \right) \right)
$$

where AdjustedImpact = min(10,10.41* (1−(1−ConfImpact* ConfReq)* (1−IntegImpact* IntegReq)* (1−AvailImpact* AvailReq))).

For each of the metric groups, an equation has been designed to calculate a score based on a set of mathematical rules. The equations are based on a rationale that varies depending on the type of metric. The merits of each of these equations are widely analyzed and debated and are of little benefit to discuss here. CVSS is explained in more detail at https://www.first.org/cvss/v2/guide.

If you want to calculate your own CVSS scores, you can try some Web-based calculators. One popular calculator can be found at http://nvd.nist.gov/cvss.cfm?cal culator&adv&version=2. You can enter whatever values you like and receive a set of CVSS scores. To understand the impact of a particular metric on the overall score, try changing only one and then recalculate. You will begin to get a feel for what score is good and what is really bad. I also suggest that you omit the environmental components so that you can become familiar with the CVSS scores you will find in the NVD, which we will discuss in Section 4.11.

4.10.1 CVSS Nomenclature

An abbreviated language is used for CVSS to make it easy to relay the details of vulnerability metrics. The letters provided in the preceding paragraphs are used in conjunction with a colon (:) and the corresponding value. Also, a slash (/) is used to separate the metrics. For example, a base group score with related metrics would look like this:

10.0 (High) (AV:N/AC:L/AU:N/C:C/I:C/A:C)

The base group score is 10.0. Next, the AV has the value of "N" for network. The next metric, separated from the first by a slash, is AC with a value of "L" for low. These values for the base metrics continue until all of the related base group metrics are provided in the parentheses. Notice in this example that the last three metrics, confidentiality, integrity, and availability impact, are "C" for complete, which is obviously really bad.

As described earlier, these entries will appear in a CVE identifier and will usually include the impact and exploitability subscores to give you an idea of the potential damage the particular vulnerability can do. Properly understood, this abbreviation system can give you some useful information at a glance. CVE identifiers have the most significant value in providing a universally shared identifier for a vulnerability for all organizations and products. Employing CVEs leaves no doubt as to which vulnerability is being handled in a product. However, the various sources of information need to be pulled together to maximize their utility in managing vulnerabilities. CVE data, OVAL checks, and CVSS scores, along with standard protocols for interoperability, are combined resources in the NVD.

4.11 NVD

The National Vulnerability Database is an online database operated by the NIST. It can be found at https://nvd.nist.gov. The NVD uses the Security Content Automation Protocol (SCAP). This protocol is a set of standards designed to support automation of VM, compliance management, and other security functions. We have already discussed some of those standards, which include OVAL, CVE, and CVSS. There are three items we have not discussed: CCE and CPE, which concern target enumeration, and Extensible Configuration Checklist Description Format (XCCDF), which provides checklists for target evaluation and standard formats for reporting.

CCE refers to Common Configuration Enumeration identifiers. These are identifiers used to correlate checks performed on system configurations with documents and tools that provide related information. CCE identifiers will not be discussed in depth except to suggest reviewing the CCE lists provided by MITRE Corporation.

4.11.1 CPE

Common Platform Enumeration identifiers provide a standard naming scheme for technology systems and components. In practical VM terms, CPE identifiers are used to indicate what systems or components are subject to a particular vulnerability. When a new vulnerability is announced, "which systems are vulnerable?" is the first question that is asked. CPE is intended to clearly document a platform so that applicability of a vulnerability announcement is easily determined through both automated and human methods.

A particular computer system can be assigned a CPE name, which represents the complete enumeration of that platform in terms of what is installed. This includes the hardware, the OS, and applications. It does not include detailed configuration options such as the status of particular switches or security policies. So, the first thing that might occur to you is that there are millions of combinations that can be enumerated. This is quite correct, but CPE has a basic requirement that addresses this issue. If a vulnerability is announced for CPE name "cpe:/o:microsoft:windows_xp::sp2," then a system enumerated with a CPE name like "cpe:/a:microsoft:office :2003::standard" is subject to that vulnerability. This is a "grouping" approach to enumeration of systems subject to vulnerabilities, which in CPE parlance is called a prefix property. The enumeration of a platform typically requires multiple CPE names since a platform can be composed of many parts.

4.11.1.1 Encoding

The encoding of CPE names is logically structured just as described in the previous section: hardware, OS, and application. The encoding format follows the Uniform Resource Identifier (URI) format although it is not officially recognized by the Internet Assigned Numbers Authority (IANA), the governing body for Internet-assigned numbers typically found in URLs. This format is used for convenience and to leverage an established convention that works well for naming a resource on the Internet. Here is the basic structure of a CPE name:

cpe:/ {part} : {vendor} : {product} : {version} : {update} : {edition} : {language}

So, there are seven parts to this format:

Part: The part is defined as either hardware "h," operating system "o," or application "a." The people at MITRE have left the door open for other parts as well, such as driver "d."

Vendor: This usually is specified as a portion of the domain name for the vendor. So, Mozilla.Org would have the vendor name Mozilla. Strictly speaking, it is the highest organization level of the DNS name of the vendor. If there is more than one organization with this DNS name, then the entire DNS name is used.

Product: CPE uses an abbreviation for the product provided by the vendor. It is common for computer users to use "IE" to indicate Internet Explorer. So, this is the abbreviation used.

Version: This is a version number for the product. For example, "5.0."

Update: These are specific updates that may be applied by the vendor to a particular version. Use of fields becomes pretty sporadic, depending on how the vendor issues releases and updates. Some vendors tend to have smaller port releases (versions) to perform updates.

Edition: The edition field typically is used to distinguish among the various flavors of a product. So, Windows Vista® would have several editions such as Home Basic, Home Premium, Business, and Ultimate.

Language: Intuitively, this is the language used in the target CPE name. This makes it easier to identify systems that are vulnerable based on their installed language pack.

4.11.1.2 Examples of CPE Names

Obviously, cpe:/a:adobe:flash_player:1.1 represents Adobe Reader version 8.1.1. But the specification is not specific to the OS. Any vulnerability using the name would apply to all version 8.1.1 instances of Adobe Reader on any OS. If we modify the name to apply only to Windows XP, then we could use the following name: cpe:/a:adobe:flash_player:9.0.20.0::windows_xp. If a specific OS is to be named for a vulnerability (e.g., Windows XP, all versions), then the following name would be used: cpe:/o:microsoft:windows_xp. However, if we wanted to be more specific (e.g., Windows XP SP1 Pro), we would use cpe:/o:microsoft:windows_xp::sp1:professional.

Hardware is identified in a similar fashion: cpe:/h:cisco:ip_phone_7960 represents a Cisco iPhone® model 7960. Notice that the model number, and not a version, is built into the product. This is because Cisco has chosen to represent product versions with a different model number. When identifying hardware, it is possible not only to identify a computer system but also a specific motherboard such as the Intel D845WN (cpe:/h:intel:d845wn_motherboard).

4.11.2 XCCDF

Earlier, we discussed the need to standardize the vulnerability testing methods using OVAL. Also, we have discussed how a data structure might look in a vulnerability scanner. Similarly, the Extensible Configuration Checklist Description Format (XCCDF) is an XML-based set of documents that specify checklists for validating security compliance for various types of target systems. XCCDF also specifies a standard format for reporting compliance and scoring. This simplifies the interoperability of various security systems. It is not a substitute for OVAL but rather a supporting technology that can actually extend OVAL and enhance its interoperability with proprietary technologies.

XCCDF has a primary use case in the definition of compliance checks, compliant machine states, and results reporting. The language is designed to allow for the definition of security benchmarks that are reflected in detailed configuration item settings. Checks can be developed and submitted to the NIST checklist program for review. If accepted, the checks will be available to anyone in the world who supports XCCDF in their product. This happens to be very few vendors. XCCDF is primarily used in U.S. government security in support of NIST publication 800-53 and FIPS 199.[6] The big benefit is that a standard mechanism has been created to validate and report security compliance to checklists and rules across multiple vendors and security systems. XCCDF supports the idea of VM as an integrated part of configuration management.

At first, you might think that any such language must be confining when it comes to defining checks and scoring. However, XCCDF is designed to be customizable and flexible for achieving consistent results for a variety of systems. For example, one option is "selectability." A particular XCCDF document will contain a set of rules describing the state of a target in order to be compliant. Those rules can be selectively turned on or off (selected), depending on the target under scrutiny. Similarly, parameters can be substituted to accommodate flexible rules. For example, the size of an encryption key for a virtual private network (VPN) configuration may be 256 bits for a system communicating insignificant data and 4,096 bits for one carrying sensitive information.

XCCDF has four types of objects:

Benchmark is a master container for everything else in the document. It is similar to the definitions in OVAL.

Item is similar to an object or test in OVAL. It contains a description and identifier. There are three types or classes of items: group (holds other items), rule (holds checks, scoring weights, and remediation information), and value (provides the previously mentioned substitution ability).

Profile provides references to item objects. It contains many of the values needed for a particular profile of a system. This significantly helps apply asset classification to the values applied to the rules, where appropriate.

Test result holds the results of the test performed. Most significant in this object are the "rule-result" and "target-facts" elements. This object contains the actual results of the tests performed and is very informative during reporting and remediation processes. The target-facts information can be sensitive information about the actual result of the test against the target that resulted in compliance or noncompliance.

An interesting attribute of XCCDF is that it can reference the content of OVAL in a rule. A child element of a rule called "check" allows the document author to reference the system from which a check is obtained. For example, '<cdf:check system = "http://www.mitre.org/XMLSchema/oval">' is then followed by the specific reference of the check within the source system: '<cdf:check-content-ref href="ovaldefs.xml" name="OVAL99"/>. This is only a reference to the OVAL rule and not the actual rule. Software that performs the checks will have to properly interpret and execute these references. The use of OVAL is not a requirement for any system unless the goal is SCAP compliance, which is discussed next.

Overall, XCCDF is a great idea for standardizing configuration compliance checks across vendors and organizations. However, its use is mostly restricted to the U.S. Department of Defense. If you work for the government or are a vendor, more details can be found in the document entitled "Specification for the Extensible Configuration Checklist Description Format (XCCDF) Version 1.1.3 (Draft)" by Neal Ziring and Stephen D. Quinn.

4.12 SCAP

Security Content Automation Protocol (SCAP, pronounced "ess-cap") is an overarching suite of the aforementioned standards that include CVE, CVSS, CPE, XCCDF, and OVAL. The NIST maintains the SCAP content, which defines how all of these protocols work together in an automated fashion. It also contains the content of all of these standards in the NVD.

SCAP also has a product validation program to assist in evaluating products for compatibility with the various open standards. NIST provides detailed descriptions of the validation areas, abbreviated here to give you a sense of the possible areas of validation:

Federal Desktop Core Configuration (FDCC) scanner: A product with the ability to audit and assess a target system in order to determine its compliance with the FDCC requirements, which were the result of the U.S. Government's Office of Management and Budget (OMB) Memo M-07-18. That memo states that the provider of information technology shall certify applications are fully functional and operate correctly as intended on systems using the FDCC.

Authenticated configuration scanner: A product with the ability to audit and assess a target system to determine its compliance with a defined set of configuration requirements using target system log-on privileges.

Authenticated vulnerability and patch scanner: A product with the ability to scan a target system to locate and identify the presence of known software flaws and evaluate the software patch status to determine compliance with a defined patch policy using target system log-on privileges.

Unauthenticated vulnerability scanner: A product with the ability to determine the presence of known software flaws by evaluating the target system over the network.

Intrusion detection and prevention systems: Products that monitor systems or networks for unauthorized or malicious activities. An IPS actively protects the target system or network against these activities.

Patch remediation: The ability to install patches on a target system in compliance with a defined patching policy.

Misconfiguration remediation: The ability to alter the configuration of a target system in order to bring it into compliance with a defined set of configuration recommendations.

Asset management: The ability to actively discover, audit, and assess asset characteristics, including installed and licensed products; location within the world, a network, or an enterprise; ownership; and other related information on IT assets such as workstations, servers, and routers.

Asset database: The ability to passively store and report on asset characteristics, including installed and licensed products; location within the world, a network, or an enterprise; ownership; and other related information on IT assets such as workstations, servers, and routers.

Vulnerability database: A product that contains a catalog of security-related software flaw issues labeled with CVEs where applicable. These data are made accessible to users through a search capability or data feed and contain descriptions of software flaws, references to additional information (e.g., links to patches or vulnerability advisories), and impact scores.

Misconfiguration database: A product that contains a catalog of security-related configuration issues labeled with CVEs where applicable.

Malware tool: The ability to identify and report on the presence of viruses, Trojan horses, spyware, or other malware on a target system.

When a product is assessed and validated, it is for one or more of these areas. The status of validation of products is posted on the NIST's public Web site. Being validated does not ensure quality or reliability of the product; only that it meets the criteria set forth by the SCAP program.

4.13 Nessus

No discussion of VM technology is complete without discussing Nessus. Some companies choose to use the open-source version of Nessus to decrease costs and have greater control over vulnerability scanning. There are many books on Nessus, so we shall not go into great detail. If it is your intention to use the open-source version in your organization, then it is advisable to acquire one of these books. Tenable Network Security can provide support and updates for an additional cost. Following is a high-level overview of the product.

4.13.1 Advantages and Disadvantages

Nessus is a popular open-source scanner for organizations that choose not to spend the money on other proprietary products. There are significant advantages to Nessus over many other products, but there are also some disadvantages.

Item	Advantage	Disadvantage
Single server performs scans and captures results to a database.	High-performance capture of data with minimum results reporting impact on the network.	Forces centralized server architecture where all scans take place from a single server.
Open-source product	Low cost of ownership. Can be customized by the end user with technical knowledge.	No support without extra fee. Requires greater knowledge to install and operate the product.
The user can compile binary.	Operates on multiple platforms: OSs/CPUs.	Requires strong knowledge about the target systems and open-source software.
Optimized version of Nessus is recommended for scanning Windows XP SP2 platforms to avoid false negatives.	Scalability problem: If your organization has a mix of architectures (e.g., Linux and Windows), then it is possible that two versions may come into use, or you are better off using a Windows version.	
Professional feeds provide immediate updates.	Receiving immediate updates for latest vulnerabilities is obviously good.	You must pay for this, but the cost is likely the same or cheaper than other products.
Home feeds provide free vulnerability updates.	This is a good way to get started evaluating the tool.	This is not for commercial use.
Plug-ins	These elements of Nessus allow for extensibility and customization commonly beyond what other products offer.	The increased complexity requires considerable knowledge and experience to deploy.
NASL*	This tool allows the user to script and run specific vulnerability checks. These checks provide a lot of control where most products do not.	Knowledge of NASL and how to use it at the command line is necessary.

*Nessus Attack Scripting Language

4.13.2 Scan Modes

Nessus provides three types of checks or scan modes:

Discovery: This process uses basic discovery protocols such as ICMP echo request/reply and TCP sweeps to identify active hosts on the network. Some products today do not have the ability to simply perform a quick discovery but instead require a full audit. This capability represents a useful tool to narrow unknown network ranges when defining networks in a commercial product. Alternatively, similar functionality can be obtained using the command-line Nmap product.

OS fingerprinting: This is performed by a handful of methods that have already been described in this book. Simple malformed packets to legitimate SNMP queries are used to gather involuntary and voluntary information, respectively. These and other methods may not always work, depending on the target. Other vendors may have developed other means to gather this information.

Complete scans: This type of scan performs discovery and OS fingerprinting and adds numerous vulnerability checks, including brute-force password attacks. It is subject to all of the same limitations and concerns discussed previously in this chapter.

One other feature worth mentioning about Nessus is the availability of Web application checks. This capability is not available "out of the box" from many vendors. In many cases, one must pay extra for the feature. Nessus provides this without reservation. It requires some configuration to be relevant to the targets but is certainly worthwhile. The user has the ability to test cross-site scripting (XSS), SQL injection, and Common Gateway Interface (CGI) vulnerabilities.

Nessus is a capable product with a greater level of control compared to most other products. However, it lacks the scalability of many commercial offerings because it's a very centralized approach to scanning. All scans take place from a central location rather than having many physically distributed scanners with a central data-collection point. However, it may be well-suited to many business/IT architectures and quite suitable at a good price point.

4.13.3 Using Nessus

This section assumes that the user has installed both the Nessus client and the server. No instruction on these topics will be provided as it is well-covered in other books and the Nessus documentation itself. Nessus has two areas in the user interface: Scan and Report. The function of each is self-explanatory. Figure 4.14 shows the scan target window. It allows the user to enter a host IP address, DNS name, IP

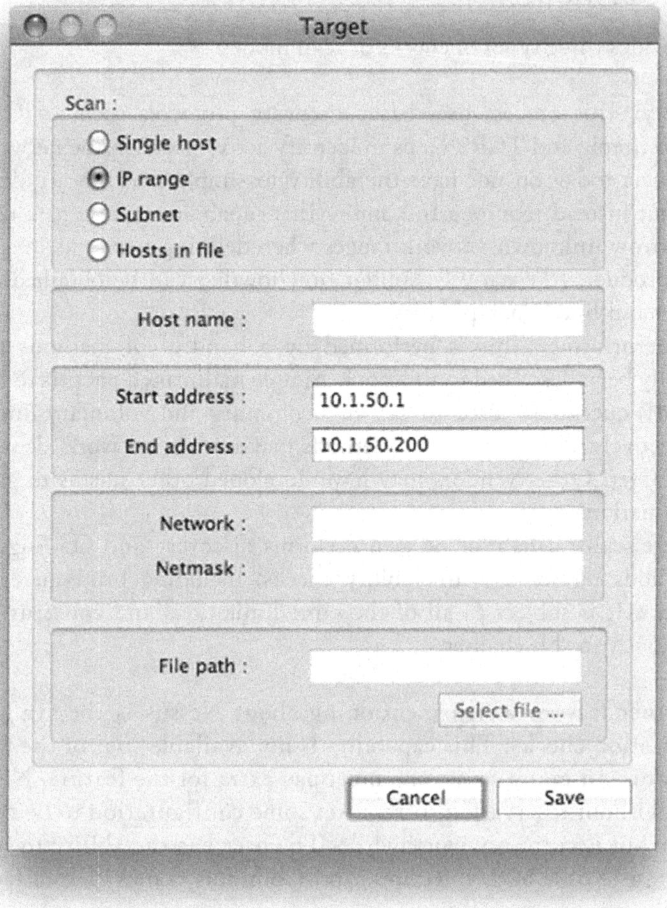

Figure 4.14 Nessus target selection panel.

address range, subnet specification, or an input file with a list of hosts/IP addresses. Each target specification is saved so that scans can be repeated in the future.

Next, the user can define the parameters of the scan by creating a scan policy. Shown in Figure 4.15, this policy contains:

Basic options about the scan (aggressiveness, packet captures, types of port scans, logging, etc).

Credentials if white box testing is to be performed.

Plug-in selection to employ the latest and most relevant checks. The library of plug-ins for Nessus is extensive. The key to efficient scanning is to select only the plug-ins needed for the target network.

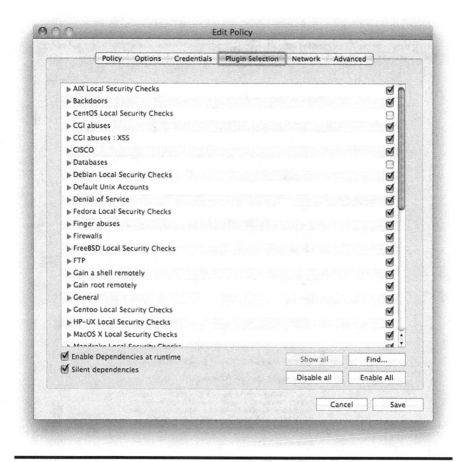

Figure 4.15   Nessus Scan Policy plugin selection.

Network congestion control settings (simultaneous connections, time outs, target disengagement rules).
Advanced parameter settings for various protocols and checks.

Once all of these parameters are selected, the scan can be performed. When complete, the report is available in a hierarchical, navigable format. This report can also be exported to HTML. The report is easy to read, as shown in Figure 4.16. This example entry from the report shows the port and protocol used to obtain the information, secure sockets layer (SSL) for Nessus (tcp/1241). Then, the report shows that the Supported SSL Cipher Suites plug-in was used to find the vulnerability. In this case, it is not actually a vulnerability but an enumeration. After that, the remainder of the report item is self-explanatory. A very nice feature of Nessus is that it shows the output from the plug-in, which in this case reveals the extent of

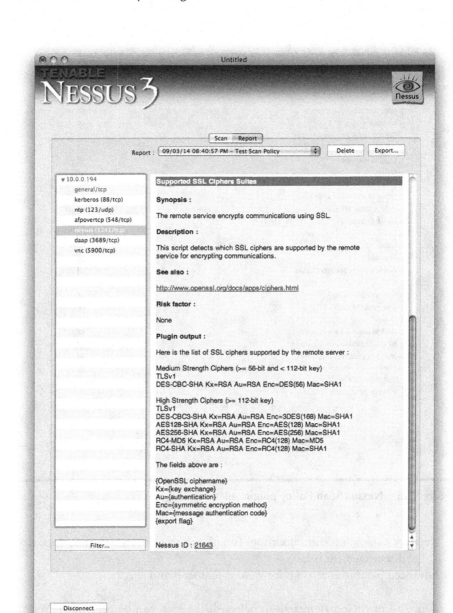

Figure 4.16 Nessus vulnerability details report.

the information that was revealed by the SSL service. Even better than this, for the technically inclined analyst, the Nessus ID will link to the details of the plug-in on the Tenable Web site. This plug-in also has a source code that can be reviewed so that the method of checking can be fully understood.

End Notes

1. Understanding this section depends on your knowledge of the OSI Basic Reference Model. A description of the OSI Model is beyond the scope of this book.
2. Tweaking TCP's Timers, CUED/F-INFENG/TR.487, Kieran Mansley, Laboratory for Communication Engineering, Cambridge University Engineering Department, July 6, 2004, 3.
3. If an application firewall is placed between the target server and the scanner, this type of fingerprinting could possibly fail because it will detect and ignore invalid HTTP requests.
4. American Standard Code for Information Interchange
5. This discussion assumes that you have a basic understanding of HTML and XML. Specifically, you should know how XML tags are constructed. It is also helpful to understand the general idea of an object in the object-oriented design sense of the word.
6. Federal Information Processing Standard Publication 199.

Chapter 5

Selecting Technology

Vulnerability management product acquisition can be a complicated process. Since reliability has increased among vendors and the time between new vulnerability discovery and check distribution has shrunk, other factors must be considered. The first and most important step in product selection is to understand the requirements. At first one may not think many requirements exist other than picking the user interface you prefer, but that is not the case. So this chapter will clarify the most significant requirements as well as some of the issues concerning the future of the industry as a whole.

5.1 General Requirements

When conducting a technology acquisition, it is important to first determine the general requirements. These requirements are closely tied to the primary goals of your firm in its Vulnerability Management (VM) program. The usual items are always present: accurately detect vulnerabilities, track remediation status, and report progress. Are there public or private clouds in operation? Those will very likely have different requirements, which will be discussed later in this book.

There are other requirements that are not always obvious. For example, are there different groups that perform various aspects of VM? In some cases, the vulnerability check parameters are defined and managed by a compliance group whereas the security or network teams control the scheduling and bandwidth settings. There are process requirements that exist in addition to the technology requirements. This is a key point; if an organization isn't ready for an enterprise VM program, regardless of the tool acquired, the program will fail.

To identify requirements, consider first the overarching goals of a VM program. Naturally, it is expected that the reduction of risk is a primary goal. But there is another goal related to reduction of risk and program governance: compliance. The entry of government regulation and private standards can cause organizations of all types to consider establishing firm requirements for compliance. Sarbanes–Oxley, Federal Financial Institutions Examination Council (FFIEC), General Data Protection Regulation (GDPR), and Payment Card Industry (PCI) standards are just a few key ones. There are also potentially numerous internal standards that must be met by IT systems. Identification of the relevant standards in your organization is a good start.

Governance serves as a measurement tool in risk management. This is where stakeholders can have assurance that the operations team is performing the right actions in support of risk management and that the outcomes of these activities are as close as possible to the plan. This does not mean that a broad measurement of risk, such as a Common Vulnerability Scoring System (CVSS) score under 9, is really reducing risk. However, when systems and practices are properly aligned with objectives, assurance becomes the observing factor for stakeholders.

5.1.1 Division of Responsibilities

A basic division of responsibilities can be critical for meeting compliance and audit requirements in a large institution. The primary concern is to avoid having the vulnerability check parameters changed by a group or individual with a vested interest in not appearing vulnerable. In addition to concealing vulnerabilities, this behavior is not unlike the age-old accounting problem where a business unit reports better results from one quarter to the next by changing the accounting rules. In the security realm, this leads to an overall security weakness that can threaten a large portion of an organization since vulnerability audit parameters can be applied globally.

Divided responsibility may not only have a compliance component but a simple operational excellence one. In the delivery of IT services to a business, various groups are accountable and yet dependent upon other groups. This is no less true for the role of VM in the delivery of IT services. For example, the network group or a cloud service provider may have service level agreements that may be impacted by vulnerability scans. Conversely, the vulnerability scans themselves may be part of the service level agreement. Those service levels are subject to change depending on customer requirements and may have many complex elements. The internal service provider, which may be a network group or server platform group, will need to exercise some control over when a vulnerability assessment takes place and perhaps how much of the provided service's resources are consumed in the process. The network team may be concerned with how much bandwidth is consumed on a particular wide-area network (WAN) link during an active scan.

A server team, however, may be concerned about the system resources required to operate an agent in different modes. Perhaps during an active assessment of the host, the agent consumes an excessive amount of CPU or conflicts with a single business-critical application service. So, limited control of the auditing process may be necessary while control over the quality elements should be restricted to security and/or compliance.

A virtualized environment can amplify the impact of an agent where multiple guest operating system (OS) instances will require the operation of multiple vulnerability assessment agents. Also, the impact risk on multiple OSs simultaneously is increased by the fact that the host OS running a hypervisor may also have an agent running. Regardless of the group managing the resource scheduling for an assessment, given the testing and management required for certain activities, a single security group may not want to have this responsibility when there are already knowledgeable individuals who would prefer to take ownership.

In summary, the message here is that each group in an IT organization is accountable for the services it provides. The introduction of a new IT function has an impact on operations in other groups. Inclusion of representatives from the affected groups will be instrumental in identifying the impacts and requirements of the VM product. One good tool to facilitate the identification of these requirements is the process dependency diagram. Figure 5.1 shows an example diagram where the VM service is the focal point. However, this diagram

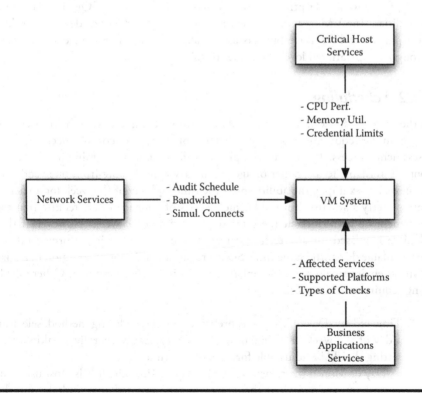

Figure 5.1   Identifying VM system requirements.

can be expanded to identify dependencies that may be created for other services where their requirements may change.

From this diagram, we should be able to quickly identify requirements for the VM system that not only achieve the objectives of identifying vulnerabilities but enhance the service levels of the affected systems. In this diagram, "Network Services" has provided requirements that affect the existing service levels:

■ Audit scheduling around business hours
■ Bandwidth consumption requirements per site or other grouping such as source network
■ Simultaneous network connections to minimize impact on routers and firewalls

The business applications services group, however, has requirements that not only affect the performance of the applications, but there is a requirement to perform certain types of vulnerability checks. This is a common result of enhancing service level agreements (SLAs) to reflect the security of a system. An SLA for an application services group may specify that tests will be performed on every new release for cross site scripting and structured query language (SQL) injection vulnerabilities. The VM system has then not only generated service delivery burdens for a particular IT service but has also enabled enhancements to existing SLAs through an operational level agreement (OLA).

5.1.2 Scheduling

In the previous section, we discussed how audit scheduling may be a requirement. This granular requirement is the specification of the type of controls needed on the assessment process. Related to the previous discussion, the timing and resource controls available to a scanner or agent can vary considerably from one vendor to the next. For example, the ability to set the time and day of the week for an active scan is pretty standard. But the business cycles of your firm may require that the assessment be performed at the same day and time each week. However, if that schedule is missed for any technical reason, the assessment is performed on the next available day at the same time. Such a requirement is not uncommon in a busy financial environment where compliance is continuously monitored. Other scheduling requirements to consider are:

1. Time of Day, Day of Week—A pretty common scheduling method, selecting a day of the week or a time of day is very typical. Generally speaking, this setting should be adjustable for a particular time zone.

   Day of Month (first, last, particular day)—This schedule is most useful in business operations where the targets must be assessed on a work day but the exact date cannot be reliably determined. Instead, the day of the week or day of the month would be specified. So, the parameter could be the first work day of the month, last work day, or even the last Monday. Some business cycles require that assessments only take place monthly or weekly on a certain day. For example, a retailer may perform collection of critical sales data on Monday mornings. In this case, it may be desirable to perform vulnerability assessment on Mondays after 12:00 noon (weekly) or on the last work day of the week (weekly) or last Friday of the month (monthly).

2. Only during/after local work hours—The assessment of desktop computers generally needs to happen during work hours when the computers are switched on. It is increasingly important to have this level of control with the focus of companies toward curtailing energy consumption.

3. Start/suspend/resume during a time/date window—This is useful when an assessment requires more time than is available during a certain time window. For example, if a scan must be performed during work hours but needs more than 12 hours to complete, the assessment should be paused for the night and resumed on the next workday/time. The process should continue until the assessment is complete. If the schedule for the assessment overlaps with the next assessment, the next one should be deferred for one cycle. This may sound like a complex requirement, but it is not uncommon and is currently not well addressed by the products available.

4. For all scheduling of assessments, the date and time parameters should be adjusted for local time zone. There are varying methods of implementation; however, the result should be that if an assessment is supposed to start at 10 am on Monday in New York, the same parameter applied to San Francisco would be 10 am Pacific time or 1 pm Eastern time. This becomes even more critical for large, globally distributed environments. I have seen systems perform all scheduling to Coordinated Universal Time (UTC) to accommodate deficiencies in local scheduling capabilities. Assuming the network is in the same time zone, a very good approach is to specify the time zone for the target network or host. Then, the schedules applied can have a parameter, which indicates whether or not the time zone of the target should be respected.

If all of a network segment were not in the same time zone, then it would be prudent to divide the network definition by time zone logically in the VM system. This will allow the system to scan on an optimal schedule for each part of the network segment. If this is not possible, then it may be necessary to confine the scan window to a common time frame during which all hosts are available.

5.1.3 Standards

Every vendor has a different approach to detecting vulnerabilities. In the early days of VM products, this proprietary approach was the primary means of distinguishing one product from another. The ability to be accurate yet fast was essential.

However, this has led to a severe lack of sharing of information among product vendors that threatens the effectiveness and consistency of security as a whole for customers. Since the results of vulnerability assessments may vary from one vendor to another, how can one be sure which results should be used to take remediation action? If one vendor detects a vulnerability by looking at a registry key and another misses the vulnerability because they use file detection, how can the security manager rely on either product since no single, reliable best-practice detection method has been employed. Discrepancies will exist if multiple VM systems are used, which can create additional work to resolve them. So that is not an efficient solution either.

Conversely, similar results can occur when software distribution methods used by organizations do not result in the common footprints on a system that result from a standard local installation. In some cases, applications on the Microsoft Windows platform can be installed with certain registry keys missing. When the vulnerability scanner looks for these registry keys and does not find them, then the vulnerability status can be misread.

A more global problem is the lack of standard vulnerability identifiers. For example, if the VM system uses proprietary identifiers for vulnerabilities and the patch management system uses Bugtraq ID numbers, how can the two be reconciled? In some cases, there is no identifier available for a particular vulnerability that was discovered by the VM system vendor, and therefore only a proprietary index is available. Some kind of standard adherence is needed to maximize the effectiveness of the overall VM process and ensure consistent identification worldwide.

There are solutions available. If it were agreeable to vendors and MITRE Corporation alike that vulnerabilities they discover can be centrally identified and described, then patch management systems can rely upon those identifiers.

Alternatively, some vendors have already integrated functionality such as patch management so that compatibility in vulnerability identification and corresponding remediation is not a concern. However, this limits the choices of products and functionality. The VM systems buyer is committed to the vendor for both functions. As of this writing, no vendor provides comprehensive patch support for all OSs and all vulnerabilities nor are they likely to do so in the future. Oddly enough, at the time of this writing, there are more than 108,000 CVEs (Common Vulnerabilities and Exposures). Yet, top VM vendors cover less than 75% of that number. Why do so many customers tolerate this obvious deficiency? If a vendor told you that their product was no more than 75% effective, why would that be acceptable? Customers need to recognize this key deficiency and demand more.

Recognizing that they cannot do everything, vendors will build in the ability to interface with key management and tracking systems such as change management and incident management. The number of compatible vendors may be limited. In that case, vendors have built an application-programming interface (API) that will allow the creation of a custom connector between the VM and other systems.

We previously discussed technology and the support for standards such as CVSS, CVE, and OVAL (Open Vulnerability and Assessment Language). There are great benefits to adopting a standard for any technology. But given the rapid proliferation of security technologies and their competitiveness with one another, the adoption of standards should become a more critical requirement. Initially, it would seem foolish for a vendor to "give away" functionality to another vendor. However, by providing the flexibility to choose the needed products, vendors can increase their chance of selection. This creates a chicken and egg problem where the vendor must support the open standard and the customer must demand it. OVAL is one of the more specific and important standards that should be seriously considered on a requirements list.

5.1.4 Reports

As you will see in a later chapter, reporting is an important part of VM and managing any process that can be measured. Before completing your evaluation of any vendor, a clear understanding among the key people involved in VM should be in place as to how the process of identifying and remediating vulnerabilities should be conducted. Then, ask critical questions about what managers, engineers, administrators, auditors, and risk managers need to know to perform their part of the process and get the most out of the system. This will lead to a definition of the reports needed. Consider distributing sample reports to stakeholders to make sure they are acceptable. Those reports have the following high-level requirements:

- Scheduling: Frequency at which the reports will be needed. In some cases, reports are needed weekly to remediate the latest vulnerabilities and, in other cases, monthly to evaluate the security posture of the organization. In still other cases, reports may be needed every time a certain event occurs such as a threshold being reached on total risk to a critical target. Having an idea about the timing and frequency of all the reports will reveal what kind of scheduling flexibility is needed in automated reporting.
- Objective: Knowing the exact purpose of the report will often help identify if the right report is present in the system or needs to be developed. Some reports produced by a system are titled differently but still may meet the objective. On the other hand, it is possible that just the reverse may happen. A report may be titled "Audit Review" where it seems that it is intended for the use of auditors. However, close observation may show that the report will not meet your specific auditor's role definition. An ancillary point here may be that one should not be too quick to check a requirement box until they have verified the details of the reports.
- Format: Most reports are not very customizable. The order of the columns, sorting and filtering options, and header and footer content may be unsuitable for your organization. The latter requirement can be a significant problem. If a vulnerability report does not have the company-required document classification statement at the footer and company logo or department name

in the header, some concerns could arise with auditors looking for compliance in document handling. Also, the utility of a report can vary greatly with the sorting and filtering capabilities. If a scan results report can only be sorted by Internet protocol (IP) address and not by severity, perhaps the prioritization process cannot be efficiently conducted.

■ Customization: When the canned reports are not available, some access needs to be given to the database and schema to allow reports to be generated that simply aren't available in the core product. This can also be provided with a report writer add-on. Any such add-on will have to be equally vetted with the requirements. Also, one must consider that additional products or consulting used will raise the overall cost of the system.

■ Types: The most common, critical areas for reporting are Remediation, Security Posture, and Process Monitoring. The type of reports you will need will naturally depend on how your process works. Remediation reports should specifically facilitate the methods by which your process remediates. This sounds obvious, but it is not. For example, a company may have a different group remediate vulnerabilities in each city or office network. So the reports should be available by location.

Alternatively, your organization may remediate by device type. For example, server administrators may all work for a global server group. Vulnerabilities for those servers would be assessed, prioritized, and work allocated by a central group. This may be the case even though the audit of those servers by the system took place as an audit of the overall network.

■ Triggers: Some reports need to be generated when a certain set of conditions are met. These reports typically are e-mailed or copied to a specific location for retrieval. The triggering event can be when the vulnerability score or a particular target reaches a certain level or when a critical host has a certain severity of vulnerability. These reports would then be automatically e-mailed to specified persons who are necessarily authorized users of the reporting system.

■ Roles: Any report should be configurable to be viewed or modified by specific roles. Those roles would be defined as: System Administrator, Network Owner, Network Group Owner, or System(target) Owner. There are two purposes for specifying which roles or combination of roles are permitted to access or modify a report: (1) Separation of duties—This ensures that reports cannot be manipulated for a favorable outcome and contradict any performance penalty that may be weighed against a responsible party who fails to remediate systems. (2) Confidentiality of the data—Each report contains a potential gold mine of information to a hacker that could surely be used to assess targets and attack vectors.

The most flexible approach to implementing roles is to allow the VM system administrator to create the roles and assign the users and user group to those roles. More about role definitions later.

■ Control: The reports should be filterable by network, IP range, system type, scanner, application or network owner. You will quickly find that once the availability of good data is known by managers and engineers, they will ask for more. Having in-depth knowledge of the structure of local networks, network managers may ask for particular subnet reports and IP ranges even through the audit process takes places on all IP addresses that can be found. Essentially, what is audited for vulnerabilities is a superset of the reports requested by the network owners.

Owners of applications may ask for reports showing the vulnerability state of the systems supporting their applications. This may include a combination of routers, firewalls, database servers, application servers, and web servers. This may be especially important for Sarbanes–Oxley (SOX) compliance or limited *payment card industry* (PCI) audits. Large organizations with very limited PCI exposure will need to assess the vulnerability of any systems directly or indirectly related to payment processing. Being able to readily identify and audit those systems without clouding reports with vulnerability data from irrelevant systems can save time and cost in an audit. The same principal holds true for non-PCI financial systems. SOX compliance should not be seen as a reason to accept or reject functionality from the VM system; however, it can be helpful in evaluating controls related to financial systems. Public companies should carefully consider the real requirements of SOX in accordance with the 2007 Securities and Exchange Commission (SEC) guidance on the topic. Vendors would be hard-pressed to provide solid advice and rationale directly related to SOX compliance and their products.

5.1.5 Advanced Reporting

Beyond the reporting discussed so far and related to customization, there are more advanced reporting capabilities that are yet to be fully demonstrated by vendors. We are discussing this in a separate section of this book because for organizations that have not yet begun to mature their processes, these capabilities may not be immediately needed. However, if you think that your organization will have a firm need for reports in support of process optimization, consider the following basic requirements:

■ The product should be able to allow for customized reporting based on access to raw audit results.
■ Summary tables of audits should be available in an open database structure (schema).
■ Add-on functionality should permit some statistical analysis of vulnerability data.
■ Beyond data analysis, the information should be combined with or readily able to combine with network topology information to assess risk by attack vectors.

These capabilities are more complex and require a greater discipline from staffing and process. They directly feed risk management functions as well as security incident management. There are already products on the market that can cull this information from the major VM vendors and combine it with firewall, intrusion protection system (IPS), and network equipment products to map and identify threats. Some vendors can even allow you to assess risks at a high level and then drill down into the specific configuration items on host, network, and security elements that can be altered to remediate an impending threat.

Assess your candidate vendor's compatibility with these advanced products to leave a path for future enhancement. As of this time of this writing, the most advanced of these risk management products are few and expensive but offer great functionality to the technical risk manager.

5.2 Automation

Automating as much of the VM process as possible will go far in having it embraced by an organization. The automation must take the form of integrating with existing systems and providing a virtually invisible footprint. More out-of-the-box integration is called for using well-established standards rather than labor-intensive customer programming. Standards such as Extensible Markup Language (XML) and remote procedure call (RPC) are very useful items to look for.

5.2.1 Ticket Generation

The creating of change or incident tickets is a key area for automation. The system should be able to interface with the ticketing system in a way that all of the required fields are supplied or synthesized and also supply the most relevant information to the ticket recipient. Make a list of the items your ticketing system requires and verify that all of those items are available in a ticketing interface or that they can be easily created. For example, some ticketing systems require a user ID of the person who created the ticket. If it is acceptable to the ticketing system users, a "vuln-system" user or equivalent can be created to accept entries from the system. Alternatively, perhaps the interface from the VM system can provide the target owner name or network owner name as a user ID. It is the small details like this that will quickly derail your plans unless they are all spelled out.

Completing the VM process is support for remediation. Once a ticket has been accepted and the remediation completed, a provisional closing of the ticket should be performed. This event should then automatically notify the VM system that the remediation has been completed and verification should take place. A follow-up scan can either be immediately performed or performed at the next scheduled time. If the target is free of the vulnerability, then the ticket can either automatically complete closure or the VM system can send a message to the ticketing system to close the ticket. If the vulnerability has not been properly remediated, then the ticket should be re-opened or a new one generated depending on the internal process requirement.

Involving the owner of the ticketing system in the product selection process is an important factor if you are considering integration. The amount of work required for the integration should be accurately assessed since it could be expensive depending on the flexibility and ease of use of system interfaces. Besides, one can never expect the integration to takes place without the support of the system owner.

5.2.2 Process Integration

Any VM system should have some flexibility in integrating with existing IT processes. Although some of these processes may not be present in an organization prior to acquisition of hardware or software, the basic idea of a VM process is unavoidable. Vulnerabilities are detected, analyzed, and remediated. Even though each step may not be thorough or well documented, they will nevertheless probably exist and should be documented to the extent necessary to validate requirements against system capabilities. In many cases, it may be easier to reengineer the process into a more standard form. Remediation through patch management is an area significantly impacted by process and technology integration and this demands greater flexibility as well.

5.2.2.1 Process and System Flexibility

Some VM systems are built around a specific and relatively rigid process. During the sales cycle, vendors often tout this process at the outset to demonstrate excellence of the product in how it delivers consistent results. Unless the buyer of these products is very flexible, efficient, and adaptive to changing critical and ingrained processes, the tool will consistently deliver poor results.

This can become a limitation on the tool's effectiveness rather than an enhancement to the vulnerability state of your organization. Having a rigid process around which the tool is built helps the product developer because it simplifies design and coding, and it also simplifies the tool for the end-user. But organizations requiring easy cultural and technological integration have much more to gain if the tool can be molded to their requirements. The type of flexibility required in technology includes:

■ Provide reports in the format suitable to your environment and culture: Some companies are averse to logging into a system and selecting parameters to receive a report. This is usually because users are so busy that they cannot include a process and system change in their daily routine. A great method for getting the important data in front of them is to send it automatically to the right manager. E-mail is a common delivery mechanism that everyone already uses.

- Alternatively, some IT managers have web portals that they use daily in their routine. Some critical information about their networks would be useful on their personalized home page. For example, a "top-10 hosts" report showing the hosts with the worst scores in their network will help them quickly assess and assign remediation tasks. For more senior managers, a "top-10 networks" or "vulnerability trend" report would help to quickly show if and where problems might exist with a 10-second review.

- Allow for individual IT managers to setup and perform audits of their area of responsibility outside of the standard, agreed-upon schedules. In active scanning, this is known as scan-on-demand. It is a valuable remediation verification tool that can minimize error in remediation. Engineers sometimes remediate the wrong vulnerability or misunderstand and incorrectly remediate one. Another common mistake is failure to reboot after installing certain patches. The verification process, driven by the system owner or IT manager, can enhance the quality of remediation results.

5.2.2.2 Patch Management Support

Patch and change management interfaces have already been discussed. If the related processes are present in your organization, then some basic data requirements should be met. But the VM system should also provide an interface that is sufficiently flexible to respond to processes. For example, internal processes may not perform a verification audit of the vulnerability and wait until the next audit. Although the change process may have completed and in doing so have informed the VM system, a verification scan should have the flexibility to be performed as part of the next, regularly scheduled audit. Anything else may demonstrate too much rigidity in the workflow of the tool.

Professional services typically are required for customization. Beware of this challenge and look deeply into the implementation requirements for your process adaptation. If the product vendor informs you that customization is only or most reliable with the use of professional services, then the cost of the deployment may be deceptively low. Include with the purchase the delivery of specific process integration requirements.

5.3 Architecture

The architecture of a VM system is an important part of its ability to work in your corporate physical structure. It also will probably be the largest factor affecting the cost of the system. Considerations such as geography, office size, network equipment, security architecture, WAN bandwidth, and government regulations will impact greatly your decision on vendors, type of product, and cost.

The last item, cost, is our starting point for making a decision on vendors. Begin with a survey of the VM market, pricing, and products. Determine what the approximate cost per active IP address would be to your organization. An estimate of the number of IP addresses would be sufficient if you can stay within 10%. Multiply the average price per IP in the market by the number of IP addresses in your organization and then add 20% for annual maintenance. Then, add 10% for shipping and customs if you have foreign offices and another 10% for consulting services if you have more than 15,000 IPs. For example, 20,000 IPs times $8 per IP = $160,000; then add 10% for shipping and 10% for consulting = $32,000. Total fixed costs: $192,000. Then calculate the recurring cost of maintenance: $32,000 annual maintenance (160,000 × 0.20). The total cost of the system for the first year is $224,000.

This is only a cost estimate, and it will be impacted significantly by the previously mentioned architectural factors. In an active scanning system, physical scanners must be purchased and installed in good vantage points in the network. In an extreme example, if your environment has 100 offices with the only good scanning point being in each office, (i.e., no strong WAN links), then you will end up purchasing up to 100 devices. These devices can be expensive depending on the product. There are sometimes less expensive solutions, including a virtual machine version of the product or the use of host agents, with no per instance charge. However, there will be some hardware costs for the buyer who supplies her own. But it may be more cost effective if there are available CPU cycles in a virtual machine.

5.3.1 Passive Architecture

Passive scanners that observe network traffic may be even more subject to this limitation since the traffic on each inspected network switch must be copied to the device. For large but complex central offices, a passive scanner is a very workable solution where connections typically are very fast and can withstand the loads that can be imposed by the RSPAN function (remote switched port analyzer, previously discussed in the technology chapter). For organizations that have several large offices with ample WAN bandwidth, active scanners can be an excellent solution. Since bandwidth is becoming less expensive and more abundant in remote areas of the world, careful planning and scheduling of audits can allow scanning to be more cost effective with fewer scanners and lower shipping and customs costs.

Centralizing the VM function as much as possible can result in considerable savings.

5.3.2 Agent-Based Architecture

With agents, it is necessary to install software on every host to be evaluated, with the exception of some agents capable of performing network-based audits of adjacent systems. In some cases, vendors will charge a higher price for server agents versus desktop agents. There is no significant functional difference in the two that merits this pricing model but rather a matter of sales volume and cost recovery. Some VM architecture strategies will deploy agents solely on servers in order to minimize the impact on the network connections, with the assumption that the agent itself will not impact other software. Vendors often recognize this, and pricing is understandably higher.

Where the use of agents can become more complex is when virtual machines are used. The agent can be installed on several guest Oss, yet they are deployed on a single physical server. The impact on the hardware is multiplied. One should seek some guidance from the vendor on how significantly the agent can impact the CPU and memory resources of a virtual machine and the underlying host OS and hardware. It is also likely that the vendor will charge for each OS and not per CPU core.

Since agents have to be deployed and maintained on every host under assessment, the solution is less prone to network limitations and more a problem of operating the software on every host. It can complicate installation and deployment but virtually eliminate the cost of shipping. Organizations with a large, mobile sales force or cloud infrastructure will benefit greatly from an agent-based system since the WAN connection speed is unpredictable and the frequency of presence in the local office low.

Agents become an essential component in cloud services when the supporting infrastructure is not under direct control. In many cases, cloud service providers would prefer that customers not perform active, network vulnerability scans. These scans can place a heavy load on virtual network infrastructure where there are several tenants possibly using the same hosts. Maintaining any specific service level becomes quite difficult.

It is also problematic when the service provider operates virtual firewalls and other hypervisor-based network services. Scanning large portions of a network can affect much more than just network traffic and certainly can consume CPU resources.

Conversely, service providers sometimes offer vulnerability scanning agents or integrated services designed to function optimally in the environment. This has the benefit of having acceptable, prepared scanning resources without the capital outlay.

5.3.3 Active Scanning Architecture

We have already discussed the basic architecture of active scanning and the considerations to be made concerning consumption of bandwidth. One other key consideration is the management of several hardware devices. While this may seem trivial to an organization with hundreds or even thousands of servers, usually the staff maintaining the VM system is limited and requires unique training. They rely on resources of other locations and departments to maintain devices with which they are generally unfamiliar. Many of these devices have command lines, serial ports, and network requirements that may not be fully understood. Although many of the administrative responsibilities can be centralized and automated, there are inevitably malfunctions in the device or the environment that need to be corrected on site.

For example, network connectivity can be lost at some point between the management server and the device itself. Despite all of the available tools, it may not be possible to determine the cause of the failure. A local engineer will have to check the physical connections, switch configuration, device power, and logical network configuration. This may involve plugging in a serial cable, configuring a terminal, logging in with local administrator privileges, and performing command line functions. In all likelihood, the engineer has not done this in the six or eight months since the device was deployed. The VM operator will have to provide written or verbal instructions and receive some feedback. The use of a network KVM (keyboard, video, mouse) device is helpful but not perfect. The physical environment may still require inspection. If the network connection to the site is lost, then little can be done remotely.

Additionally, replacement of devices that have failed may be difficult—but not for want of technical expertise. Some countries have import duties and restrictions on technologies that can extend the replacement cycle for months. Certain locations seem particularly unfriendly to commerce, particularly where technology is concerned. Russia, Venezuela, and even Mexico can be very resistant to receiving technology to the detriment of their own citizens. It is even possible that final delivery in some locations may call for a small bribe to the delivery person. Ultimately, a virtual machine version of a product, if available, can be sent electronically and made operational overnight.

With an understanding of the aforementioned issues, your plan will have to carefully consider the number of devices, location of each, skills of local personnel, languages, reliability of network, available bandwidth, power requirements, environmental conditions, customs procedures, and vendor presence and inventory. There are some clever ways to accommodate deficiencies in many of these components. Depending on your specific challenges, one or more of these strategies will help.

5.3.3.1 Determining the Number of Devices

Determine the number of devices required and include a growth factor. Volume is simply more difficult to manage. Determine the number of networks, strength of network connections, and number of targets. From this information, a total load for scanning can be estimated. Scan Load = Bandwidth/Target + 10% Overhead + 15% Growth. Then estimate the amount of time required to scan a set of those targets with the candidate vendor's product. A test of a scan under specific conditions provides the average time per host. Extensive testing is recommended since every environment is unique and will respond differently to the various approaches of vendors.

For example, a company has several networks in separate physical locations as shown in Figure 5.2. This table shows the amount of bandwidth provisioned, used,

XYZ Corporation - Audit Schedule																											
	Mon				Tue				Wed				Thu				Fri				Sat				Sun			
GMT	0	1	2	3	0	1	2	3	0	1	2	3	0	1	2	3	0	1	2	3	0	1	2	3	0	1	2	3
HQ		■																										
HQ-Servers					■																							
HQ-Intranet			■																									
HQ DMZ																										■		
HQ-VoIP			■																									
Dallas						■																						
Dallas-Servers						■																						
Hong Kong										■																		
HKG-Servers																							■					
Santiago																		■										
Santiago-VoIP																						■						
Mexico City											■																	
Mexico-Servers														■														
Mexico-VoIP												■																
Chicago																			■									
Chicago-Mfg																		■										
Atlanta															■													
Atlanta-Servers														■														
San Francisco											■																	

Figure 5.2 Audit schedule GMT chart.

and available. In order to get an accurate estimate of the amount of time required to audit a network, there are two tests performed with these sites to determine the average amount of time required to scan a host. Some simple math gets a close estimate of how much time is overhead for gathering and transmitting results to the reporting server. Two tests are required with the largest practical target sample size. The key is to make sure the difference between the two samples is substantial enough to meaningfully calculate the difference, indicating the time required to scan a target. The overall process of determining the number of scanners required is as follows:

■ Review the networks and select a representative sample of sites, WAN connection types, bandwidths, and host types. The type of WAN connection and bandwidth will impact the response time of scan activities and, on a large scale, impact the total time. Connections such as Frame Relay will show longer response time than dedicated private lines. Bandwidth will have an impact as well but only up to a limit. Scanning activity has limits in device hardware and protocol connection limits.

■ Select a sample size (S1) of targets to scan in the representative networks. This sample size should be at least 10% of the total number of hosts but not less than 10. A second sample size (S2) should also be taken that is larger than the first by at least 50% and not less than 20. This will ensure that the sample size is sufficient to show a meaningful difference in the results.

Table 5.1 Scan Time Estimation Chart

Location	Targets	Bwdth	Util	Avail	Audit Time		Time Per Target	Estimate 20 Targets
					10 Targets	20 Targets		
HQ	450	N/A	N/A	N/A	9	11.5	0.25	119.0
Dallas	260	2000	72	560	13	15	0.2	63.0
Hong Kong	241	4000	45	2200	12	16	0.4	104.4
Santiago	75	384	80	76.8	11	15	0.4	37.0
Mexico City	245	4000	52	1920	8	13	0.5	125.5
Chicago	325	4000	62	1520	11	14.5	0.35	121.3
Atlanta	175	1544	70	463.2	13	16	0.3	62.5
San Francisco	310	4000	55	1800	9	12	0.3	99.0
						Total Hours Required		12.2

- Capture measures to complete the Table 5.1. In the table, calculate the time required to scan each target (ST) by subtracting the time to scan the first sample (T1) from the time to scan the second sample (T2) and dividing by the difference in the sample number of hosts. This is the total time required to scan a single host (TT) absent the overhead for gathering, formatting, and transmitting results.

- Calculate the amount of time required for the scanning overhead (OH) mentioned previously. The overhead for the larger sample is the amount of time required to audit S2 minus time to scan all of the S2 targets. S2 - (S2-hosts * ST). The point is that there is a significant difference in the amount of time to scan targets versus to complete all of the activities of the audit.

- Extrapolate and estimate the time to scan the entire network by multiplying the number of the total hosts in the network by TT and add overhead: X = TT * OH. The final column in the Table 5.1 shows this number. The sum of these figures shows the number of hours required if a single scanner were to audit all of the networks from a single location one after another. Although this scenario almost never happens with this broad of a geographical distribution, it does provide a "feel" for the amount of device time required.

- Decide on how often an audit of every target in the organization is needed. This will indicate the amount of time you have to allocate a single scanner for scanning targets and ultimately lead to the total number of scanners that are needed. A typical network should have audits performed at least weekly to be sure that newly discovered or reported vulnerabilities are captured on reports and that remediation activities are taking place in a timely fashion.
- Create a proposed schedule for auditing. Since many targets will have to be in use during a scan, a schedule will have to be created with the information from the previous step. With a schedule, you can determine how many targets can be audited by a single scanner over a day or week. Note that you will have to consider local time, office customs, and target availability when making this schedule. Figure 5.2 shows a sample schedule. Looking at each time slot for audits will show how many audits must take place at a given time. This sample has 4 time slots per day, with each spanning a 6-hour period on a Greenwich Mean Time (GMT) clock.
- Get the vendors' recommendation on how many simultaneous audits can be performed by one device and how much impact that will have on scan performance. For example, a scan of network A will may take 45 minutes when performed alone. But when performed with another simultaneous scan of a network of equal specification, the scan may take 30% longer on average, assuming none of the other network devices in between introduces more delay.
- Estimate the number of devices needed. Referring again to Figure 5.2, you can assess how many scanners are required by counting the recommended number of simultaneous audits to be performed and dividing by the number recommended. In some cases, you can reduce the number of scanners by rearranging the audit schedule. NB: Always leave room for error and growth. This arrangement shows us that if an audit of networks is performed from a central location, it is probably manageable with a single device provided that the device can conduct two audits simultaneously without significant performance degradation.

If it were determined that due to operational constraints, the audit of "Chicago-Mfg" could only be performed on Wednesdays, then there might be contention for a time slot. Negotiating compromises among the operational requirements of each site can resolve such issues and further minimize devices. Also note that server networks can often be audited on weekends and late evenings, thereby providing some relief to audit user workstation networks during the daytime.

Every network is unique, and results may vary. Testing is an effective tool but not perfect in predicting the idiosyncrasies of networks and systems. Leaving some flexibility in requirements for adaptation is essential. Some advance planning and testing can save a lot of money when making a purchase. It will also enhance the credibility of the system and its operators in the eyes of the user population. Once the scanners are deployed, any top-end VM system should provide a means to report on scanner resource utilization so the system manager can reallocate in a changing environment.

5.3.3.2 Select Locations Carefully

The location selection should be based on:

- The number of targets to be scanned locally
- The bandwidth available to other adjacent networks
- The availability and skill level of the support staff for the location
- The regulatory restrictions on IT issues such as privacy and union work rules

Other factors such as shipping costs, taxes, and other import considerations should be made. Also, basic deployment logistics such as power supplies, rack space, and network physical layout should be considered but typically are minor factors.

5.3.4 Secure the Platform

Requirements should also stress the importance of a secure design. The least desirable situation is to introduce greater threats into the environment with the intent of improving security. Any hardware or software introduced into the environment should be vetted for security. Certainly no vendor has an interest in providing a vulnerable system, but any acquisition calls for the exercise of due diligence. It seems natural to expect all hardware appliances to be well locked down and software to have been securely developed. However, the VM program manager would be negligent if she did not verify the state of these systems at a minimum through reference checking.

Furthermore, vulnerability results may be stored on an appliance or other external storage device. I recommend checking the security design of any appliances. If there is local storage on the appliance, such as a hard drive, determine if and how scan results are stored on the unit. Find out how long the data are stored and how they are removed. When the unit is returned or lost in transit, could this represent a threat to the organization by exposing the dirty laundry to hackers? The appliance should be subject to the same data retention, backup, and secure storage policies and standards as any other system with only minimal deviation to accommodate product limitations.

5.3.5 System Integration

It is not unusual that many organizations purchase and install technology without consideration of its active role in the rest of the IT infrastructure. The end result is often a system with greatly limited functionality requiring significantly greater effort to integrate with other systems or major process changes to compensate.

There are numerous ways that a VM system can provide data to maximize the benefits to security and operations. Among those systems to be considered are change and incident management. These systems commonly are found in mid to large organizations trying to maturely and consistently extract higher performance from IT services.

With the use of agents in the cloud and active scanners in the organization-owned data centers all on the same management platform, it is quite practical to gather a much more complete view of the vulnerabilities in the operating environment. Subsequent integration into other tools such as those used for threat mapping, security information and event management (SEIM), and security governance monitoring, one can formulate a very strong, active technical risk management program.

5.3.5.1 Change Management

Change management is a critical component of the remediation process. As previously discussed, when a vulnerability is found, the details can be sent automatically to a change management system to initiate a change process.

The ability of the VM system to be interfaced with change management is never as straightforward as vendors tend to suggest. Some custom development is almost always needed. Development of this type is typically for the conversion of data types, format, and communication method. The vendor's product may deliver Simple Network Management Protocol (SNMP) traps for newly discovered vulnerabilities, yet the change system will require XML or use an e-mail listener process. Someone will inevitably have to code an interface between these two completely different technologies. Whatever the interface method, the common data elements exchanged are:

- Vulnerability details sent to the change system
- Vulnerability event identifier sent to the change system
- Change status update sent to the vulnerability system once remediation is complete
- Re-open or re-creation of the change, if the vulnerability is still present

One method for sharing and aggregating security information is through the use of open source technologies such as Grafeas. This is an open source specification for an application program interface (API) to share or transfer metadata from various technologies concerning the security state of the environment. It is particularly useful when collecting metadata about vulnerabilities, containers, operating systems, packages, and code. Some cloud service providers have cloud security advisory services that can ingest vulnerability information using the Grafeas specification.

One provider has APIs using Grafeas that allow the customer to take vulnerability scan data and other findings into a "findings API" that can capture the occurrences, provider name, resource name, type of finding, severity, network connection, remediation steps, certainty, and context. This information is then integrated with the other metadata that the service provider has to produce meaningful and robust reports on the security posture of the environment. This helps companies with multi-cloud or hybrid cloud environments and a variety of security tools to work toward a single picture of the fully integrated security posture. It also has the benefit of reducing the amount of custom coding and reporting needed to achieve this integration.

5.3.5.2 Incident Management

Similar to interfacing to change management, incident management may be a part of the portfolio of the operational support system in your organization. Interfacing issues are similar and will vary by process. In some cases, organizations prefer to handle changes in a change system, but incidents are reserved for a very specific set of circumstances.

On the other hand, it is not unusual to generate an incident for tracking the vulnerability and remediation process and then use the change management system to track only the impact on systems, resources, and processes when that change is made.

In either case and as previously mentioned, the completion of a change will initiate either the closure of an incident or the immediate notification of completion to the VM system. The VM system will then reassess the target to determine successful compliance.

5.3.5.3 Intrusion Prevention

Some vendors have attempted to integrate their products with intrusion prevention systems only to find that IPS vendors have dreams of competing against the VM vendor. This has led to a few failed attempts by vendors that would have otherwise benefited the customer greatly. If you are lucky enough to have an IPS that is compatible with vulnerability data from a selected vendor, then by all means have a hard look at the benefits, as there are many obstacles.

Standards or format compatibility are a significant obstacle. Although we discuss standards at length in this book, few vendors fully support them in the IPS world, or in the vulnerability world for that matter. At this time, the two industries are so far apart in interoperability that only a demanding customer base will be able to influence change. However, the basic idea is that if a new vulnerability is discovered on a target system, then the appropriate upstream IPS will be notified to activate the signature that would protect the asset until it is properly remediated.

There are two major benefits to this type of integration. First, a vulnerability is protected until full remediation can be complete, which lowers the overall dynamic vulnerability level in the environment. Second, the IPS optimizes its performance since only the necessary rules are activated above the standard policy implementation. This is particularly important when a very expensive IPS is heavily loaded on a busy DMZ (demilitarized zone) segment and a hardware upgrade does not offer sufficient cost benefit.

5.3.5.4 Security Event and Incident Management (SEIM)

SEIM integration is generally easier to accomplish. SEIM vendors make compatibility with myriad data sources an important selling point. The collection of data is their strongest suit, and it is very likely that they will accept data from VM systems with little modification.

If your organization has a SEIM, it would be remiss to not accept this important data feed. Where the IPS integration is not possible, the SEIM can at least use the data to determine the severity of an incident and escalate it accordingly. If your vendor does not easily support one of the major vendors of VM products, then they have likely chosen poorly.

5.4 Application Programming Interface (API)

Although frequently overlooked or treated as an afterthought check box, custom development is a significant area for specifying requirements. Very often, those who implement VM initiatives discover too late that significant customization is needed to maximize the potential of their security systems. This can happen when there are change management systems, often custom developed, around which entrenched internal processes are built. Since it is unlikely that a new change management system will be purchased, the ability to efficiently extract information from the VM system and initiate a change and/or incident process is critical.

At a high level, as previously described, when interfacing to a change or incident management system, the following items will need to be managed by the interfaces:

- Extract vulnerability data from the VM system.
- Initiate a change or incident in the internal system while retaining the reference provided by the VM system.
- Take a provisional closure of the incident and update the VM system. This will optionally start a verification assessment.

■ An event from the VM system will trigger closure of the incident or re-initiation of the incident depending on the outcome of verification.

Depending on the process and systems in your enterprise, the aforementioned steps can vary the data structures and processing required in the interface code. A clear understanding of the interface capabilities of the candidate vulnerability systems is essential prior to purchase. Once understood, assess what coding requirements there will be for each candidate. This will help highlight any potential shortcomings that may significantly limit overall effectiveness. For example, the planned internal VM processes may require that the detailed recommendations on remediation be transmitted from the VM system to the change management system. If this critical data element is not provided in the ticket generation process, then this may result in a critical gap in achieving IT security service goals.

5.5 Scoring Method

A close examination of the scoring method employed on the VM system is essential. The basic requirements of a scoring system as it relates to security operations may be:

■ Take asset value into consideration. More valuable assets in your organization should definitely receive higher priority handling than those with little value. Somewhere in either the scoring method or alerting capabilities should be a consideration of an asset value in either numeric or category terms. The process of valuing assets may be time consuming if it cannot be obtained from an existing asset management system.

■ Severity can be logically or intuitively determined from the score. If the number seems arbitrary or relative to zero, then it is difficult to determine if a score of 300 is severe, moderate, or informational. At some point, either from experience with the system or from knowledge of the method by which the score is derived, it should allow you to determine the category of severity.

■ Current knowledge of available exploits should be included in adjusting the severity. Vendors would have to revise their scoring method if a new, easily scriptable exploit is released to the general public. The score should be dynamic to keep pace with a dynamic threat environment.

■ A standards-based, either primary or secondary score such as CVSS should be included for comparison to public databases. This will prevent any confusion about the meaning of a score that may be derived from a proprietary scheme.

■ Optionally, a score should have a cardinality component. This means that the score will vary depending on the source of the assessment. If a vulnerability can be detected over the network from the public Internet, then it should have a higher score than one detected from the local segment.

Determining the appropriate score for a vulnerability is partly mathematical and partly a matter of requirements. It is not unlike the computation of risk:

$$Risk = p(x) \times \varepsilon \times \rho$$

where $p(x)$ is the probability of occurrence, ε is the loss expectancy from a single event, and ρ is the rate of occurrence per year. An example of a vulnerability score computation might be based on the following variables:

Severity of compromise (α)	Remote Control of System = 100 Remote Access to System = 75 Remote Reconnaissance = 50 Local Control of System = 50 Local Access = 40 Local Reconnaissance = 30
Ease of attack (β)	Easy (Scripted) = 1 Medium = 0.75 Difficult = 0.5
Existence of exploit code in wild (χ)	Exists = 1 Proof of Concept Only = 0.5 None = 0.25

So, the computation is a simple multiplication formula:

$$Score = \alpha \times \beta \times \chi$$

This simple approach to creating a score confines the score to a value between 3.75 and 100. That is, if "Local Reconnaissance" (30) is the severity, "Difficult" (0.5) is the ease of attack, and "None" (0.25) is the state of exploit code availability, then the final score is

$$Score = 30 \times 0.5 \times 0.25 = 3.75$$

Should the severity of compromise become remote control of the system, which is very bad, and all other factors remain the same, then the score rises to 12.5. By extension of this simple approach, the worst possible score is 100 with the β and χ factors equal to 1 and remote control of the system being the outcome.

Many scoring methods are more sophisticated that this and consider additional factors such as the length of time the vulnerability has been in existence. Furthermore, other scoring methods do not confine themselves to a simple scale of 0 to 100 but rather have no upper limit. This will naturally occur when unbound numbers such as age of vulnerability are considered. Also, the simple example given here has very limited bounds because it uses simple multiplication, but other methods prefer to make a clear distinction between that which is really bad and that which is of low risk by comparison. Operators such as squares and factorials can drive the score very high for greater risk distinction. But such scores may be more difficult to interpret. Whatever method is preferred, be sure that it can be transformed into a form suitable for input into any risk assessment methodology that is in use.

5.6 Access Control

Access control is an essential feature of any application. Depending on the infrastructure standards, it is valuable to insist upon an external authentication mechanism. Roles and access rights will have to likely be defined in the VM system but external authentication should be possible.

5.6.1 Active Directory

Active Directory (AD) is one of the most commonly used authentication mechanisms for Windows systems. Later versions support Lightweight Directory Access Protocol (LDAP) and LDAP over secure sockets layer (SSL) for directory loading. Kerberos and NTLM (Microsoft's NT Lan Manager) are common options for authentication. Since AD capabilities are so common in the corporate environment and standards are available to interface with other systems, this is a good choice. However, any LDAP directory service should work. There are two common approaches to AD integration.

One method synchronizes directory information periodically, looking for additions and deletions. A copy of the directory entries is stored in the VM database for quick reference to access privileges. This is the most common and compatible approach that will use LDAP. Usually, special credentials have to be created to log into the directory systems and retrieve the basic information about the users. Using LDAP also affords the system the option of portability to other directory services platforms.

Later, when a user attempts to log into the VM system, the credentials supplied by the user are sent to the authentication system using NTLM or Kerberos. Once the credentials are accepted, the VM system will apply the privileges stored in the VM database for that user.

A second approach is to natively integrate with AD using the Active Directory in Application Mode (AD/AM) capability that comes with Windows. Net Server 2003™. This enables the VM application to have its own instance of a directory service with schema extensions and built-in attributes but still participate in the security structure of the AD domain. Naturally, the services that support this capability must run on a Microsoft technology-based server. This provides a tightly integrated directory product for Microsoft directory-committed organizations. A significant advantage of this approach is that AD groups can be used to grant privileges in the VM system rather than creating an internal set of roles or a user group. The disadvantage is that you may be committed to the Microsoft AD platform.

5.6.2 RADIUS and TACACS

In a more network-centric environment, RADIUS (Remote Access Dial-In User Service) is a very common protocol option. It is an old method system typically used for dial-in systems. However, the protocol is no less useful for network equipment. With RADIUS and TACACS+ (Terminal Access Controller Access Control Service Plus), however, the user ID must be entered into the VM system since no directory service is provided. This user ID must exactly match that which is expected by the authentication server. The most significant difference between RADIUS and TACACS+ is the use of User Datagram Protocol (UDP) versus Transmission Control Protocol (TCP), respectively. TCP has the security advantage of being able to communicate with an authenticating source without spoofing since there is a handshake process in the protocol.

Some vendors of network authentication products go so far as to support RADIUS, LDAP, Kerberos, TACACS+, and other methods. These authentication products are able to effectively "glue" together various authorities and protocols, allowing a variety of methods to be employed.

Changing from one authentication method to another can be difficult depending on the implementation. To avoid complications in the future, select a method from the beginning and stay with it.

5.6.3 Authorization

Authorization capabilities should be able to meet the various roles you have planned for operations. This is one key reason that requirements must be defined prior to beginning the RFP process. One of those requirements is a definition of who will perform what functions and what capabilities are needed. Role-based access control is the mechanism that will have to be vetted during the selection process. Some of the capabilities to consider are:

- Separation by network—some users will be permitted to only take actions against certain networks. Local IT personnel in Mumbai should not be able to examine any vulnerability reports for Chicago, for example. Scan parameters should not be modifiable by anyone except the VM administrator.
- Actions—Closer to the definition of a role, these are the specific activities to be performed, such as:
  - Defining a network or administering IP ranges.
  - Running reports: Many people are likely to be able to perform this function. Being able to generate a report is fundamental.

Table 5.2   Permissions Grid

Role \ Capability	Report	Scan	Schedule	Maintenance	Parameters
System Administrator	N	N	Y	Y	R
Local IT	Y	N	N	N	N
Regional Security Manager	Y	N	N	N	N
Global Security	Y	Y	Y	N	RW
Global Compliance	Y	N	N	N	R

– Conducting a scan: Few people should be able to conduct a scan. Active scanning capabilities are potentially disrupting to operations and therefore should remain in the custody of those who are qualified to assess the impact on the network and the need for current audit results.
– Maintaining the health of the overall system and available audit parameters: The parameters of audits should rarely be tampered with unless extensive testing has been done. Adding TCP ports or additional checks can impact the entire scanning schedule. Only a few people should be able to make changes to the parameters. These people likely have a combination of security and compliance roles.

A good way to document authorization requirements is with a permissions grid. This grid should indicate the roles across the top and the capabilities down the side. See Table 5.2 for an example.

Where a particular function can be performed, a Y or N is indicated. If access type is specified, then an R and or W are specified for "Read," and "Write," respectively.

5.7 Deployment Methods

There are many ways to deploy a system, and what is needed for the operating environment possibly will affect the solution chosen. In some ways, this is related to architecture as discussed earlier in this chapter. But there are other considerations to be made related to how you will deploy a system. In this section, we will discuss the major issues affecting deployment. The goal in the approach to deployment is to achieve maximum effectiveness in the shortest period of time with the least investment. The basic deployment strategy to achieve this is:

1. Establish a foothold with maximum access to target systems.
2. Test processes on a small scale and refine.
3. Expand deployment by adding targets until the foothold is 75% deployed.
4. Simultaneous to item 3, create and refine management reports at all levels.
5. Take additional footsteps in other locations.

Each of these steps will be reviewed here for active physical scanners, active virtual scanners, passive analyzers, and agents.

5.7.1 Active Scanner Deployment—Physical

The first step in implementing a strategy for deploying physical scanners is to select a central location to which all scanners will report in the future. In the case where there may be multiple central reporting servers, select a location with the most hosts on the local network and preferably one that has unfettered network access to other major locations. Verify that there is sufficient bandwidth available to support a schedule structured using the method previously discussed. Then follow the iterative process:

- Perform test scanning and remediation reporting on the local network where the reporting server is installed or on another less critical network. A 24-bit classless inter-domain routing (CIDR) block would be sufficient.
- Review the report results and any unexpected impact on the environment.
- Adjust the system and scan parameters to compensate. Be sure that any adjustments you make are scalable to hundreds or even thousands of networks once the deployment proceeds.
- Add as many similar network ranges in the local office as possible, one at a time.
- Repeat the previous steps to validate the reports and the impact on the environment. Adjust accordingly.

While waiting for a few cycles of this activity to complete in the local area, plan and coordinate the next phase of scanning over the WAN to other offices in the scope of your scanning strategy. These are offices that will not receive equipment but that have the capacity to be scanned through their WAN connection without impact to operations. Again, repeat the evaluation and refinement process and update the scanning standards documentation accordingly.

As the expansion of scanning begins outside of the local office, begin generating and refining the management reports. At this stage, management will become quite curious about the results of the new system. Be sure that the reports are reconcilable and that questions about their content can be addressed. If the pre-acquisition testing has been done properly, this should be easily done with possibly minor assistance from the vendor. Having an executive sponsor who is willing to preview these reports before they go to a wider audience can help identify discrepancies and questions earlier.

At this point, as much as 75% of the initial zone of scanning should be deployed and processes beginning to take firm, repeatable shape. The next zone of deployment should then be planned by selecting another major office with as many good connections to other target offices. Then, repeat the gradual expansion process discussed in the previous steps.

5.7.2 Virtual Scanners

Active scanners that are created using virtual machine technology generally follow the same strategy as physical machines with some minor differences. VMs can be deployed much faster in many locations with less reliance on WAN links. The locations chosen to not have a VM are those that do not have hardware, personnel, and licensed software sufficient to support it. On the other hand, each VM instance requires a license, maintenance, and support so their number should be kept to a minimum.

It will also be important to get a clear definition of the hardware requirements to operate a virtual machine. Most vendors have ported the software that typically runs on an appliance to a VM. Doing so can have unpredictable performance results when the host OS running virtual machine software separates the scanner from the hardware. A completely separate round of testing is in order for a virtual version of a hardware product.

Sometimes it is more practical to use both a physical appliance and a virtual appliance rather than just one. This is especially true when shipping a product from one place to another is impractical. Furthermore, rack space and power consumption can be problematic for devices that are used only during business hours for auditing desktops or only at night for auditing servers. The growing emphasis on power conservation makes the prospect of virtual appliances appealing to senior management.

5.7.3 Passive Analyzer Deployment

Passive analyzers typically are hardware appliances, as described in our section on technology. They have unique requirements for the environment in which they are installed and can limit the choices of location. Where active scanners behave as hosts connected to a network switch, the passive devices are completely unseen, depending on their implementation. The target installation network must have the ability to copy the desired information to the network port of the scanner. Not all switches have this mirroring or switched port analyzer (SPAN) capability and should therefore be assessed as a part of the requirements for selecting sites.

If a network tap is used instead of the port mirroring function, then only a limited amount of traffic may be visible to the device. This is because not all devices are exchanging packets with devices outside of their own network segment. When port mirroring is used on a switch, all packets from all members of a particular network segment can be copied to the analyzer. But a network tap is used on a single network cable to observe whatever may pass by. But the conversations between two devices on the same network would remain unobserved.

It is possible through some creative network configuration to overcome this problem within limits. The mirroring solution is limited in the completeness of traffic that can be examined because the aggregated bandwidth of all source traffic cannot exceed the bandwidth of the link connected to the vulnerability analyzer. For example, if a DMZ has 20 hosts that consume an average of 50 Mbps each, then the link to the analyzer will have to be a minimum of 1 Gbps and preferably greater. Furthermore, the device and software of the analyzer will have to have sufficient capacity to fully consume the traffic. If not, the result will be errors and potentially missed information. If the device doubles as an intrusion detection system, then the performance requirements will be much more stringent.

Locations that are good candidates for passive traffic analyzers are those that communicate primarily to parties outside of their own network. Internet DMZs and internal server farms are good candidates. Anywhere a network gateway or an advanced network switch with port mirroring can be found is helpful. Furthermore, the location typically cannot perform port mirroring for too many devices. So the target network should preferably not use this technique to implement other technologies such as intrusion detection systems. Any planning of this type of deployment will require close coordination with the network manager and the switch vendor to determine if the site is a good candidate for the particular implementation.

5.7.4 Agent Deployment

Agents are a very effective means of testing for vulnerabilities with minimal network impact. They are constantly aware of the local system state and often can perform scheduled audits of surrounding devices. Common strategies employed depending on the vendor's capabilities are:

■ Install agents on certain workstations or servers that are always active so that scans can be performed with a minimum number of agents. The disadvantage here is that if you depend on a particular workstation, then you are at the mercy of the user of that workstation when and if they shut it down. This can be mitigated in some locations by installing on a server.

- Install agents on all devices in a network to avoid excessive network traffic for audits. This has the disadvantage of creating more traffic to update the vulnerability information on each agent. However, such information typically is small if updated on a weekly basis.
- Install agents on domain controllers in each office since they are always active. This can, however, affect the performance or reliability of the domain controller. An advantage to the selective deployment of agents is that they can provide a view of vulnerabilities from a network perspective. That is to say the vulnerabilities can be assessed through the network and security infrastructure components to provide a better idea of the real exposure. Note that a lot of planning is necessary to make this strategy work well. Thorough testing is again essential.

Whatever method of agent deployment is selected, note that agents are beginning to fall from favor in the industry due to compatibility and manageability concerns. Planning can be complex, and overall impact on the infrastructure is less predictable than with other methods.

5.8 Summary

As always, we can see that process and planning are essential to the selection of VM technology. By developing and agreeing upon the process that is to be followed in selection, the key participants will have a sense of ownership. Planning for the most complete and expected implementation is also important. Too often, companies will start by evaluating products and looking at vendor evaluations without considering the concrete use cases most relevant to the environment. The needs of risk management and security should be of paramount concern while remaining compatible and acceptable to the supporting infrastructure and user groups. The essential principles that should guide activities in the selection process are:

1. Be inclusive of all groups that will be affected by the system.
2. Visualize together how it will work.
3. Capture the requirements by drilling into the details of number 2.
4. Develop an evaluation approach.
5. Be transparent about the results.

It is not uncommon for the planning to center around identifying a product with the most effective vulnerability results and getting it to work to serve the known security requirements. However, given the potential deployment complexity and the dependency the organization can build around such a system, it is important to consider the future use cases from both an operations process perspective and a technical one. An overly simplistic view of the future application and implementation of the system will only lead to dissatisfaction.

Chapter 6

Process

6.1 Introduction

Process is a critical component of any successful security program. It is integrated into the organization to support policy and, by extension, the program charter. Process guides the use of technology but is not a servant to it. This distinction is important because, too often, processes are designed purely to operate technology rather than produce the outcome that supports the organization's objectives. The result is a series of ad hoc revisions to processes once they are implemented.

Process development need not be a long, drawn-out affair. With a basic framework of process, 90% of the work can be done quickly. In this chapter, we will discuss the steps in the vulnerability management (VM) process and how each interacts with the rest of the organization.

As previously mentioned, VM is a process and not a technology. Developing excellence in creating a process and refining it for optimal performance will build confidence that the greatest threats will be identified and remediated. Process development begins with determining the elements that are compatible with the organization. One must answer the question: What are the attributes and activities in the organization that must be accommodated in the process for minimal impact and maximum achievement of the VM program results? You can choose one of two ways to structure process, depending on the current practice standards of the organization. You can choose to employ an Information Technology Infrastructure Library (ITIL)-centric approach or a unique, customized approach without following a published framework. The approach is largely dependent upon the maturity of your current processes and whether or not you have adopted an ITIL-centric methodology. Many large organizations are choosing to follow the ITIL service management process model in order to maintain a high level of business-requirement-focused, measurable results. Other than ITIL, there are really few practical choices outside of a custom, in-house developed framework.

The elements of process that must be evaluated for organizational compatibility are the activities, inputs, and outputs to be integrated. Each of these elements should be implemented in a particular way that allows for optimal performance of the VM function while controlling the impact in cost and performance on existing, related processes.

6.2 The VM Process

The steps are closely aligned with what typically is seen in "life-cycle" frameworks by starting with definitions at a high level and expanding in depth to complete a task. Along the way, interfaces to other processes are created. A typical VM process that we assume for this book is shown on the right side of Figure 6.1. It includes the steps outlined in this section.

6.2.1 Preparation

Some knowledge about the targets to be audited is necessary before beginning. The general Internet protocol (IP) range and any authentication mechanisms must be defined for an audit to be effective.

Scope of audit: Determine the approximate number of hosts to scan at a time, types of scans depending on target technologies, and length of time for audits.

General rules of engagement: Identify targets and determine which networks are to be audited first. Consider a delineation by virtual local area network (VLAN), IP range, or target type. Also, review a list of any known negative interactions of active scanning systems to avoid causing problems with a similar configuration.

Identify remediation managers: Agree on who will own remediation and to whom they are accountable.

Develop scanning schedules: Agree on the time of day and day of the week with the manager of the networks and systems. This decision largely depends on the type of host and business operations patterns. Performing an active audit during the day may have a potential impact on production but may also be necessary for desktop systems since it is typically when they are switched on.

Survey environment: Review types of hosts in the environment, and determine whether special exceptions are needed. For example, some appliances may not permit authenticated active scans for vulnerabilities. These systems should be identified and possibly excluded from the audit.

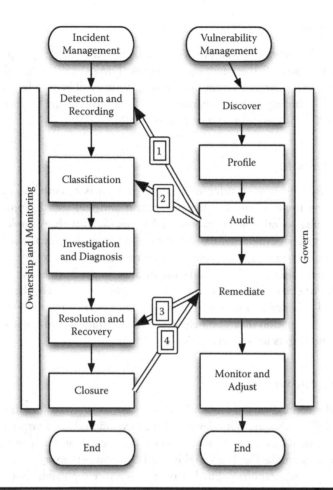

Figure 6.1 Incident management/VM process interaction.

Name and asset value: Each network and/or host may have a name and an assigned asset value. In active scanning, credentials typically are assigned to log into the target to perform a more thorough audit.

Basic architecture: The position and number of audit system components must be determined in advance. This topic of architecture is discussed more in each relevant section of this book.

6.2.2 Discovery

Identification of all targets in the environment is done through a combination of technical and manual processes. Automation helps inventory what is out there, but asset owners must identify the business function and relative value of each target.

6.2.3 Profile

Get a view of how complex your environment is and the basic security posture. You should know where all the demilitarized zones (DMZs) can be found as well as what security measures sit in front of each target. This will help to further plan the vulnerability scanning and remediation steps. Two activities are performed in this stage of the VM process: evaluate and contextualize.

6.2.3.1 Evaluate

Understanding the relative value of a target or asset is essential at later phases. Depending on the maturity of the environment and real security process needs, you may choose to value assets in financial terms ($) or with a simple numerical ranking. A financial evaluation should take into account the cost to the business of losing the use of the target for a period of time and the cost of recovery. A numerical valuation would simply be the relative importance to the business of the function performed. For example, a scale of 1 to 10 may suffice. Ultimately, the valuation of the asset will help determine which targets get remediated first when resources are limited. Asset valuation may also help decide the frequency and order with which you check the targets for vulnerabilities.

6.2.3.2 Contextualize

Defining the context of the vulnerability is essential to avoid focusing resources on vulnerabilities that are not relevant in the environment. If a target is found to be vulnerable to attack X but either the attack is extremely unlikely or the controls around the target make the attack highly unlikely, then perhaps resources are better spent on other vulnerabilities. Furthermore, it is entirely possible that the vulnerability is a configuration item necessary to allow an application to function properly. The following list gives examples of items that may contribute to the context of a vulnerability:

Existing security controls: As previously cited, the security controls surrounding the vulnerability may sufficiently mitigate the risk, making the vulnerability of little significance.

Application requirement: Some applications require what may be considered vulnerability configurations. A very common example is the ability for anyone to read from a directory unauthenticated. While this may seem to be a vulnerability, it can be understood by reviewing the classification of the accessible data.

Change management operations: Some vulnerabilities may already be scheduled for remediation by other change activities. For example, if a vulnerable system is to be upgraded to a new version or replaced altogether, then the vulnerability may be remediated as a consequence. The most important consideration here will be timing versus the threat. If it will be six months until the change activity is performed and the severity of the vulnerability is high, then it would be unwise to delay remediation.

6.2.4 Audit

This is the ongoing scanning process to detect vulnerabilities. This process will also feed information into the previous two steps for refinement of what is often a very dynamic environment. Audits are performed frequently and, to be most effective, require access privileges to the target.

6.2.5 Remediate

This is where you will fix what is found in the audit phase. These activities sometimes require careful planning and testing to avoid disrupting business activity but, many times, the solution is as simple as automatically applying a manufacturer-supplied patch. Although patching is a presumed solution, this frequently is not the case. The configuration of the machine may be at issue, or perhaps a default password requires change. Such changes can often impact other systems that rely on the particular configuration of the target.

6.2.6 Monitor and Adjust

By reviewing the results of the audit, problems can be identified and parameters altered to prevent potential disruptions of service and to increase accuracy. Networks, target configurations, and organizations are dynamic. What worked today may not work tomorrow. So, some amount of monitoring of results and performance is necessary to ensure smooth operation. It is not unusual for a network manager to add VLANs and remap IP addresses of hosts, with the change going unnoticed by the security and audit groups. These types of changes should be identified and addressed quickly or the accuracy and coverage of the VM system will degrade.

Another example of how degradation can take place is in the type of protocols and services used. Today, much of an organization may use typical Web transmission control protocol (TCP) ports 80 and 443. While these are certainly monitored, new application architectures can cause the use of additional ports such as Structured Query Language (SQL) Server or a more obscure port for Web services. As these changes take place, the VM operator will have to adapt and make sure that risk is adequately considered when setting audit parameters. Active scans are particularly susceptible to these types of changes.

6.2.7 Govern

Mid- to long-term trend analysis is essential for gauging the overall performance of the VM program. If at least the first five phases are completed, you are 70% of the way to an excellent program. However, governance will drive more consistent results and greater reliability. Without this step, the program runs the risk of atrophy and degradation. Just as one regularly performs maintenance activities on a motor vehicle to keep it in top operating condition, so too must a manager maintain a VM process.

The entire process we are discussing is repeated constantly but at varying intervals that meld with business cycles. Most commonly, the audit and remediate phases should be repeated as frequently as the infrastructure can manage without degradation of any services. This frequency should be no less than once every two weeks and every week if possible. The reason for this is to discover new targets attached to the network and to apply new vulnerability checks, which are released continuously by the software industry.

Following is a list of some useful activities to perform in the governance phase:

Regular report reviews: A summary report of the vulnerabilities found and a comparison with reports from the previous cycle can be instructive about the changing security posture.

Evaluate the worst performer: A "top 10" list of the networks with the most severe vulnerabilities is an excellent tool to apply pressure to the IT managers who need incentives.

Identify the best performers: These best performers are doing something right. Find out what their practices are and communicate them in a case study to all the IT groups. Being in the spotlight is beneficial to all concerned.

Monitor trends: When the trend for the entire organization or a particular network seems to rise in vulnerability count or score, escalation may be necessary before the network makes the top 10 list. A word of caution about trends: It is important to make sure that the cause of the trend is poor performance and not the effect of newly discovered vulnerabilities. Chapter 7 on reporting and analysis will cover this topic more.

6.3 Baselines

In any continuous VM process, the refinement of assessment results to the risk-based requirements of the organization will optimize overall process. A baseline is a known, accepted secure configuration. This baseline reflects what is currently understood as a good configuration and patch state for a particular combination of platform and purpose. A good example is a standard desktop computing platform for the general user population. This platform is a set of software components configured to run on a specified range of hardware components. It is configured to meet the security requirements of the organization in a computing environment definition. The following attributes define a baseline configuration:

User group: This defines the users of the system both locally and remotely. For desktop computers, this definition would include the local, general users of productivity software such as word processing and e-mail. For the remote users, this definition would likely refer to the desktop administrator or help desk using remote access applications and various administrative utilities.

Use case: An extension of the user group, the use case defines exactly how the platform will be used. For example, a general Web server baseline may have the use case of executing publicly facing Web server software with Java™ server applications connecting to back-end data sources. The use case will specify areas that are or are not included in the application functionality. This may include financial applications, infrastructure control systems, or building security systems.

Environment: Every computing platform operates in a particular environment that has considerable effect on the risk potential of the supported applications. General Web servers will run in a public DMZ with a different risk level from database servers holding critical customer data in an internal database tier. Industrial control systems may be connected to a manufacturing network in a harsh physical environment.

Supported hardware: With every computer, a certain range of hardware components require supporting software and drivers. These supporting software components, as we have previously discussed, have vulnerabilities that need to be managed. If the hardware platform is outside of the expected range, then management of those vulnerabilities can become more complex. That is not to say that we should avoid variation; but if the job can be done with an established secure configuration, then there is no point in increasing risk by injecting more exotic hardware without business justification.

With all of these attributes and possible combinations, the risks, impacts, and mitigation costs vary. By defining them in advance and minimizing the number of baselines to what 95% of the organization requires, the process of identifying and remediating vulnerabilities can be very manageable. Following is a list of key benefits to the baseline approach:

You will avoid being forced to make the regrettable decision to accept higher risk because an application is not running on a baseline platform.
The baseline minimizes the variability in analysis and patching. If the remediation solution is the same throughout most of the organization, then the impact to supported applications and hardware can be more easily assessed.

Support of the solution is also simplified when local IT personnel contact the systems engineers to understand what must be done.

Overall risk analysis is simplified and allows for the rapid and reliable update of metrics for the security manager.

Baselines should be updated on a reasonable schedule depending on the risk environment. The support staff should be able to identify and update older baseline installations as the new ones are tested and qualified for introduction into the environment.

6.4 ITIL-ITSM Processes

From http://www.itlibrary.org:

> The Information Technology Infrastructure Library (ITIL) defines the organizational structure and skill requirements of an information technology organization and a set of standard operational management procedures and practices to allow the organization to manage an IT operation and associated infrastructure. The operational procedures and practices are supplied independently and apply to all aspects within the IT infrastructure.

In this section, we will explore the ITIL process known as IT Service Management (ITSM) only as it relates to VM activities. A more complete discussion of the service management aspects of ITSM would consume at least an entire volume and is outside the scope of this book. If you are interested in more content on this subject, I recommend that you find one of the many books available. The concepts discussed here will be based on ITIL version 2 since it currently seems to be the most broadly accepted. Although the ITIL framework is evolving to version 3, it would only be confusing to introduce it here. Service support and service delivery are the two broad areas relevant to VM.

6.4.1 Service Support

This area of ITSM is the most active for security because it is the primary objective of VM to provide an aspect of support for existing IT services. Service support consists of the following activities:

incident management,
problem management,
configuration management,
change management, and
release management.

As described in an earlier case study, incident management and change management are often used in even the most basic ITIL-focused operations. But, a more complete discussion of each of these processes is necessary.

Incident management is supposed to focus on restoring normal operations as quickly as possible. Usually, this means getting back to normal service levels as specified in a service level agreement (SLA). For those who are unfamiliar with the concept of SLAs, the idea is that an agreement based on business requirements is drafted between the business managers and the IT services group. This agreement has specific objectives and metrics that must be met in the delivery of IT services. Some measurements are performed in order to ensure that the terms of the agreement are met.

Regular reports to the business are made so that the business managers can see that service levels were met. This is a very responsible approach to delivering consistent service to the business and providing continuously measured operational objectives to the IT team. The most significant strategic benefit of the SLA is that IT operational objectives are directly tied to business objectives, thus ensuring a tightly coupled value chain.

The same kinds of service levels are provided for VM services. Although many organizations choose not to create SLAs for VM, it is certainly beneficial to position the entire discipline as a service to the business that has a measurable outcome. The value of the measurable outcome is discussed in the description of the business case and charter for a VM program in Chapter 3.

For now, let's consider some basic metrics for VM as a service:

list of highest-risk business units,
percentage of all vulnerabilities remediated monthly and quarterly,
percentage of estimated number of targets audited quarterly,
percentage of critical vulnerabilities remediated versus discovered monthly and
    quarterly, and
average time to remediation of critical vulnerabilities.

Following are a few basic characteristics of these metrics:

Measurable: This is essential if you are to report on the metric to the business.
Relevant: They are real indicators of the IT security organization's performance.
Realistic: Most vulnerability systems should be able to provide these metrics,
    with the exception of estimated number of targets, which must be obtained
    from other systems.

In many organizations, individual vulnerabilities are managed as incidents when their severity reaches a certain level. This is not a bad approach if you prefer to drive your SLA to a granular level rather than to an overall security posture level. The vulnerability audit function acts as a monitor for SLA compliance.

Responsibility for the SLA falls to the group responsible for remediation and proper configuration of the targets.

After a considerable amount of time getting to a level of predictability in the number and severity of vulnerabilities, you may choose to provide an operational level agreement (OLA) to the rest of IT and, by extension, the business, or perhaps directly to the business as a part of an ongoing IT risk assessment. When there is a deviation from SLAs, an incident is created to track resolution. So, the incident in this case is a high-level incident showing a failure to adhere to the SLA.

If incidents indicate exceptions in service levels, then the position of security is one of proactive hardening of IT services. If incidents are used to indicate the presence of vulnerabilities that need to be remediated, then the position is one of reacting to vulnerabilities as small fires to be extinguished. It may seem like a subtle distinction but the important lesson is to avoid counting new vulnerabilities, over which the IT organization has little control, as a failure to meet an SLA.

If your SLA is focused on remediating a vulnerability of a particular severity through certain means within a given amount of time, then an "event" will be necessary for every discovered vulnerability that meets the agreed-upon criteria.

6.4.2 Service Desk

The service desk is the single point of contact responsible for managing incidents. As you will see from the discussion that follows, the creation and management of incidents and related communications are the primary purposes of a service desk. It acts like a central communication hub that maintains relationships with all the key parties necessary for resolution.

6.4.3 Incident Management

If an SLA specifies that the severity of vulnerabilities on a given target will not exceed a certain level, perhaps as indicated by a numerical score, then incidents only need be created when vulnerabilities cause the system to go outside that value.

The benefit of this approach is that every vulnerability that violates the SLA is raised to a status of formal recognition. However, the workload can be significant for tracking and remediating so many incidents, which can be arguably insignificant to the security posture of the target. Conversely, this approach may create fewer incidents to manage that may not be so important to the security posture but could allow one or more relevant vulnerabilities to expose the system unnoticed.

Incident management fits perfectly onto a VM process because it deals with direct solutions to what would otherwise be classified as problems. The vast majority of all vulnerabilities detected through automated means can be considered incidents because the cause and solution are readily identifiable. Figure 6.1 (left side) shows a basic incident management process in parallel with a VM process. Each of the connecting lines between the two processes shows exactly where there is either communication or process interaction:

The vulnerability audit is the detection and reporting mechanism that generates incidents.

Part of the audit data also contains critical input into the classification process. This is usually a definition of the vulnerability and the severity.

Additional remediation details, typically recommendations from the vendor of the vulnerable system, are provided in the incident report.

When the incident is finally remediated, the closed or remediated state of the system is communicated to the VM process to verify success in the monitoring process. This step may be automated.

6.4.3.1 Problem Management

One of the great things about aligning the VM process with ITIL/ITSM is that incidents can become problems if they repeat sufficiently to cause a disruption in service. This would most often occur in configuration errors that may result in disruption of service. Blank system administrator (SA) passwords in an SQL Server database are a good example. This is clearly a vulnerability of high severity and, if globally distributed due to some error in process or standards, a problem may be declared. Problem management focuses on the incidents that cause the greatest risk when the cause of the problem is unknown.

In this example, it is possible that several servers were implemented without following standards or perhaps as the result of malicious activity. The cause and solution are unknown. However, the problem is the result of an incident generated by the vulnerability scanner. The resolution may be to set the SA passwords according to standards. If the cause is an error by the IT administrative staff, then this problem is a known error. If the cause is malicious activity, then this problem is a severe security incident.

In most cases, VM systems and processes perform the problem management function in determining the root cause. The output, therefore, typically is not a problem but an incident.

6.4.3.2 Configuration Management

Configuration management is substantially aided by VM systems because they are able to provide a large amount of configuration data to the configuration management database (CMDB). For those who are unfamiliar, the CMDB is a database containing all of the configuration details of assets in an IT infrastructure. These details are known as configuration items (CIs). This database is used throughout the change, release, and event management processes to verify the impact of changes and events.

The CMDB is also informed by the problem management function previously discussed. In the previous example of blank SA passwords, if the problem turned out to be a known, nonmalicious cause, it is then classified as a "known error." The results of the discovered vulnerability are recorded as such in the CMDB. More specifically, the SA password CI is noted as having this known error. In the future, such errant changes can be minimized by following the standards for the CIs as stated in the CMDB.

To summarize the effect of VM in the configuration management process, it minimizes the recurrence of known errors on a CI that may present vulnerability.

6.4.3.3 Change Management

Similar to configuration and problem management, change management allows for changes to the environment with the goal of minimizing the negative impacts to IT services. In the case of VM, this means the instantiation of vulnerabilities when performing changes. Change management also provides the process for remediating vulnerabilities by following a standardized process that provides for prioritization, monitoring, and reporting of completion.

The key benefit of a change management process is that it facilitates a major portion of the remediation process. Part of the ITSM process for change management is development of a business case for performing the change. This is where deviations are likely to be, depending on the culture and business priorities of the organization. Much of the input to the business justification of a vulnerability remediation comes from the potential impact should the vulnerability be successfully exploited.

However, there is a cost to implementation. Typically, a patch to a Web browser on a desktop system is innocuous with little cost, especially if it can be performed automatically by a patch management system. However, the cost can be substantial if it is a Java virtual machine update that could break the functionality of existing applications. This is because it could require extensive changes to the underlying application, which results in extensive regression testing. Time and effort equate to higher costs and can result in seeking more cost-effective means of remediation or avoidance.

6.4.4 Service Delivery

Service delivery primarily is tasked with staying ahead of the business to keep the services operating at or above service levels. Ensuring that service levels, capacities, and availability mechanisms are in place and operating correctly keeps IT services running smoothly and seamlessly with the business even as it changes.

6.4.4.1 Service Level Management

Service level management can be just as applicable to VM services as any other IT service. Since the goal of VM is to identify and remediate vulnerabilities and reduce risk, the SLAs that may be created will require a certain amount of service level management. When the VM program is operating under the ITSM framework, there will be SLAs identified as well as OLAs and underpinning contracts (UCs).

Briefly, OLAs are the agreements that the VM program has with other services in the organization that support the SLAs to the business. UCs are the contracts that the VM program has with vendors to provide supporting services. For example, the network group may have allocated a certain amount of bandwidth dedicated to active scanning of targets or a dedicated switch port with copies of traffic on particular VLANs for passive analysis. This would be detailed in an SLA they would provide.

Additionally, the vendor of a VM system would have a contract that underpins the SLA provided by the VM program to provide updated vulnerability checks on a weekly basis that would include the latest Microsoft vulnerabilities within seven days of announcement. It is not common for VM providers to supply such a restrictive SLA because there is no way to determine how much time and effort will be required to address a particular vulnerability that is reported at random with unknown severity. It is, therefore, more practical to provide an SLA committing to resolving a false positive within 30 days of reporting or accepting a trouble ticket at the service desk within 24 hours.

6.4.4.2 Capacity Management

When managing capacity of the VM system, there needs to be some continuous monitoring of the number of IP addresses that are analyzed for vulnerabilities and the amount of time required to perform that analysis. This is particularly true in active scanning versus passive analysis. In active scanning, there are many limiting factors to capacity such as bandwidth, business hours, and network response time. These factors can be managed with OLAs for the most part; however, occasionally, as the enterprise grows, more auditing resources will be required to continue to deliver at established service levels.

For example, more active scanners may be required to target new locations that may be opened in the near future. It is the job of the VM team to identify and respond to these changes in the business and maintain the same level of security. This is something that can be easily missed in an SLA when the VM service manager fails to recognize that the business group with which he has an SLA is opening a new office.

An example of capacity management as it relates to passive assessments is the ability to capture vulnerabilities with consistent accuracy up to a certain data rate. This rate may occur in megabits per second or in connections per second. In any case, the vulnerabilities for which checks are in effect should apply with any amount of traffic within an agreed-upon range. Additionally, it may be desirable to only check for a set of critical vulnerabilities at higher traffic levels. The ability to deliver on these SLAs will depend on the capabilities of the traffic analyzer and any limitations imposed by the network.

6.4.4.3 Availability Management

Although availability management is a discipline of ITSM that is applied in sustaining the VM service, it is more important to understand what VM contributes to availability management. One aspect of availability management is security. The part of security that deals with the availability of services contributes information that can be used to keep systems running. The detection of a vulnerability whose exploitation could result in a denial of service is definitely of interest. Such information must be provided on a timely basis to the managers of systems to maintain this effort.

So, those who are responsible for availability management can be recipients of reports of vulnerabilities related to availability of their services. If a network manager must monitor and support the availability of network services, then audits of those network devices should be provided to that manager in furtherance of his responsibility.

6.4.5 Other Areas

The following areas of ITSM are not discussed because they have little relevance to VM:

release management,
financial management for IT services, and
IT service continuity management.

6.5 IAVA Process

Separate from ITSM and as a substitute for other VM processes used in the private sector, the U.S. Department of Defense (DoD) employs the Information Assurance Vulnerability Alert (IAVA) process. It is database-centric, as stated in the memo from the Office of the Inspector General, DoD Report No. D-2001-013:

> The policy memorandum instructs the Defense Information Systems Agency to develop and maintain an IAVA database system that would ensure a positive control mechanism for system administrators to receive, acknowledge, and comply with system vulnerability alert notifications.

IAVA is a basic process whereby a flaw in software results in the release of one of three notifications:

Information Assurance Vulnerability Alert (IAVA),
Information Assurance Vulnerability Bulletin (IAVB), or
Technical Advisory (TA).

The severity or impact of the vulnerability will dictate the type of notification issued. This approach is similar to the "threat level" notifications provided by vendors and security organizations such as the Internet Storm Center at SANS Institute.

The IAVA process closely mirrors the typical VM process, only with more DoD-centric language. The strength, however, of the IAVA process is that it begins with a system or target that is known to be fully patched and properly configured to have all required flaws addressed. This is known as being "in a compliant state." Then, future vulnerability assessment actions are used to determine whether the system remains in a compliant state. This is a much stronger approach than trying to discover everything that is broken and simply decrease risk by remediating vulnerabilities—an approach that most businesses take until they might be fortunate enough to reach a fully compliant state. In the private sector, this compliant state is the equivalent of establishing a baseline configuration.

The IAVA process has the following basic steps:

1. Establish an IAVA-compliant system.
2. Assess compliance.
3. If the system is compliant, return to step 1.
4. If the system is not compliant, remediate.
5. Return to step 1.

When a target is found to have a relevant vulnerability, the system is said to be out of IAVA compliance. It is possible for a system to have a vulnerability that is not relevant in that it does not create an unacceptable risk.

6.5.1 Managing the IAVA Process

The Defense Information Systems Agency (DISA) is responsible for maintaining the IAVA process. The primary tool for this process is the IAVA database with which every DoD system registers. The information in this database enables DISA to track the compliance of those systems and generate reports. The IAVA database is a tool that allows for the tracking, reporting, and monitoring of compliance in the previously described process.

When a security researcher discovers a new vulnerability, it is called an IAVA requirement. This requirement is compared against the contents of this database to determine the compliance status of any registered system. If a system is found to be out of compliance, then according to the process definition, notifications are sent out to system administrators. It is then the responsibility of the system administrator to bring the subject system into compliance.

But, the issuance of an IAVA alert, bulletin, or technical advisory is not that simple and not necessarily fully automated. The following must be determined by the Computer Emergency Response Team (CERT):

the type of operating system affected,
the vulnerability of the application affected,
the ease of access to the system,
the type of threat imposed,
whether the infrastructure will be affected, and
whether the vulnerability has already been exploited.

If it is then deemed necessary, CERT will issue one of the previously described communications. If an alert is issued, the subject systems administrators must acknowledge receipt within a specified period of time. This is the equivalent of an SLA in the private sector.

The DoD entity must report the following conditions upon receipt of an IAVA message:

number of systems registered,
number of systems compliant, and
number of systems with waivers.

Waivers are ostensibly used to allow for non-remediation when an application can be broken. A simple tally will reveal the amount of risk that has gone unmitigated due to lack of remediation.

Although this process makes sense for the DoD, it is not accepted in the commercial environment. Perhaps in the future the output of such government standards can be properly applied and adapted to industry. The biggest impediments to broad adoption of the IAVA process are probably the lack of standardization among VM product vendors and the lack of incentive to impose such rigid positive controls over the vulnerability state of systems. If every vendor and security researcher used standards such as OVAL® Open Vulnerability and Assessment Language) for encoding checks for vulnerabilities, and if the process of vetting and accepting vulnerabilities in the Common Vulnerabilities and Exposures (CVE) and the OVAL library were more efficient, then perhaps adoption of standard processes would follow.

As for the effectiveness of IAVA, it is far from perfect. Problems can occur in several places:

The quality of the content of notifications can be poor and make remediation more difficult. This further creates delays in patching activities while revisions are made to messages and more detailed information is sought.

Lack of standards adoption (previously discussed) among VM and configuration management tool vendors makes identification all the more difficult for personnel. Each tool may use a different method to identify a flaw, with some more reliable than others. Efforts such as OVAL are valuable in establishing vulnerability check standards that not only can enhance DoD processes but those of large corporations as well.

Personnel who feel they have other priorities can easily abuse the existence of a "waiver" and use this mechanism to apply those priorities. In some cases, it is possible to eliminate the need for a waiver with a little additional work. But, the resources simply are not available to do so.

The waiver can be a vulnerability. A clever attacker working for a foreign government who wished to target certain systems by exploiting a vulnerability can tamper with the IAVA database application to issue waivers for those systems under certain circumstances. Those systems may then never get remediated.

Notification processes can be vulnerable, too. Under the same circumstances as the previous item, the IAVA message system has several hierarchical links in the chain that may provide an attack vector to tamper with the content or routing of messages away from vulnerable systems. Compliance messages might also be tampered with, either from the origination point or in transit.

One must ultimately ask the question: If IAVA is so great, then why do we continuously hear about the compromise of government systems using common exploits? This is not intended to condemn the process itself but perhaps the implementation. A key item that is lacking is the incorporation of policy compliance into the IAVA process. It is no more difficult to check for technical policy and standards compliance with an automated tool than it is to check for vulnerabilities. This ultimately leads us back to a discussion of standards because so many disparate VM systems may not apply the same methods or language for the checks they perform. This makes centralized, positive control much less effective and more vulnerable to manipulation.

6.6 Data Classification

Although policy is a very important step toward implementing a VM program, having a strong foundation of security operations is another. Many companies fail to properly classify data, but doing so will make a VM program all the more successful. Understanding the various levels of sensitivity of data and the related threat levels will enable security managers to more effectively monitor and manage risk.

6.6.1 Case Study: Big Tyre Corporation

Big Tyre Corporation, known as the Big T, is a global manufacturer and distributor of heavy truck and construction tires with offices in 12 countries. All critical computing facilities are redundant at HQ, and each country head office has its own enterprise resource planning (ERP) and accounting systems. Manufacturing systems are managed by a separate IT group based in Chicago, with local management and maintenance groups in each country. Other sales and marketing systems vary by location, often several within each country due to the gradual acquisition of other tire manufacturers. None of the sales systems were ever integrated because they were low priority and high workload at the time.

When the VM system was planned, scanning for vulnerabilities seemed simple. All of the policy and processes were in place. Senior management supported the effort, and line managers were eager to demonstrate their willingness to excel. During the initial discovery of hosts, many of the ERP systems had basic patches missing, and priority was quickly given to getting the problems remediated. Because of their complexity and integration with other internal systems, the process went slowly. Many IT resources were tied up with what turned out to be long-term projects (six months to a year).

During that time, several other vulnerabilities were found in systems that were not well understood. A random investigation by an internal security auditor revealed that sensitive design data for a new model of tire were stored on a home-grown marketing system in China. This was apparently necessary to develop sales templates for when the tire would be available for sale. However, the system was riddled with vulnerabilities and missing patches. The existence of these missing patches was well-known for several months, but no action was taken because it was believed to be a non-critical system.

The security director was concerned that the system was too vulnerable with such information stored on it, and further investigation was conducted by a forensic analyst. After one week of probing, it was determined that the host had been compromised for at least one year.

The sensitive data were on the host for three months, and it was not certain whether a copy of that data had been improperly disclosed to an external party. Apparently, a host external to the company had been exchanging data through a specially scripted Hypertext Transfer Protocol (HTTP) to get requests in China. The Web server code had a special script added to look for the specially formed request and provided directory information and file downloads.

6.6.1.1 Analysis

At this point, the chief information officer (CIO) should have ordered a review of all data considered sensitive to the company. A new project should have then been started to identify classified data and find any instances of that data on all hosts. The proper standards for handling of each class of information would be used to bring hosts into compliance. Since the vulnerability scanning process had already begun, each host would have to be reassessed for its criticality based on the classification of data and business processes handled.

Current remediation projects would continue, but the hosts being remediated and those scheduled in the near future would be classified first in order to shift priorities where necessary. As the hosts are valued and data they handle classified, the classification would be added to the VM system to weight the vulnerability scores and help refocus remediation priorities.

These activities are clearly more work than anyone would like. But, since they are being performed after the deployment of the VM system, it will be more work than it would have been had asset valuation been performed ahead of time.

6.6.2 Data Classification Process

Classifying data is a critical part of determining the appropriate security controls necessary for any particular target. During the vulnerability assessment process, the data classification is instrumental in prioritization. It can be used to help determine the asset value and to perform risk assessments. The asset value is instrumental in prioritizing remediation activities. We will not discuss data classification at length except to stress that it is an essential contributor to the VM process. Numerous articles and books address this topic in more depth. To stimulate your thinking on the topic, I list the following basic steps to classifying data:

1. Assess business requirements/impacts: Mission-critical applications, uptime requirements, outage sensitivity (rank from 1 to 10), impact of data corruption, period of time data are to be retained, regulatory restrictions, and civil penalties.
2. Develop classification levels: Determine number of levels (keep limited for simplicity) and assign appropriate names to the levels acceptable in the culture (public, internal use only, restricted, confidential, private, etc.).
3. Develop a change management process for adjusting the classification of data as time and usage continue. Classification information is dynamic. As it is used more widely and the business changes priorities, the importance of the data can definitely change. When this change takes place, usually at pivotal moments in the business strategy, a process for identification of related data and reclassification must be in place.
4. Identify assets affected by the classification levels: Some assets store or handle more than one classification of data. If multiple classes of data are handled by one asset, then the highest level handled applies.

6.7 Risk Assessment

A VM system will greatly help in performing an ongoing risk assessment for an organization. However, some preliminary steps must be performed to get information about the assets and the business. The risk assessment will provide a strong understanding of the threat environment, which will help prioritize remediation work and the overall VM deployment schedule. Vulnerability assessment and risk assessment are two intertwined activities that are both more effective when performed together. Although there are many approaches to risk management such as operationally critical threat assessment and vulnerability evaluation (OCTAVE), Central Computing and Telecommunications Agency (CCTA), CCTA Risk Analysis and Management Method (CRAMM), and security officers management and analysis project (SOMAP), the basic goals are the same. It is not necessary to detail these approaches, but a basic review of risk assessment will put the role of vulnerability assessment in perspective.

When tying vulnerability scores to the risk management process, the net result is a security posture in the form of a numeric value that can be ascribed a descriptive condition (more about this later). Following is the process to arrive at this value:

1. Get the vulnerability score of a particular target.
2. Sum the value of the assets on the target to get a total value.
3. Evaluate the security controls between external and internal sources and the target.
4. Calculate the threat profile and asset risk.

6.7.1 Information Collection

Risk assessment involves the collection of information about assets, threats, vulnerabilities, and controls to determine the total state of risk in an organization. This state is understandably fluid since organizations and the environment in which they operate are seldom static. VM assists in supplying the key information to the risk assessment process.

It is imperative that a risk analysis includes a detailed understanding of the operating environment. Understanding the organization structure, business units, network designs showing internal and external connection points, and asset inventories will make the identification and measurement of risk all the more effective.

A key part of information collection from a technology perspective can come from existing asset inventories and configuration databases. If such databases do not exist, then the vulnerability system may be able to help collect such information. However, it will still be necessary to identify the business functions or requirements of each asset discovered. The information from a VM system is "raw" in that it may tell you all about the configuration of a host but not how it meets business needs and what critical applications are running.

When identifying assets, do not forget to include outsourced operations and related information assets. These are often overlooked when company personnel do not directly operate and monitor them. The sum of the value of the assets on each target equals the total value of the target. This value is not the liquidation value of the target but the exposed value—that is, the value that is at risk. A particular asset can be at risk at multiple locations in the organization.

A VM process supported by properly configured software can supply many of the key data necessary to perform a risk assessment. Not only can basic asset data be provided as previously described but the security state as well. This security state has three relevant components:

Asset value: The value of the asset is entered into the VM system to support risk assessment. The value can be determined by a variety of methods. Such a method is described later in this chapter.

Asset security configuration: Most VM systems are able to check the state of security CIs. These items can be more precisely checked for compliance with a policy or standard. This is sometimes performed automatically through add-on tools.

Vulnerability state: The overall vulnerability state of the asset is calculated according to the rules prescribed by the VM product vendor.

6.7.2 Assess Security Controls

A complete understanding of policies, procedures, and standards will also paint a clearer picture of the risk environment. Policies may not reflect the changing needs of the organization or, conversely, operations may not adhere to policy or standards. In the risk assessment process, it is necessary to quantify the value of the security controls employed between potential threats and a target as shown in Table 6.1. The threats come from two sources: internal and external. So, there are two security posture values to calculate: security posture-external threats (SPe) and security posture-internal threats (SPi). The following steps are used to determine the value of the access controls:

1. Build a checklist of security controls required by policy and standards between the target and the internal and external threats.
2. For each control in place, assign a value of 1; otherwise, assign 0.

Table 6.1 Target Control Assessment List

Control	Internal (CI)	External (CE)
Strong passwords on accounts	1	1
Local access controls to data	1	1
Encrypted storage	0	0
Firewall	0	1
Network intrusion prevention system	0	1
TOTAL	2	4

3. Sum the value of the controls separately between the internal and external threat sources and place that value in the denominator and 1 in the numerator.
4. For each SPi and SPe, multiply the value in step 3 by the vulnerability score from the vulnerability system.
5. Multiply the value in step 4 by the asset value of the target to get the total exposure.

This process leaves us with the following equation:

$$SPe = \frac{1}{\sum\limits_{e=1}^{n} C(e)} \times V$$

$$SPi = \frac{1}{\sum\limits_{i=1}^{n} C(i)} \times V$$

where C is the value 1 or 0 for the presence of control 1 through n, and V is the vulnerability score from the VM system.

This process assumes that internal and external threats are of equal value. Although industry statistics are constantly changing, the fact is that there typically are fewer controls between the target and internal threats than external threats.

> *Example:* A server in an organization processes payroll data. Because the payroll data are considered to have a high confidentiality value, 85 out of 100, a number of security controls are required. (There will be an example later about a method for calculating asset values.) In this example, let's assume that security policy and standards dictate the presence of the security controls in Table 6.1. For each of these controls, we indicate their presence with a 1 or absence with a 0.
>
> The data from the VM system show a vulnerability score of 75 on a scale of 0 to 100. So, the security posture from internal and external perspectives is
>
> $$SPe = \frac{1}{4} \times 75 = 18.75$$
>
> $$SPi = \frac{1}{2} \times 75 = 37.5$$
>
> Interestingly, this example is the not-uncommon result that the internal security posture is higher than the external one. Since the firewall and intrusion protection system (IPS) are not present between internal threats and the target, the posture is lower. The risk manager will have

to decide from this analysis whether further controls are necessary for internal threats or additional vulnerability remediation is necessary. The threshold for triggering action should be determined by the risk analyst and should consider many factors such as the value of the target or other impact characteristic. Characteristics such as significance of the business unit to the overall enterprise or future plans for the target system or network may be outside of the quantifiable realm as well.

6.7.3 Business Requirements

As an extension of the first item, understanding the business requirements will help a risk analyst to align the current state of risk with business needs. In many cases, the exposure of data to risk does not meet the needs of the business. In the turmoil of doing business, sometimes assets get positioned where no business requirement had previously existed. This leads to unnecessary risk-taking since the data classification does not meet the security controls applied to the asset. Usually, this is the result of a mismatch between the business requirements that dictated the protection of the asset.

See the example in Figure 6.2. The value of the asset was increased when classified data and associated applications were placed on the system. But, the protection of the asset remains low. As a result, the real risk to the asset has become high, yet the security organization, unknowledgeable about the new deployment, considers

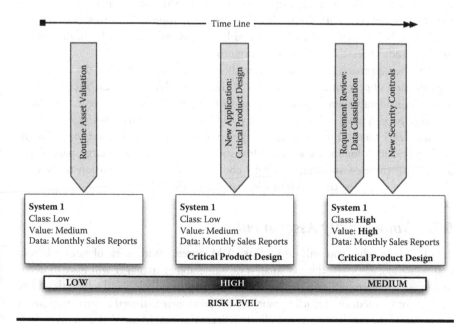

Figure 6.2 Changes in risk over time.

the value of the asset as medium and the data classification still low. This is the result of a failure to inform the VM process of the new business requirement; therefore, the asset valuation has not been revised and, consequently, neither has the risk assessment.

Eventually, a review of the business requirements for the applications and data running on the asset has revealed the discrepancy. A reassessment based on these new requirements results in the application of new security controls and finally a lower vulnerability and, by extension, a lower risk profile for the target.

6.7.4 Asset Valuation

Knowing the relative value of an asset seems to be a difficult thing, but it is crucial for determining overall risk. Asset values can be denominated in several ways. They could be represented with a monetary value or an index of some sort, perhaps from 0 to 1.0 or low/medium/high. This is where the classification of data previously discussed can become important. Some prior assessment of the data has been done to give the data a classification. The assets handling that data will have a higher value if they handle highly classified assets. Data classification becomes yet another factor in valuing the asset.

Some organizations have shown a preference for an approach that encompasses more factors related to the impact of a risk. A common method is to develop a scale for confidentiality, integrity, and availability (CIA). This scale can be bound to a maximum score such as assigning a portion of 0 to 100 to each category so that the sum may not exceed 100. Figure 6.3 illustrates this approach. In this example, the total value is 70 out of 100, which could be considered medium-high, depending on the standards established for your organization.

Another approach is to take a more difficult route of estimating the cost to the organization of certain levels of breach of the three CIA categories. Such methods require considerable development and effort to complete the assessment. Simplicity is generally preferable as is compatibility with the vulnerability scoring system.

Whatever method is selected, this type of information will go far toward identifying priorities for future security investments. It makes up a large part of the overall risk value of an asset. A critical contribution to asset valuation is the classification of data. See the previous discussion on this topic.

6.7.5 Vulnerability Assessment

This is part of what you will do with the VM system. With a list of vulnerabilities that apply to each asset, the risk analyst or vulnerability manager will have to determine which vulnerabilities really require immediate remediation and which should be deferred or ignored. By including much of the previously gathered information into a risk score for the target, reports can clearly reflect priorities. Many VM systems include the ability to insert a value or metric that gets included in calculations and reports.

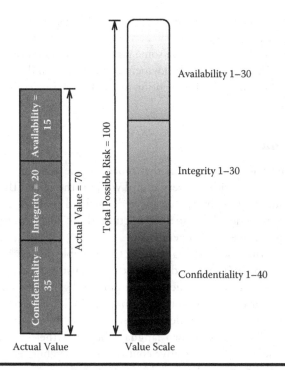

Figure 6.3   Valuation scaling method.

In the earlier example of calculating the security posture of a target, the results can be improved by remediating more severe vulnerabilities so that both the internal and external security postures reach an acceptable level. This is generally a more cost-effective solution than applying additional security controls.

6.7.6 Control Effectiveness Assessment

This step reviews internal security controls to determine their effectiveness in meeting the risk requirements of the business. Technical and procedural elements are evaluated for their ability to address the current threat environment, which is derived from the threat profile. But, effectiveness against the current threats is insufficient at this stage.

The effectiveness in VM comes from the ability to adapt to a changing threat environment. The ability to get updates for the latest vulnerabilities must also be assessed. This includes the following three key attributes:

Timeliness: Updates have to come frequently and soon after the discovery or disclosure of the vulnerability.

Accuracy: Nothing wastes more time than a false positive; so many steps must take place before it is realized that a vulnerability does not exist. This is especially true for those present on some targets and not on others.

Automation: The receipt and deployment of new vulnerability checks should be automated to minimize intervention and delay.

6.8 Summary

From this chapter, it should be clear that process is the skeleton of VM, while the technology is muscle. Neither is very useful without the other. The success of any process is measured by its ability to achieve the defined goals. By aligning the VM process with organizational design and function, those goals can be achieved with minimal disruption to existing operations.

We have seen that there are many paths to a suitable process for any organization. Private enterprise is largely dependent upon custom processes fitting existing ones. These processes have much in common and generally are versions of the process indicated in this chapter. For mature, ITSM-centric operations, the VM process can fit very nicely alongside and intertwined with the service management definition. The military has its own language but nevertheless achieves the same result through the concept of "positive control" of vulnerabilities.

Ultimately, the success of any VM process is dependent upon transparent implementation and broad acceptance. Transparency will address concerns about the goals and methods of the process, thus reducing the perception of VM as a threat to anyone's performance image. Inclusiveness will give all key participants an opportunity to optimize results by becoming an owner of the process with a vested interest in its success.

Chapter 7

Execution, Reporting, and Analysis

7.1 Introduction

What should be obvious by now is that the vulnerability management (VM) process and technology cannot be managed without accurate and actionable information. By the end of this chapter, you should be able to decide what kinds of reports you will need for your organization. You should also be able to specify the contents and format of the reports to make your processes more efficient. In the previous chapter, we discussed process. These processes must be supported and monitored with actionable information as input. When a manager responsible for VM needs to determine the most important areas of the IT infrastructure to remediate, the information must be readily available. The engineer who must perform the technical remediation tasks will need to know exactly what to remediate and how to do it. It is not sufficient to simply state that system X has critical vulnerabilities. Similarly, the manager cannot simply assume that because systems are being scanned and tickets are being opened that the overall process is working.

This chapter walks through key phases in the VM process and discusses what information is needed. The phases of most interest are discover, evaluate, profile, remediate, and govern. We have omitted the audit phase because this is a technology-automated step. It is not that this phase is unimportant, but the machine does not require reports. On the other hand, the effectiveness of the audit step is heavily influenced by the actions taken on the reports that we will discuss.

7.2 Discovery Reports

The discovery process is typically a combination of manual and automatic tasks. The basic goal is to understand the following:

■ How many targets are in the environment?
■ What kinds of targets (operating systems) are there?
■ What are the configuration items on the targets?
■ Where are the targets located?
■ What is the value of each target to the organization?

The basic idea behind these questions is to understand (1) what systems and components compose the IT environment and (2) how exposed those systems might be. The first consideration is important but only in the context of the others. Knowing how many of anything can give you some sense of scale and effort required to manage the VM program. Knowing that there are 2,000 hosts is interesting but less useful than knowing there are 1,000 Windows® hosts, 800 Linux® hosts, and 200 network switches and routers.

To make this information even more useful, we add in the configuration of each target. It is helpful to know that 400 Windows® hosts are on the network but even better to know that, of those 400 Windows machines, 300 have QuickTime® installed. If it is not obvious, the reason this is more useful is that you know QuickTime vulnerabilities will have to be patched and they are possibly not part of the standard enterprise desktop disk image. The number of different versions of QuickTime may also be useful to determine whether it is necessary to bring all systems up to the same later version to make it easier to identify and patch as well as reduce overall risk.

The configuration details and installed software are called configuration items (CIs). Those items can tell you a lot about the state of security. It may be that your organization already has this information in a configuration management database (CMDB). These terms typically are used in the configuration management discipline. VM is closely related to configuration management in that it seeks to establish the state of CIs on a system. Configuration management deals with the issue of monitoring and assessing the impact of CI changes on the system. The primary purpose, of course, is to maintain a consistent level of performance of the services provided by the target.

Another important consideration is the location of the target system. The significance of this piece of information cannot be underestimated. The aspects of target location are more complex than most people realize. Consider the publicly disclosed fact that the Department of Defense (DoD) lost laptop computers containing personally identifiable information (PII). In a 2008 report,[1] the Inspector General of the DoD stated, "Although the Defense Privacy Office determined no public notification was warranted, a risk of unauthorized disclosure of PII still exists if laptops still remain unaccounted-for." From this statement, it seems absurd to have the assumption that risk was sufficiently low to avoid notification when the whereabouts of the assets were still unknown. The report goes further to state, "A review of 50 DSS property records showing custody of electronic devices such as laptops showed only 23 of 50 property records were accurate. DSS internal controls were not adequate." Simply knowing the vulnerability is useless if you cannot find the asset. Furthermore, a missing asset is a vulnerability in itself.

There are four types of location:

1. Physical location: This location is pretty self-explanatory. It specifies in what address, building, floor, room, and the rack/shelf the asset is found. This is often important when a piece of firmware or hardware must be replaced. It may seem inconceivable that a vulnerability could require hardware replacement as a remedy, but it happens. One common cause is obsolete hardware with supporting software drivers that have reached the end-of-life stage and are no longer updated by the vendor. Vulnerability researchers still do testing on such products after that time. The degree to which vulnerabilities are likely to be discovered often depends on the ubiquity of the device.

2. Beneficiary location: This location is relative to the business owner or cus-tomer. It is the group that derives direct benefit from the services provided by the system. They typically are the reason for the existence of the system and collectively, by extension, all of IT in any organization. This is an important consideration when assessing the impact of loss or change. If your firm is operating a business where critical suppliers use a system to receive orders for parts or services that go into key products, then the impact of loss might be very high. On the other hand, a system that delivers static catalog content to casual inquirers will have little impact if disrupted. However, the latter example is seldom the case.

    The beneficiary is often a critical constituency to the VM service. Vulnerabilities generally are ignored by the beneficiary until they are exploited. Then, there is nothing but punishment for failure to remediate in advance of an incident. On the other hand, this group has little patience for downtime to correct problems. Politically, this is a group to work closely with and keep informed of risks and current issues.

3. Financial location: The financial location is similar to the beneficiary. These are the people who pay the bills for installation and maintenance of the sys-tem. Their interest is in satisfying the requirements of the beneficiary. The constituencies in the financial location derive an indirect benefit from the system. This location is defined by an accounting code. The individuals who support this accounting code will have to be informed of the potential impact of vulnerabilities and can assist in convincing the beneficiary that a change is necessary.

Depending on the structure of the business, the financial location and beneficiary may be the same. It would be so reflected in the accounting codes for related asset costs and reflects are IT strategy of distributing IT resources into the beneficiary organizations. For example, the organization responsible for paying for systems housing data (financial location) may also be the same organization receiving revenue from the use of the data (beneficiary). This is not always the case.

4. Architectural location: Very important for risk assessment is the architectural location. This refers to the position of the asset in terms of accessibility. A DMZ (demilitarized zone) is a good example of an architectural location. A DMZ is a network segment that is located between two security gateways. Knowing where an asset or target is positioned can help to determine the real threat levels. If the target sits between two properly configured firewalls and corresponding intrusion prevention system (IPS) devices, the probability of compromise might be very low. If a vulnerable service answers on a transmission control protocol (TCP) port that is not permitted in through the security devices, then again the risk might be very low. On the other hand, if a simple firewall or router sits between the Internet and the target with vulnerabilities in the Hypertext Transfer Protocol (HTTP) service, the risk might be quite high. Knowing as many details as possible about the architectural location is essential. There are numerous configurations that can result in serious threats.

The output of the inventory process is a list of devices and configurations that either validates or populates a CMDB. Knowing what assets are present and their configuration helps the staff to understand and manage a complex environment. Change management, configuration management, and incident management processes benefit greatly by allowing administrators, engineers, and managers to more quickly and accurately assess the impact of events on normal operations.

Figure 7.1 shows a possible device inventory. This report displays, at a minimum, the name of the asset, the software installed and version numbers, and the hardware components. This inventory helps engineers and planners in two ways. First, it helps the planner assess the complexity of the environment and possibly the amount of effort involved in maintaining and replacing the functionality. Second, it helps engineers replicate the functionality with similar components by identifying potential compatibility and configuration issues.

Depending on the technology used to discover the asset, the accuracy of this information may vary significantly. Identifying assets through automated means can be a very challenging task for any technology. Not only is the variety of available versions and brands of products extensive, but the similarities and methods of identification are a daunting challenge as well. Agents generally have performed better in this area than agentless discovery technologies.

Asset Configuration Report		
Domain: xyzcorp.com		**Date: 2 August 2010**
Name	Software	Hardware
acctg.xyzcorp.com	Windows 2003 Server IIS 5.0 ASP.Net Java 1.5	RAID Controller 8 GB RAM 5 X 750 GB DISC 2 X1 GB Ethernet 2 X 3 GHz 64-bit CPU
webinside1.xyzcorp.com	Apache JRun	Intranet Server 1
loadbal1.xyzcorp.com	SuperBalance 1.0 Application Security Module	8 X 1 GB Ethernet 1 X 100 MB Ethernet
asw10-5	SuperSwitcher 2.1 Firmware	ASW Backplane

Figure 7.1   An asset configuration report.

7.3 Evaluation Reports

The inventory is also used in numerous risk management activities and requires evaluation. The inventory will, at some point, include an asset value, which is collected in an evaluation process. Two kinds of value need to be gathered during evaluation. The first is the direct cost of replacement of the device and all internal hardware and software components. This includes the purchase of the same or similarly performing components and the cost of effort to assemble, install, and test the replacement. The obvious reason is to determine the cost of replacement should some disaster befall the target.

The second value to be captured is the benefit derived from use of the asset. This is where beneficiary location is important. Knowing who the beneficiary is and the location inside or outside the organization will draw the attention of the evaluator to the value that beneficiary receives. Ultimately, it is the company operating the asset that incurs the loss should the asset be lost or the service it delivers be disrupted. An external entity loses the benefit of the asset for which the entity ostensibly pays. A good example would be advertisers on a Web site. Those advertisers pay the operator to run ads. The advertisers lose that benefit when the site is destroyed or operationally disrupted.

The operator or owner of the device who gets revenue directly from the asset constitutes the financial location, which is defined by a code that represents a financial accounting unit. On paper or in reality, this unit is taking a risk by providing the direct funding of the device of the associated risk. If the device is insured, the insurer will incur a direct loss according to the terms of the insurance contract.

The value is combined with various risk metrics to assess risk on those assets and to help all of the parties specified by the locations understand the impact to their business. Knowing the physical location of the asset helps with assessment because the level of risk can vary with the attributes of that location. To do this, each location in the company should be assigned a category of location that represents the risk of certain events. For example, a computer and related CIs placed on an undersea oil-exploration platform would be considered to be in a high-risk environment with a high probability of total loss.

When managing the same assets day to day, a basic understanding of the location, owner, and value of each will allow engineers to prioritize remediation and maintenance efforts. It also can be used as input into the severity assessment of an event. Figure 7.2 shows such a report. The name, exact physical location, financial value, and operational criticality to the business is shown. These factors can be quickly used to prioritize actions. For example, "acctg.xyzcorp.com" is the asset with the highest depreciated value in its location. In response to the risk of a sprinkler system malfunction, this server might be the first to be secured against water damage.

On the other hand, a computer found on the 10th floor of a Midwest office building would have a low probability of encountering a total loss. Assessing the risk to the physical environment provides a risk rating, perhaps high/medium/low with an associated numerical value. What is needed in the risk assessment process is a report detailing the inventory of assets discovered, their value, and the physical

Asset Valuation and Location Report					
Domain: xyzcorp.com					Date: 2 August 2010
Name	Physical Location	Rack/ Shelf	Depreciated Value	Criticality	Description
acctg.xyzcorp.com	25 Water St. 4th Floor Computer Room	3C/12	$150,000	High	Accts Rec Server
mail01.xyzcorp.com	25 Water St. 4th Floor Computer Room	5A/2	$50,000	Medium	Internal Mail Server
webinside1.xyzcorp.com	100 Main St. 2nd Floor Computer Room	6A/4	$50,000	Low	Intranet Server 1
webinside2.xyzcorp.com	100 Main St. 2nd Floor Computer Room	6A/6	$50,000	Low	Intranet Server 2
webinside3.xyzcorp.com	100 Main St. 2nd Floor Computer Room	6A/8	$32,000	Low	Intranet Server 3
loadbal1.xyzcorp.com	100 Main St. 2nd Floor Computer Room	7A/10	$32,000	High	Load Balancer 1/2
loadbal2.xyzcorp.com	30 Ocean Av. 5th Floor Equip. Closet	7A/11	$30,000	High	Load Balancer 1/2
asw-10-5	100 Main St. 2rd Floor Equip. Closet	5	$30,000	Medium	Access Switch
asw-10-6	100 Main St. 3rd Floor Equip. Closet	7	$30,000	Medium	Access Switch

Figure 7.2 An asset valuation and location report.

risk level. Having identified the physical location, we can assess the risk to that location from disaster, attack, or random accident. These factors can be combined in a very effective assessment report that is useful to facility owners and operators when taking appropriate mitigation steps.

Figure 7.3 shows a sample of a physical exposure report at a summary level. At a glance, this report helps the asset manager to quickly see the risk exposure and

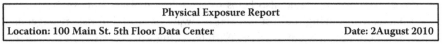

Physical Exposure Report	
Location: 100 Main St. 5th Floor Data Center	Date: 2August 2010

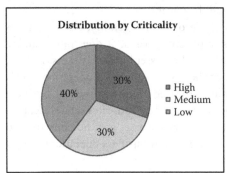

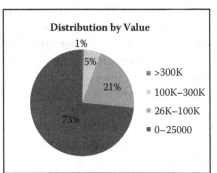

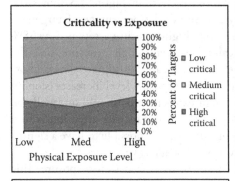

Top 5 Most Exposed Systems	
Name	**Owner**
acctg.xyzcorp.com	Joe Smith
mailhost.xyzcorp.com	Jerry White
theapp.xyzcorp.com	Miles Kendrick
currency1.xyzcorp.com	Mary Alice
personnel.xyzcorp.com	Joe Smith

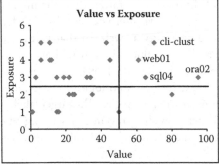

Figure 7.3 A sample physical exposure report at a summary level.

the top assets to monitor more closely. Knowing who the owner is will help with communication of the risk to the asset. This report is used to facilitate negotiation to lower the risk where possible. The distribution by criticality chart will show the relative weight of critical assets in the environment. Ideally, the number of critical assets should be kept to a minimum, while the impact of loss also should be minimized. This is a difficult kind of optimization, but this chart will help a risk manager find an appropriate balance.

The distribution by value also helps to assess the replacement cost impact of physical loss. Minimizing the cost of assets is always beneficial in risk management as well as making good business sense. With fewer high-priced assets in the organization, the potential replacement impact will be lower.

Figure 7.3 also illustrates the risk exposure of assets overall. Criticality is an index rather than a precise value. This is important because it does not quantify the precise or even estimated cost of loss of use of an asset by the business. It does, however, convey the general importance of the asset to business operations. This type of information is less disputable when provided from a survey of business owners and stakeholders. In such a survey, the respondent indicates on a scale, perhaps 1 to 5, the criticality of the asset: 1 means that the asset is of no consequence should it cease to function, and 5 means that essential business operations would be disrupted.

The x-axis of the Criticality versus Exposure chart in Figure 7.3 shows the exposure level: high/medium/low. The y-axis shows the percentage of targets in each exposure level. The number of high-value, high-exposure assets is near 38% of total. Another 22% of medium-critical assets have a high exposure, and the remaining low-critical assets have high exposure. Ideally, this chart should show the high-critical assets decreasing in number as the exposure level increases (sloping downward). The largest percentage in the high-exposure area should optimally be the low-critical assets. The use of criticality in the charts focuses attention on the impact of the loss of the asset to business operations. It is possible to have a significant impact on the business by losing a relatively inexpensive asset.

Another view of loss is to compare the value of an asset with its exposure. This presents a more focused view on the loss of the asset itself rather than the impact to the organization's operations. Figure 7.3 also shows alternate visualization for value versus exposure that can be applied to criticality as well. In that view, one is interested in assets with high exposure and high value. These would appear as points in the upper right corner. These points are identified specifically as "cli-clust," "Web01," "sql04," and "ora02." So, these hosts should logically have more priority when assessing risk and developing mitigation strategies. The target labeled "cli-clust" is a client-facing application cluster providing revenue-generating services. The server obviously has a high value and, in the case of this report, has considerable physical exposure.

One might question why this server and the others are in a physically exposed location with so much value at stake. The report has specifically identified hosts that should be reviewed for relocation to a less exposed environment. In an active IT environment with servers being added, changed, and moved on a daily basis, weekly review of this chart and indeed the entire report is merited.

7.4 Profile Reports

The profile reports seek to provide an understanding of the environment in terms of architecture. Quantity, criticality, and value of an asset are shown in the context of architectural or business area. It can be very instructive, for example, to quantify the number of critical hosts residing in a public DMZ versus noncritical hosts. A similar metric indicating how many hosts are deployed overall for back-office purposes versus direct revenue generation is helpful to understand the amount of administration and monitoring necessary to maintain different aspects of the business. It also provides an opportunity for senior management to see whether the assets by category are appropriately aligned with business priorities.

If the business managers have determined that the top priority of the business is to maintain a current revenue stream from online sources, vis-à-vis an online sales effort, then one would expect a large percentage of hosts and network equipment to be focused on this outcome. On the other hand, if more automated back-office operations were a priority to reduce dependence on higher staffing levels, then a greater portion of hosts would be located internally for operational efficiency. These are only two coarse examples of metrics that can be gathered at the profiling stage. More detailed metrics can be created to more precisely monitor the state of the environment in the context of business goals. Remember that processes in a VM program are intended to align with business goals as articulated in the program charter.

Figure 7.4 shows an IT asset alignment report. This is useful to senior IT management in gauging the level of spend or asset commitment to a given business

IT Asset Alignment (Operational Area)				
Name	**Qty Alloc.**	**Qty %**	**Value Alloc.**	**Value %**
Accounting	4	12	170	6
HR/Payroll	6	18	130	4
Manufacturing	9	27	900	30
Order Fulfillment	2	6	600	20
Engineering	12	36	1200	40

Figure 7.4   Sample IT asset alignment report.

segment. It is generally considered common business practice to rely on annual budget and expenditure reports to determine whether they are aligned with business priorities. However, it is more effective to examine what is present in the business after years of spending to understand whether the current state of the infrastructure matches priorities. This report has two basic types of information: quantity allocation, which is a count of the number of hosts in a given asset group or network, and value allocation, which sums the assigned value of the asset in a network or group. These values are expressed as both percentages and absolute numbers. In this example, the largest percentage of assets in quantity and cost is allocated to manufacturing and engineering. These locations are properly suited to a typical technology-product-driven business model. However, a sales and marketing model would be better focused at delivering IT assets and services to order fulfillment and sales.

Figure 7.5 shows an example of an asset value/vulnerability alignment and deviation report, which combines profiling and audit data. This report serves two purposes. First, it shows the IT manager the distribution of hosts and their average values from one network to another. An asset manager can quickly identify from this report where excessive value is placed in fewer numbers of hosts. When looking at a list where the networks have numerous hosts, that is, in the hundreds, one should expect that the value of the hosts typically will not vary greatly if similar functionality is provided. To make this task easier, a chart is also provided.

The chart in Figure 7.5 shows the deviation in host average value to average number of vulnerabilities. In a perfect world, the average number of vulnerabilities in all networks would be the same regardless of the number of hosts, thus reflecting the uniformity in all factors that may affect average score such as complexity, configuration, process, software installation, and technology selection. If all locations, functionality, and processes were consistent, the average value of the assets should be almost identical. Where this chart is most useful is in showing when the average values of the hosts in a network vary greatly from the others. Also, the average number of vulnerabilities should inversely follow the valuation of the hosts when the process of prioritization and remediation are aligned. That is, when the values of hosts are high, the vulnerabilities should be remediated first on those targets, as indicated by the number 2 over "Mumbai." However, when there is a network with hosts of lower average value, less priority is given to remediation. One would expect that the average number of vulnerabilities might be higher, as in the example where the number 1 is over "Paris."

What an IT manager should be concerned about in such a chart is when the high-value networks have numerous vulnerabilities. It is this scenario that represents a significant increase in risk to the organization. Should that be observed on this report, then a close examination of the vulnerability trend report for the particular network is called for. Later in this chapter, we will discuss a more sophisticated approach to prioritizing vulnerabilities that will turn this concept upside down.

IT Asset Value/Vulnerability Alignment (Network)			
Network/Location	Hosts	Avg Value	Avg Vulns
New York	627	532	35
Hong Kong	310	475	37
Chicago	200	530	40
Los Angeles	190	522	37
London	462	458	34
Paris	355	620	39
Mumbai	280	498	45
Tokyo	170	445	34

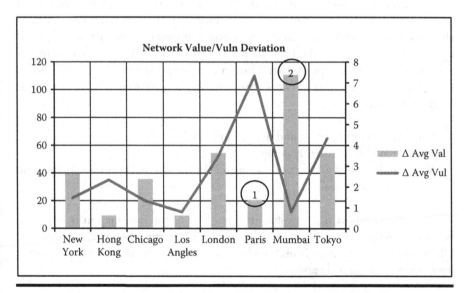

Figure 7.5 Sample asset value/vulnerability alignment and deviation report.

7.5 Audit Reports

The process of auditing is highly operational. Audits are being executed automatically and on demand as remediation activities take place on a daily or hourly basis. Audit processes have little to provide to managers outside of progress reports on the total volume of audits and their overall success and failure rate. There are, however, two general kinds of reports that are needed during the audit phase: current audit status reports and audit schedule reports. Of course, these reports refer to an active scanning technology using stand-alone appliances or agents. A passive vulnerability technology would have different information to indicate the status of each data collector and a different view of performance.

7.5.1 Active Scanning Audit Reports

7.5.1.1 Audit Status Report

With active scanning, the current audit status report exemplified in Figure 7.6 shows several networks currently under audit. Each network has been assigned a specific scanning configuration, which defines the parameters applied for the particular scan. The name of the configuration, as a good practice, indicates the parameters that are key to the planning and organization strategy applied by the system manager. The Internet protocol (IP) range, though not as important, serves as a more specific verification to the operator of which network is being audited. The status answers three important questions related to current vulnerability operations:

> Which audits are running and near completion?
> Which audits have recently completed?
> Which audits will start in the near future? (In the case of this example, the time frame is ± 24 hours.)

The sample report is a snapshot in time. Part of the information is historical but not so old as to be useless in quickly assessing the impact on the environment. Older historic information is useful when analyzing the results of audits that may have failed for technical reasons.

7.5.1.2 Audit Schedule Report

This report helps to track the usage of active scanning resources. When the networks in an organization are widespread with varied accessibility, bandwidth limitations, and few scanners, planning can be facilitated by reporting on the current

Current Audit Status/Schedule (+/- 24 Hours)					
Network	IP Range	Status/ Schedule	Configuration	Last Scan Time	Hosts
New York	10.30.8.0/22	Complete	High-Friday	1:20	430
Mumbai	192.168.70.0/24	Complete	2Mb-Friday	2:45	612
Frankfurt	192.168.1.0/24	25%	High-Weekend	0:59	181
Dusseldorf	192.168.50.0/24	30%	High-Weekend	2:07	210
Paris	192.168.55.0/24	75%	6Mb-Weekend	1:19	167
Karachi	192.168.85.0/24	01:00	256K-Weekend	9:52	140
Osaka	172.16.100.0/24	14:00	1Mb-Saturday	11:31	202
Shanghai	192.168.3.0/24	16:00	2Mb-Saturday	12:44	287

Figure 7.6 Combined current audit status and schedule report.

allocation of scanning resources. Figure 7.6 shows a sample report with two key columns that will help greatly in scheduling scans to available resources: last scan duration and hosts. These columns can help set performance expectations. Since scans need to be performed during a certain time window when the business will be least affected and yet the targets most available (online), knowing how long the scan will take and the schedule can help allocate resources and discover constraints.

For example, the three networks shaded on the report (Karachi, Osaka, and Shanghai in Figure 7.6) take an unusually long time to complete. This is possibly due to bandwidth limitations at the location from which the scan is being performed or target network limits. Note that the same device is performing these two scans during overlapping intervals. From this information, we know that we will likely have to reschedule one of the networks for scanning.

7.5.2 Passive Scanning Audit Reports

With passive vulnerability assessments, where network traffic is analyzed, the impact on the environment is negligible. This leads to different requirements that are immediately more relevant in managing vulnerabilities and inventory rather than monitoring the impact on operations. Figure 7.7 is a sample real-time report of the status of various passive vulnerability analyzers. The metrics found here are very different, and this is only one possible conglomeration of metrics. For the purposes of this discussion, let's assume that there is a device on each network in a physical location. The devices are named for the networks monitored. Shown are three types of networks and likely metrics to be seen, depending on variability of the operating environment.

Current Audit Status - Window: 24 Hours					
Device	New Targets	Proto	New Vulns	Peak Util	Avg. Util
New York-Fin	7	8	54	60	20
New York-DB	1	2	6	90	54
Mumbai	15	16	7	25	18
Frankfurt-LAN	25	8	82	65	30
Frankfurt-DMZ	2	4	14	73	52
Dusseldorf	14	24	96	60	18
Paris DMZ	0	3	221	90	72

Figure 7.7 Sample real-time report of the status of various passive vulnerability analyzers.

Run for a specified time window, this report has the following columns: the device name of the network/device performing analysis, new targets seen from the previous time period, network protocols observed during the time period, new vulnerabilities seen, and peak and average utilization of the analyzer.

"New York-Fin" is a finance network with relatively low average utilization and cyclical peaks, depending on the time of month and year. Since hosts are added and removed with moderate frequency, the number of new targets is relatively low. Similarly, the "Frankfurt-DMZ" is a public DMZ allowing many users to access the provided resources. Peak utilization of the analyzer is quite high (90%) when the site is extremely busy. Since it faces the public, average utilization remains high as well. However, such an environment does not change often, and the number of new targets remains very low. The changes in this figure should easily be reconcilable with change management processes. Later, trend reports on utilization will help determine whether the capacity of the unit in place is sufficient to meet the changing business technology environment.

The "Frankfurt-LAN" device shows a large number of new hosts discovered. This is very common in a physically public environment allowing many users to travel through, connecting to the network wirelessly. These can be guests or traveling employees in a global company. In some businesses, the trend is to allow anyone to connect to any network with a qualified device. This presents new challenges for security, and one of the effects can be observed on such a report by noting an unusually large number of newly discovered hosts. Monitoring the number of new hosts discovered on a daily basis will give an analyst or system operator a "feel" for the technical behavior of the work environment.

Finally, the "Paris-DMZ" item in Figure 7.7 shows no new hosts, which is not unusual. However, there are a number of new vulnerabilities. This type of result is usually because of either a new discovery by a researcher or a fundamental change to the configuration of one or more hosts. This is where alignment with the change management process is important. If a configuration change or new software installation created a vulnerability, remediation should have been considered in the change process. Alternatively, if a new vulnerability has been discovered, it may merit more attention from a systems engineering team. This counter on the report can be a red flag, depending on the operation's activities.

7.5.3 Audit Trend Analysis

7.5.3.1 Vulnerability Trend Report

As mentioned earlier, when there is suspected misalignment of host value and remediation priorities for a given network, then a review of the vulnerability trend is in order. This report is a raw count of the number of vulnerabilities discovered over time and the average number of vulnerabilities per host. The raw count will suggest the level of overall vulnerability activity in the network, but the average will tell us over time whether remediation efforts are keeping pace with new discoveries. *Note:* This report is a substitute for a remediation tracking report with key performance indicators.

Figure 7.8 shows a vulnerabilities and targets report, which displays important trends in a specific network or in the entire organization over a 20-week

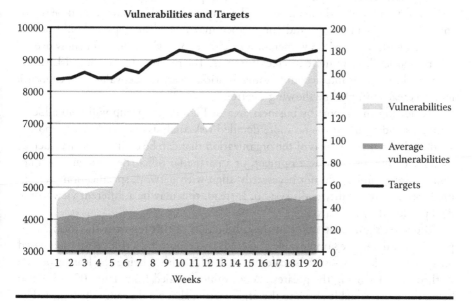

Figure 7.8   A vulnerabilities and targets report shows important trends in a specific network or in the entire organization over a 20-week period.

period. This report generally should be used for any networks or groups of hosts that are managed and remediated by the same team. The report is intended to identify areas where trends show an unhealthy rise due to operational challenges or unexpected changes to the environment. In this example, the number of targets is steadily increasing but not at an unusual rate for a growing business. However, there is a dramatic increase in the number of vulnerabilities. This information alone could possibly be explained by the addition of more complex hosts and applications in the environment. But, this phenomenon typically would be shown as a spike in the absolute number of vulnerabilities rather than a continuous upward trend.

It is possible that the introduction of new targets is simply increasing almost linearly with the number of hosts, that is, maintaining the same average number of vulnerabilities per target. To check this, we include a line showing the average. As we can see, the average is steadily increasing. This trend typically shows up when the staff is unprepared to maintain the additional load of new systems. Generally, it is a result of the inability to remediate at a higher pace, or when the new hosts have been deployed in a way that monitoring and control systems have not yet been configured to perform patching and other automated remediation tasks.

7.5.3.2 Network Risk Trend Report

This report is a fundamental representation of the risk trend for a given network or group of targets. Although it is simple, it is important in assessing the overall risk to IT infrastructure and the business. The audience for this report would be senior to mid-level risk managers and compliance managers. This report should not be confused with the previous vulnerability trend report, which does not show overall risk but rather deals in more discreet numbers. The risk trend report is a risk assessment tool that takes into account vulnerabilities, severity, asset value, and exposure level to create a single line showing the trend.

Reviewing this report by business area or IT security group will help allocate resources and focus efforts on more detailed risk analysis. Typically, this report is produced to represent areas of the organization that can be easily identified such as manufacturing, product development, or a particular office, department, or function. These groupings do not necessarily align with network specifications configured into a vulnerability audit system. Instead, this may be a different view of the data produced by such a system.

The most significant factor in the production of this report is the formula for plotting the data. The sample table that feeds this report has a risk calculation based on specific scales. Exposure is scaled from 1 to 5, with 1 being the least exposure to threats and 5 being the greatest. Asset value is scaled from 1 to 100, with 100 being the most valuable assets to the organization that would cause the biggest loss if damaged, lost, stolen, or otherwise rendered inoperative. The vulnerability score for the network is scaled from 0 to 100, with 100 being easily exploitable, remote privileged access to all targets. Risk is calculated as follows

$$Risk = vscore \times \frac{ex}{5} \times \frac{av}{100}$$

where *vscore* is vulnerability score, *ex* is exposure, and *av* is asset value.

The basic idea is that the vulnerability is multiplied by some fraction of the total exposure and the relative asset value. Exposure, in this example, is measured on a scale from 1 to 5. This needs to be reduced to a fraction from 0 to 1 so that the final result does not exceed 100. Similarly, the asset value (*av*) is expressed as a fraction, *av*/100, which again gives us a fraction from 0 to 1.

The example trend report in Figure 7.9 shows the risk for the engineering area of a company. The amount of risk is clearly rising over time, while the risk from month to month fluctuates. The fact that it fluctuates from one month to the next tells us that there is an active remediation process but for some reason risk is not fully addressed. More importantly, we can see from the linear risk trend line that risk is increasing, where in some charts this would otherwise not be clear. The engineering area clearly needs some attention to discover why risk is increasing.

A look at the detailed data in Figure 7.9 shows an increasing asset value, but more interesting is the increased vulnerability score. The score begins in January at 75 and increases over the next 18 months to 92 in June of the following year. Also telling about this data is that the vulnerability scores are respectably under control for the first eight months. Then, the scores begin to increase in September and make little progress toward decline. Furthermore, beginning in July, the risk scores increase because asset values have increased. This suggests that there is probably an infusion of new, more expensive assets that have also created higher vulnerability scores, possibly from greater complexity. In many cases, such a pattern is due to an engineering or security staff that was ill-prepared for the net assets. An examination of the remediation effort and the specific vulnerabilities affecting the host is in order.

7.6 Active Scanning: Scheduling and Resources

When using active scanners either with agents or appliances, the process of scheduling and resource management can be critical. When an active scan of a network segment is performed, as previously discussed, there are impacts on networks, targets, various infrastructure components, and possibly, by extension, business operations. In order to properly manage these factors, a certain amount of information must be readily available to the system operator and program manager to make intelligent decisions about scan parameters and schedules.

	Engineering			
	Vuln Score	Exposure	Asset Value	Risk
Jan	75	3	40	18.00
Feb	77	3	40	18.48
Mar	78	3	40	18.72
Apr	78	3	40	18.72
May	75	3	40	18.00
Jun	74	3	45	19.98
Jul	76	4	45	27.36
Aug	77	4	45	27.72
Sep	79	4	45	28.44
Oct	79	3	45	21.33
Nov	80	3	47	22.56
Dec	82	3	47	23.12
Jan	83	4	47	31.21
Feb	85	4	48	32.64
Mar	88	3	48	25.34
Apr	90	3	49	26.46
May	90	4	49	35.28
Jun	92	4	48	35.33

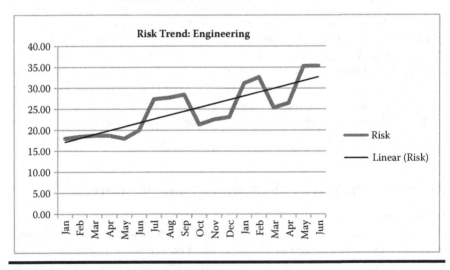

Figure 7.9   Sample risk trend report.

7.6.1 Audit Parameters

Audit parameters refer to the set of rules and limits that are paired with a network's specification to perform an audit. These parameters include but are not limited to:

bandwidth,
protocols,
ports,
vulnerability sets, and
authentication.

Each of these can have a significant impact on the performance, duration, and impact of an audit on the infrastructure.

7.6.1.1 Bandwidth

An easy example of the potential impact of a vulnerability scan on infrastructure is bandwidth. The amount of network bandwidth consumed on a weak wide-area network (WAN) link during business hours may definitely impact one or more critical service levels. To avoid these impacts, adjusting the time during which the audit takes place can make a significant difference. However, the consequence of this decision means that many desktop and laptop computers may not be available for audit. We will discuss scheduling in the next section.

7.6.1.2 Protocols

Protocols are a key decision to be made when performing an audit. Knowing which are most relevant to your business and which are likely to reveal the most vulnerabilities with the least impact is critical. In most companies, the choices in high-level protocols are TCP and UDP (User Datagram Protocol). The use of TCP is unavoidable except for specialized applications that only employ UDP. For example, many market data systems are strictly UDP for performance reasons. There is no two-way handshake in UDP and, therefore, no guaranteed delivery. But, network resource consumption is a small fraction of what occurs with the application of TCP.

7.6.1.3 Ports

On the other hand, it is not unusual to have a business use 95% TCP for applications and services with the exception of domain name system (DNS), which uses UDP port 53. Therefore, excluding UDP in an environment is a viable option for many companies. By doing so, an entire range of checks can be bypassed, thus decreasing the amount of time required to complete an audit.

An even greater impact on the results of an audit is the selection of protocols to be assessed over a particular port. This is an exercise in compromise for maximum effectiveness. If too many protocols are selected, the impact to the infrastructure can be severe. But, if too few are selected, some hosts and vulnerabilities may be missed. A good way to assess the requirements for protocols is to conduct a scan of a sampling of targets in the environment using as many protocols as you think likely to be used. Then, review the audit results to see what protocols are found to be active on the targets.

The common protocols such as HTTP/S, File Transfer Protocol (FTP), and server message block (SMB) are to be expected in nearly any environment. But, there are more obscure protocols for streaming media, peer-to-peer, and Web services that may be unexpected. Those should definitely be included in the list for general use. On the other hand, there may be platform-specific protocols that simply do not apply. For example, an all-Microsoft environment may exclude Novell protocols. Additionally, if the use of Oracle® is non-standard in your business but Sybase® is common, then the commonly used ports for the right vendor should be observed.

Alternatively, for compliance reasons, it may be desirable to check for all protocols for major database vendors. This can lead to the discovery of rogue or noncompliant products in use for which the IT operation is unprepared to provide support. Following is a list of the most common TCP/UDP ports found in a typical enterprise:

FTP data	20	This port is used as a channel for the transfer of data to and from an FTP server.
FTP control	21	Controls the flow of data to and from the FTP server. Client/server connections are established on this port while data is transferred using a different band (TCP-20).
SSH	22	This is an authenticated, encrypted protocol for accessing systems remotely at a command line. It is also used for file copying.
TELNET	23	This is a common method for accessing systems at a command line through an unencrypted channel.
SMTP	25	Servers use this protocol to receive e-mail from other systems. It typically is found on mail servers and not clients.
DNS	53	Typically used with TCP for zone transfers but not standard queries. With UDP, this port is generally used to field requests for domain name resolution.

HTTP	80	The most common protocol on Web servers, this port receives in-bound requests for Web pages.
POP3	110	This port receives requests to collect mail from a mailbox usually held on the listening server. It is referred to as a store-and-forward protocol for mail where the e-mail is removed from the server once it has been delivered to the client. It is generally unencrypted content served from the server to the client with basic authentication.
RPC	135	This service allows other computers to contact and execute programs on the local machine. There are numerous vulnerabilities associated with the handling of requests on this port.
IMAP	143	This allows users to view and manipulate e-mail uniformly on any host supporting the protocol without simply collecting and deleting the mail. The e-mail remains stored on the server after being viewed.
SNMP	161 (UDP)	This port is used to manage SNMP-enabled devices, which can be just about anything connected to the network.
HTTPS	443	Similar to HTTP, this port listens for requests for encrypted Web pages using SSL certificates.
SMB	445	This protocol is used for file-sharing and is most commonly used in Microsoft-based systems. It is also found in UNIX® and Linux systems under the name SAMBA.
IMAP over SSL	993	The same functionality as IMAP but with the added benefit of encryption.
ASP.net session state	42424	Microsoft's ASP.net® platform uses this port to communicate session state information with a Web server so that Web applications can track the state of a transaction without maintaining cookies on the client computer.

7.6.1.4 Vulnerability Sets

The selection of vulnerability checks to be performed can also have an impact. While it is natural to check for any and all possible vulnerabilities, in some cases there is reason to avoid a particular class of vulnerabilities. Some active VM systems have specialized checks for applications. Those applications can be adversely affected by the check. For example, security policy on a target may be set to disable an account after five unsuccessful log-in attempts. However, vulnerability scanner routines test the strength of SNMP community strings and passwords through brute-force means. If these checks are performed against a service account used by a business application to access a remote system, then a locked-out account will cause the application to fail.

Certain kinds of scans of hosts have been known to cause failures in the network equipment supporting those hosts. This is sometimes related to the way the switch or router participates in monitoring the state of the connections between the scanner and the target. The exact reaction of the network device is not predictable but is usually known and documented by the vendor.

7.6.1.5 Authentication

Also discussed earlier on the subject of stand-alone vulnerability scanning, authenticated scans of a target can reveal considerably more information about vulnerabilities present. However, it may be sometimes desirable to have a "hacker's view" of the target. Since credentials typically are not available to intruders, performing aggressive scans from an external vantage point can be informative. The impact on the target is generally lighter as well. This kind of reconnaissance is very fast but will likely be affected by firewalls and IPS devices in between. On firewalls, it is advisable to avoid logging or even possibly blocking such scans to maximize information for the scanner and reduce noise on firewall log analysis.

When applying authentication, using as few credentials as possible globally is easiest to manage. Directory services such as Active Directory® can be used to create and distribute credentials specifically suited for authenticating to a host and reading critical system information. These credentials should have the minimum privileges necessary to perform the tasks and no more. Very strong passwords are a good practice, as well as good handling procedures for such an account. Furthermore, the credentials should be changed on a regular basis but not so often that audit operations are disrupted. This typically means every six months to a year. Also, some business units may require a different set of credentials be used for systems than those in other units. This is a matter of governance practices and policies.

7.6.2 Scheduling

The planning of active scanning resources can be critical when the intensity of scanning activity can affect operations. As previously discussed in Chapter 5, an active scan can affect host performance and network performance, and it can cause denial of service on critical infrastructure components such as firewalls and routers. Also, the cost of scanning devices can be significant for more reasons than acquisition alone. For these reasons, it is important to determine an appropriate schedule for use of these devices and scanning of the specific targets.

It is desirable to scan desktop and laptop computers while they are powered on and connected to the network, which means during business hours. Servers typically are running 24 hours per day so timing is less important for availability reasons but more important for service impact when in use. Some servers operate for the benefit of customers 24 hours per day so only periods of low utilization are appropriate for vulnerability scanning.

Three strategies are common for placing and using scanners. First, scanners can be centrally located and treated as a farm to audit all target areas. Second, additional scanners can be placed on the sites with the highest number of hosts per unit of bandwidth to minimize disruptions to network traffic. Finally, a combination of the previous two approaches can be used for optimal results.

It is not unusual for a mid-size to large organization (20,000 to 100,000 targets) to deploy as many as 30 to 50 scanners. Planning the use of these scanners is a lot like building a train schedule. Unfortunately, VM vendors still are not adequately addressing this area so some careful planning may be required.

7.7 Audit Trend and Performance Reports

Trend and performance reports are the essential information tools for a security manager, technology manager, or vulnerability manager to monitor processes, systems, and personnel performance. It is this information that will provide ongoing performance monitoring enabling each user to identify deficiencies and address them. In this section, we will discuss two types of reports: (1) basic reporting that shows trends in vulnerability processes and (2) advanced reports that can help identify sources of interference with normal organizational behavior.

7.7.1 Basic Reports

These reports define the VM process or perhaps more specifically the remediation process. You should already have done this if you have gotten this far in this book. Figure 7.10 shows an abbreviated process with key functional areas. The shaded items are data elements that flow into and out of the steps.

Determine the inputs and outputs from that process for each step. The process in Figure 7.10 has inputs and outputs in each phase, as indicated by arrows. Not all of these originate directly from the VM process. Instead, there is input from other processes in the organization as well as those developed and delivered by security researchers and vendors. As inputs, "discover vulnerabilities" has the total set of vulnerabilities discovered by researchers worldwide that are relevant to the

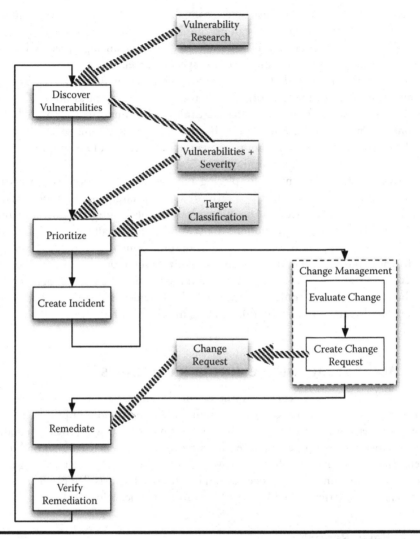

Figure 7.10   Abbreviated vulnerability management process and data flow.

organization. The outputs are the set of vulnerabilities discovered within the organization's IT infrastructure on each target. The latter information set is input into the next phase, "Prioritize."

Also, inputs into the next phase are the classification level of each target (potential impact) and the severity of each of the vulnerabilities. The output from "prioritize" is the list of vulnerability/host combinations to be remediated in order of priority. Setting priorities is either a manual process or a manually controlled process. Manually controlled processes have automation to produce the priorities list with inputs that are adjusted by the administrator.

The output of this process can take the form of a change control ticket or incident ticket, depending on the way your organization has planned operations support systems. In our example, an incident is created and assigned to the appropriate change manager or owner. In the change management process, other activities outside the scope of VM are performed to coordinate changes with other IT operations.

Finally, as input, the remediation process has tickets from the change management system. When the remediation is complete, there should be some verification of the vulnerability. The results of that verification are outputs of the process along with a "clean" system.

Determine the important variables that can affect the process performance. Although there may be variation within your customized processes and your organizational requirements, there are a few basic measures to be considered. They should be evaluated over varying time frames, depending on your operational cycles. For most businesses, this is usually weekly, monthly, or quarterly. These metrics should also be grouped from one business or IT area to another. For example, if your organization has separate IT groups in each business unit, then it is highly instructive to look at the metrics by business unit to make processes more uniformly efficient with more predictable results. Process performance is likely experiencing wide variation caused by different management styles and cultures that influence its effectiveness.

This information is ultimately used to construct the critical reports necessary for performance trend analysis. The following is a list of reports that are commonly useful in managing a typical VM process:

Configuration vulnerabilities by operational area: An operational area is some part of the technology or security organization that performs a function—for example, messaging systems, Web server management, or desktop management. Each of these areas has the ability to significantly influence the number and severity of vulnerabilities, and attention should be drawn to their performance in affecting the overall organizational risk. For example, network switches may consistently show a vulnerability resulting from improperly configured SNMP services. This might suggest that there is a problem in following standards or the requirements for a revision to standards.

Vulnerabilities by severity across operational areas: Knowing how many vulnerabilities are present for various severity levels in each operational area of the business can help identify problems with prioritization.

Configuration vulnerabilities discovered versus remediated by severity and/or type: The order in which vulnerabilities are remediated or avoided is important to get the most impact from the remediation and configuration processes. For example, the number of weak passwords (a configuration item) discovered compared to the number remediated tells us how proactively this particularly insidious vulnerability is addressed in advance—that is, during configuration versus late in the process during remediation. The metric can be applied to specific vulnerabilities or to broad categories or severities. This metric will help identify when process phases fail to address the broad prioritization requirement.

Configuration of remediated vulnerabilities by target classification: Similar to the previous metric, knowing the vulnerabilities for each type of host in terms of business criticality will focus attention on the prioritization of VM activities toward critical hosts. When configuration and remediation processes are performed, priorities in resource allocation should be properly directed. It is very common to have different IT groups involved in managing critical hosts—for example, servers versus less critical targets such as desktops. This type of measure will help identify deficiencies in ability to prioritize, often within particular technology management groups.

Extending this metric, the report can be ordered by asset value multiplied by the vulnerability score. Although not perfect, it can help prioritize the remediation effort by value to the business rather than simply data classification. This may be necessary because asset value does not always follow data classification, which happens because asset classification is not applied uniformly (nor is asset value). And even though data classification should follow asset value, the asset owner may view them differently since the perception of value throughout an organization is not consistent.

Vulnerabilities by remediation type: This metric provides information about how either patches or configuration corrections are the remediation methods of vulnerabilities. The numbers can be further broken down into operating groups to identify where the resources are needed. For example, messaging systems may encounter a large increase in patchable vulnerabilities, and therefore require better patch management or a review of patching processes to give them more emphasis.

New vulnerabilities: All of the vulnerability metrics have to be viewed in the context of the overall vulnerability environment. It is possible that more new vulnerabilities were discovered in packaged software; therefore, the amount of remediation will increase. The other metrics have to be considered in this context to avoid falsely determining that a process flaw in your organization created the change in metrics. If the number of vulnerabilities in a particular area increases at the same rate as the total discovered, then it is less likely that internal process deficiencies are the root cause.

Remediated vulnerabilities failing verification: From the last step in our example process, a verification of the remediated target is performed prior to permitting the change or incident ticket to be closed. This metric can go directly to the effectiveness of the remediation process.

Vulnerabilities per application: This is the top number of vulnerabilities per application over a period of time. It helps to understand the complexity of the environment and identify any applications that may be particularly more vulnerable or require more remediation than others. This information can be used to identify the true cost of operating an application and possibly trigger a reassessment of the viability of the vendor's products in the organization. For example, if packaged application XYZ were very expensive and had numerous vulnerabilities found over a six-month-to-one-year time frame, this may indicate poor security quality. Identifying this application can lead to an assessment to determine whether the cost of remediation is becoming too high. Perhaps an alternative vendor should be selected or some credit from the existing vendor sought.

7.7.2 Advanced Reports: Control Charts

All of the audit reports thus far have provided information on a short time frame and are used to manage the daily operations. However, trend reports can be more telling and assist greatly with strategic security planning. Understanding, for example, the number of new hosts found over a four-month or even a year-to-year time frame can reveal important yet uncommunicated changes in business cycles. Trends can also help manage the overall VM program by identifying deficiencies in processes.

Every process has some range within which it operates. By measuring certain outputs of the process and describing them statistically, we can determine the normal distribution or operating range of that process. This is called process capability. Anything outside of that range can indicate a malfunction in the process or an opportunity for improvement. In VM, we might measure the number of vulnerabilities found or remediated over time. Significant changes in these numbers without a change in the number or classification of targets can be a red flag on configuration management or VM processes.

One of the most common tools for monitoring the statistical variance in a process is a control chart. This chart in a manufacturing process, for example, will show the number of defects over time for a part. For the purposes of a VM application, we will look at the number of vulnerabilities for critical hosts over time. There are two lines that show the "control limits" for vulnerability discovery. These are called the upper control limit (UCL) and the lower control limit (LCL). Anything outside of these limits shows that things are not in "statistical control." This means that there is a source of variation in our results or performance that is unanticipated. This is known as special cause variation. More commonly, when there is a pattern of variation within the upper and lower control limits, this is called common cause variation. This represents the level of variation inherent in any process. And, what often happens is that people look at short-term charts, see a blip, react, and try to fix a problem that in fact is not a problem but part of the normal variability of the process. Only once it is outside the control limits, that is, special cause, should it be addressed.

In the context of VM, common cause variation might show up as a spike in critical vulnerabilities on Wednesdays of every month. This is likely because new vulnerabilities were reported by a vendor on schedule and included in the checks from the VM system. On the other hand, a significant spike above the upper control limit might suggest a flawed process introducing excessive vulnerabilities. But how can we find these variations and determine the root cause? Here are the basic steps necessary:

1. Collect the basic data required. The three basic types of information needed are the count of number of vulnerabilities and the average number per a unit of time, the average score for a target or group, and the count of targets passing or failing a particular requirement.
2. Construct control chart. Once you know which of these types of data you wish to analyze, construct the charts to identify special causes. These causes of variation will show on a properly constructed chart after some research. In many cases, the cause is obvious from the chart; but in others, you will have to interview and study process steps to discover it. Constructing the control chart requires a few basic steps.
3. Select the group and subgroup to be analyzed. If you want to analyze the number of critical hosts that have a vulnerability score below a certain level across business units, then the group is critical hosts, the subgroup is the business unit, and the data element is the count failing a standard. If you want to analyze the average score per host for a particular network over time, then the group is all hosts, the subgroup is the network, and the data element is average host score.
4. Determine the average score for the entire network for each month. Simple enough: average the score of the network for the last 12 months. The single resulting value is known as the X-Bar, and it forms a straight line across the chart known as the center line. This gives the user the ability to tell at a glance the variability of the scores from one month to another.
5. Determine the UCL and LCL. The control limits tell us what the statistical upper and lower tolerable boundaries are for the data. If a data point reaches or passes this control limit, we should be interested in why this has happened and investigate. Determining the UCL and LCL is a little more complicated than calculating an average. It requires the following steps:

    Step 1: Determine the difference in score from one month to the next (monthly delta): Score(Jan) − Score(Feb), Score(Feb) − Score(Mar), etc. This will produce 11 numbers for a 12-month period since there is no number from which to subtract the last month. To keep the resulting monthly delta value positive, use the absolute value of the difference.

    Step 2: Average the 11 scores from the previous step. This value is known as R-Bar.

Month	Tokyo	Monthly Delta
January	547398	64651
February	482747	7109
March	475638	1691
April	473947	18802
May	492749	27825
June	520574	63953
July	456621	45133
August	501754	22727
September	524481	23927
October	500554	140046
November	640600	144497
December	496103	N/A

Average = $\overline{R}$

Average = $\overline{X}$

Upper Control Limit (UCL) = $\overline{X} + (2.66 * \overline{R})$

Lower Control Limit (LCL) = $\overline{X} - (2.66 * \overline{R})$

Figure 7.11   A table showing the monthly vulnerability scan scores for Tokyo.

Step 3: LCL is X-Bar − (2.66 × R-Bar).

Step 4: UCL is X-Bar + (2.66 × R-Bar).

Consider the example in Figure 7.11, which shows the monthly vulnerability scores for Tokyo. It is the average of these scores that is the X-Bar value. The last column is the absolute value of the difference in the scores from month to month. The average of these values is the R-Bar value. Finally, these values are used in LCL and UCL equations to generate our boundaries.

A chart is created from this data, as shown in Figure 7.12. The vulnerability analyst can discern an important finding from this chart. It is most obvious that the X-Bar value rose to near the UCL in November. This suggests that something has happened beyond what would be expected based on past performance. Processes that are properly managed generally do not generate this level of variation. Some investigation will be necessary to determine the cause. The results of this investigation can be instructive to avoid such an increase in overall risk. Some of the possible causes might be one of the following:

A failure to remediate previously discovered severe vulnerabilities: This is a common phenomenon when a serious vulnerability is discovered in a large number of systems. The overall impact to the risk score is quite high.

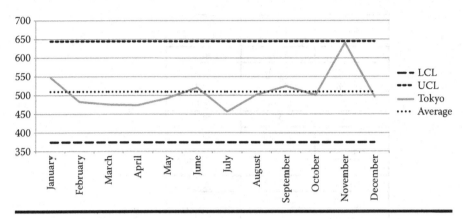

Figure 7.12   Chart: Monthly vulnerability scores for Tokyo.

Further interviews with IT managers responsible for remediation will help identify the cause.

A vendor release of an abnormally high number of critical vulnerabilities: In some cases, the list of discovered vulnerabilities from the software manufacturer are batched together and released all at once. Many risk managers consider this approach to be harmful because it reveals a significant amount of vulnerability with little time to remediate before public exploits become available. Checking other reports to see whether the number of vulnerabilities per host company-wide has increased makes for quick identification of this cause.

A vendor release of a batch of new checks, some of which may be relevant and severe: This is another common cause that can result in anomalous scores. Methods to address this issue include holding the new release until the impact can be evaluated or a simple communication to the risk manager of the expected result.

Vulnerabilities released for systems that are unique to the environment: A particular network or organization, in this case Tokyo, may have several new, severe vulnerabilities released, which may be related to a Japanese language character set or a special type of software in use that is not found in other parts of the company. However, it is necessary to determine whether the problem is confined to the one area or company-wide.

In addition to the event where variation in vulnerability score goes outside of the control limits, other patterns may indicate problems in process:

seven points in a row are on one side of the average vulnerability score;
seven points in a row are found that show progressively increasing scores;

over 90% of the plotted points are in the middle third of the control limit region
  or fewer than 40% are found there; and
random patterns.

7.7.3 Introducing Vulnerability Swarms: Controls Performance Report

Vulnerabilities are not always obvious and discreet. Most of the VM practice to
date and indeed in this book has centered around two central management themes:
(1) front lines (identify and remediate) and (2) leadership (optimize and manage
process). However, there is another level of vulnerability I propose to identify and
remediate for which no formal methodology has yet been proposed.

The concept is called vulnerability swarms. It is common to see many low-
to mid-level vulnerabilities that are not given priority because either the severities
or asset values are low. These vulnerabilities generally go unremediated because
the organization is preoccupied with higher severity items. What is missing is the
appreciation of the collective threat of these vulnerabilities, especially when they
are of the same category, technology, or specific software product. The ubiquity of
the vulnerable technology is what makes what would otherwise be innocuous very
dangerous.

For example, the security standards may state that all file shares require authenticated access. However, a specialized "swarm analysis" vulnerability report shows
a high vulnerability score for a category called access controls. Drilling down into
this area, the security manager finds numerous instances of file shares allowing
write access to everyone.

Knowing that security awareness training has not resulted in any greater level
of compliance, a technology alternative can be considered. In this example, a group
policy object (GPO) in Active Directory might prevent further creation of such
open file shares. This is a no-cost solution to what could be a critical vulnerability
problem.

One might wonder why such vulnerabilities are not detected through more
granular reports such as the vulnerability reports discussed earlier. The simple reason is that these reports are provided in a fashion that facilitates remediation of the
most severe vulnerabilities. However, a low-value asset such as a common desktop
with a relatively low severity vulnerability would not be a priority. What might
be a configuration requirement for certain applications may go ignored in many
locations. A large number of these types of vulnerabilities can be crippling to an
organization when a virus uses the poor configuration practice to spread. So, a very
good way to detect a swarm of low severity vulnerabilities that add up to a high
severity one is through analysis of results aggregated by type of control and further
by commonality of a specific vulnerability.

A controls performance report allows the security manager to assess the effectiveness of internal controls. When security controls are deployed, they must be configured to a certain standard. Also, there are security controls required to be configured as a part of any software component installed. The controls performance report breaks down the categories of compliance items that are lacking by the organization. Some of the compliance categories are the following:

authentication and access control,
storage and backup,
malware management, and
logging and non-repudiation.

By ascribing a value or vulnerability score to each of these areas for a target network or organization, the security or risk manager can determine how effectively current controls are being used. It can guide the actions of a risk manager to investigate current processes to improve control usage or to revise the tactics to achieve the same security value.

Addressing the earlier example, let's look at a report showing the authentication and access control category. This report will show a vulnerability score for the entire category. But, this score should not simply be a sum of the score of each vulnerability in the category. This can provide misleading results since the vulnerabilities may be unrelated outside of the category characteristic.

For simplicity, we will use Common Vulnerability and Exposures (CVE) numbers as an identifier of a vulnerability. Some vulnerabilities can cross technologies or hardware platforms, but CVE generally takes this into account.

File shares allowing write access to everyone is a poor practice and a vulnerability to be sure. Since some applications may require this capability, it is not given a significant severity in comparison to what are likely more severe problems elsewhere. This vulnerability may exist on multiple systems running both Windows and UNIX operating systems. Normally, these would go unremediated. To draw attention to this widespread vulnerability, we sum the number of such vulnerabilities and express it as a percentage of all systems using the underlying technology, the SMB protocol.

So, if we have 100 systems using SMB and 30 of these systems have the vulnerability, then the "swarm score" for this vulnerability will be 30. But, this does not sufficiently communicate the scale of the problem since the overall impact to the organization might not be clear. If there were 1,000 systems, then the percentage of affected systems would be much lower and, therefore, the assumed severity much lower. Using this simple math, in theory, only 30 of 1,000 hosts would be vulnerable. But, the vulnerability may be greater than just the percentage of affected systems since those affected may have a greater value than the remaining 970 systems.

What is needed is a more accurate representation of the impact. For that, we must take into account the value of the assets or systems affected as a percentage of the total value of all systems. This is because the value of affected systems might be greater (or less) than the value of unaffected ones. We can do this with the following formula:

$$S = 1 + \frac{\sum Vx}{\sum Vt} \times \alpha$$

where Vx is the value of vulnerable systems; Vt is the value of all systems in the network, organizational unit, or other division; and α is the score of the individual vulnerability.

This equation finds the value of the affected assets as a percentage of the total value of all relevant hosts being compared. This value is then used as a multiplier of the score of a single instance of a particular vulnerability. So, if a vulnerability had a low score of 10 and the value of affected host expressed as a percentage of the total was 52%, then the result would be $1 + 0.52 \times 10 = 15.2$.

This number is still far too low to be noticed on a report of common vulnerabilities. However, these types of vulnerabilities are better left to a separate report or a separate section of a vulnerability summary. This report may resemble Figure 7.13 for XYZ Corporation.

In this report, there are five vulnerabilities of relatively low significance when evaluated individually. However, they are nevertheless exploitable. En masse, the

XYZ Coporation
Vulnerability Swarm Report   15 September 2009   Page 1 of 1
Network: San Francisco

Business Unit: **Widget Design**	Thresholds	
	Volume: 5	Score: 2

Vulnerability	Volume	Score
0001 – SMB Share allows write access to everyone	30	15.2
0045 – SQL Server weak SA password	6	18.0
0133 – SMB Null Session Enumeration	82	14
0227 – Weak SNMP community string	18	9.2
1472 – SMB Share allows execute access to everyone	41	6.1

Total Vulnerability Swarms: 5

Figure 7.13   A common vulnerability report.

impact could be much more significant. The weak SNMP community string is a good example. It can be used for reconnaissance. However, it is very common and relatively safe to have such a string in printers, depending on your printer maker and position in the network. Consequently, it is easy to lose sight of these vulnerabilities when there are so many. Sometimes, they are completely ignored because they are so numerous on printers. As a result, the same vulnerability goes unnoticed on servers. This report will take the higher value of the servers and elevate the seriousness of those vulnerabilities en masse.

7.8 Compliance Reports

The other important item monitored by a vulnerability audit is policy compliance. This is currently an emerging addition to VM that helps organizations not only meet security objectives but monitor compliance with policy and standards as well.

Generally, compliance reports require a policy specification related to the CIs on the target systems. Those CIs are checked and a tally of compliance is made. The resulting reports serve three primary purposes:

Indicate the level of compliance of each host, network, or organizational unit.
Identify the configuration items that must be corrected.
Historically show compliance performance for systems and organizations.

7.8.1 System Compliance Report

This report identifies the systems that are out of compliance with a particular policy in order to facilitate bringing the systems back into compliance, that is, remediation. This report is not unlike the detailed vulnerability report, only not as much detail is necessary. Following is a list of the essential elements of this report:

overall policy report name, date, and network;
host name and IP address;
number of policy and standards items out of compliance; and
owner or administrator of the system.

This report will allow the compliance manager or security manager to quickly identify the most noncompliant systems and networks to concentrate remediation efforts. An example can be found in Figure 7.14.

An additional, more detailed report is necessary or can be combined with this one to show the detailed state of each system. This report will further enable the

XYZ Coporation
Policy Compliance Report   10 September 2009   Page 1 of 3
Network: Chicago-Main

Business Unit: Widget Distributors

Compliant Targets: 2   **Noncompliant Targets: 3**

System	Noncompliant	Compliant
SERV01.widget.net (10.1.2.30)	2	4
SERV02.widget.net (10.1.2.31)	1	5
NET-SW.widget.net (10.1.2.2)	0	6
EDG-RT2.widget.net (10.1.2.1)	3	3
EDG-RT3.widget.net (10.1.2.3)	0	6
TOTAL	6	24

Figure 7.14   Sample systems compliance report.

administrator of each system to concentrate remediation efforts on specific CIs. For example, if antivirus software is required on a host, but having file-sharing with write access open to anyone turned off is only a best practice, then the antivirus software item would be the first to be remediated. Following is a list of the required report elements:

policy report name, date, and network;
host name and IP address;
policy item number and description; and
compliance state.

Figure 7.15 shows a sample page from a system compliance report. It is a positive assertion report, which means it tells you not only what is not compliant but also what is compliant. This will leave no doubt for an auditor about the state of the target, which is a common requirement for Sarbanes–Oxley (SOX) audits.

7.8.2 Compliance Executive Summary

The executive summary report assesses the degree of compliance in the organization to specific IT management goals. For example, IT managers may set the goal of having 95% of all systems compliant with PCI standards by the end of the year. A template of these standards can be compared against collected data from the

System: Cust-Web01.XYZCORP.COM (10.2.3.4)

Compliant: 4   Noncompliant: 1

Policy Item	Compliance State
4.1 Use strong cryptography and security protocols such as secure sockets layer	Compliant
5.1.1 Ensure that antivirus programs are capable of detecting, removing, and protecting against other forms of malicious software, including spyware and adware.	Compliant
6.1 Ensure that all system components and software have the latest vendor-supplied security patches installed. Install relevant security patches within one month of release. • MS06-11 Patch not installed • MS07-15 Patch not installed	Non-compliant
8.5.10 Require a minimum password length of at least seven characters	Compliant
8.5.11 Use passwords containing both numeric and alphabetic characters	Compliant

Figure 7.15   Sample page from a system compliance report.

hosts and the report generated on a regular basis. Such a report would contain the following, at a minimum:

number and percentage of hosts out of compliance,
number and percentage of hosts in compliance,
average number of compliance items missing per host, and
for each network or organizational grouping, the number and percentage of hosts in and out of compliance.

This information shows the IT managers which groups are most successful at compliance and which are the least. It helps allocate resources to bring the most deficient groups to a greater level of compliance.

7.9 Summary

It should be obvious from this chapter that easily accessible and organized information is essential for managing a VM program. Vulnerability assessment products are information-gathering systems. Many people miss this point and expect little from these systems. These systems typically are planned and implemented by technologists whose comfort zone ends at the details of target configuration. I theorize that this is the reason reporting functions are so lacking.

It makes little sense to collect so much detailed information and yet mine the data in minimalistic fashion. The value of the information is far beyond technological, and it is the responsibility of the program manager to bring these benefits to the enterprise. If you review the contents of this chapter, you will see that much more of the reporting to be generated can support excellence and efficiency in process. Ultimately, this will lead to superior, faster, more reliable remediation, and by extension, better security. The ability to identify a vulnerability not only in one target but in a collection or swarm of targets as well can shift priorities and save the business real money. It is not very exciting to make a global configuration change that fixes a relatively minor vulnerability. But, it is even less exciting to clean a worm infestation off the same targets and then remediate the same exploited vulnerability.

End Note

1. Accountability for Defense Security Service Assets, Inspector General, U.S. Department of Defense, Report No. D-2008-114, July 24, 2008.

Chapter 8

Planning

8.1 Introduction

Up to this point, I have discussed the various aspects of vulnerability management (VM) and their relevance to the overall VM process. I have also described the broader role of VM in an organization's risk management function and maintenance of security posture. Many of the individual stages of implementing VM have been described, such as the development of policies, processes, and requirements. But what is needed now are a project plan, checklists, and strategies to get the program off the ground.

This chapter will provide you with the checklists, plans, strategies, and advice to help you develop a complete VM program in a large, globally distributed company. Some selectivity and tailoring will be required to match specific program needs, which may include the following components:

- VM program charter,
- business case,
- requirements document,
- security architecture proposal,
- project plan,
- request for proposal,
- implementation plan,
- operations process document,
- asset valuation guide, and
- vulnerability and remediation policy.

Each of these documents informs the subsequent one. The process is not linear but rather a series of feedback loops of decreasing iteration over time. When you write the program charter, it will set the tone for the business case. Research for the business case may provide discovery that will modify your charter. As the requirements are developed, you may find additional benefits not originally articulated in the business case that will increase the scope of the project but are essential to the organization. Then, you may decide to adjust your business case and present it to management for additional funding.

In any project, we must acknowledge from the outset that you are not going to create and operate a perfect project plan from the beginning. Every project is a learning process and, although I have provided you with advice for the framework here, more complete documentation and project management will be required. This is not a chapter on how to manage a project. We will instead discuss critical characteristics of a VM project.

8.2 Charter Development

The VM program charter is a very important document that sets the goals and objectives of the program as well as the business rationale. The former point is obvious but the latter is the most important. For the program to be successful, senior management must understand and accept that there is real business value.

8.2.1 Introduction: Business Value

Business value must be articulated up front in the introduction of a charter. It answers the critical question: "Why should I spend money on this?" This value can be presented in many ways; for example:

- Provide tangible examples of what typically may be broken and why it must be fixed. This can be a short list of vulnerabilities that have been exploited at other companies and have caused quantifiable damage. It is also important to make the case that the potential damage from vulnerabilities has a cost to the business in downtime and added labor beyond that which would be required for a VM program. This topic is more exhaustively explored in Philip B. Crosby's book *Quality Is Free: The Art of Making Quality Certain*.[1]
- Keep examples and descriptions in a business context. Anything that is explained can be articulated as a threat to:
  - the viability of the business model;
  - consistency of revenue streams or growth rates; and
  - profits, since they are net of post-incident cleanup costs.
  - VM can lead to operational efficiencies by making what could be a difficult and time-consuming task more routine.

▪ Quantify the benefits wherever possible. It is common to have costs associated with implementation of a program, but if senior management cannot see the financial benefits, they will be far less likely to accept any proposal. By including the financial goals of the program in the charter, it shows a focus on what is important to the company.

8.2.2 Goals and Objectives

Another part of the charter is a description of the program goals and objectives. These should be two separate sections. Keep in mind that goals are the broad outcomes or benefits expected from a series of actions. Objectives are specific items that you wish to achieve and typically are quantifiable.

Here's an example of a goal statement: "Accurately identify and report the vulnerabilities and the status of their remediation." This tells us what we want to achieve but is not really quantifiable. One or more actions or even objectives can be used to reach this goal.

Here's a more concrete example of an objective statement: "Remediate a minimum of 75% of critical vulnerabilities on noncritical targets connected to the XYZ network." This statement is very clear and fully qualified. It is something by which the project can be measured on achieving.

8.2.3 Scope

The scope section of a document will articulate the extent of the project in terms of:

resources required,
networks and hosts affected,
locations affected physically (hardware installed) and logically (scanned or monitored),
processes created and modified,
systems modified (typically to accommodate remediation activities),
types of products purchased, and
types of services required (e.g., systems integration).

8.2.4 Assumptions

This section requires great care when crafting. This is usually a table or a set of short sentences reflecting the assumptions you are making. Many of these statements may be high level if you are uncertain of specific elements. If you know what kind of VM system you will purchase or who will operate that system, those specifics need to be listed. On the other hand, you may not know these things yet, as evidenced in the scope statement, and the only assumption that can be made is that someone will be responsible for administering the system part-time or full-time. Following are some other possible assumptions:

General	Specific
A full-time administrator will be responsible for operation and monitoring of the system.	A current senior security manager in London will be assigned to monitor and operate the system part time.
Vulnerability scans will take place on a regular schedule sufficient to meet the objective of identifying and remediating vulnerabilities within 30 days of discovery.	Weekly vulnerability scans will be performed and critical vulnerabilities immediately assigned to a party responsible for remediation.
Additional, minor development will be required on the change management system to accommodate tracking of remediation activities.	Two developers will be required for a total of approximately 100 hours to make changes to the XYZ change system.

Notice that the general statements can cause fewer problems when scrutinized by senior managers. The more specific statements, however, will better clarify your expectations and also may show what is built into your budget. The choice of which statements are general and which are specific depends greatly on management attitudes and the culture.

8.3 Business Case

The business case, if necessary in your organization, should focus on risk management practice and not on quantifying probabilities. If you suggest the probability of a vulnerability being exploited, the reader will quickly challenge this figure, and rightly so. It is an argument that one can only lose. The reason is that you will likely have no solid numbers specific to your business model, organization, or industry that can reliably predict such an event. The variables are simply too complex to go unchallenged. When constructing a business case, use these tips:

■ Focus on the impact: The impact of loss is well-documented in the field of security. This is difficult to calculate but much easier than probability. Great sources of this information are computer security publications, the FBI, and the Computer Security Institute's Computer Crime and Security Survey. Senior managers would be hard-pressed to say that a broad survey of many companies showing the average loss per security incident in *x* dollars is wrong or not applicable.

■ Intangible risks: The reputation of the company is a very valuable asset. It has goodwill value as well as marketing value that has been carefully built up by marketing and sales organizations for years. The image of the company in the industry and among customers is very difficult to repair but easy to destroy. Some tips on getting the business case viewed favorably:

- Some of those who review the business case should have experience in sales and marketing so they will have an understanding of the value that is at risk.
- Reviewers should be senior enough that they can influence the decision-making process and the budget.
- Include examples of other companies damaged by incidents where vulnerabilities were exploited (e.g., Petco, T.J. Maxx).
- Make the point that loss of or damage to systems and data is bad even if there was no malicious use. The mere public exposure of the incident is sufficient.

■ In some states, the punitive damages for customer data compromise can be significant. If this is relevant to your business, highlight it.

8.4 Requirements Document

Anyone who has worked on a formal IT project knows the necessity of a requirements document. This document will align the goals, processes, and systems in the organization with the functional capabilities of the target solution. These requirements may extend beyond system specification and include the related processes that must be developed or changed. Following is a list of some of the key components of the requirements document:

■ Functional requirements: Explain in detail what all software and hardware components should do. These requirements may include the following:

type of vulnerability detection,
tunable parameters,
vulnerability report elements,
report types (management, executive, risk summary, remediation, etc.),
system interfaces (change and incident management systems, ticketing),
network and group definitions,
authentication capabilities for active scanning,
external database requirements,
backup and restore capabilities,
audit scheduling features, and
security and privacy (encryption and high-availability features).

- Process requirements:
  what steps must be performed,
  who should be able to perform each step,
  inputs and outputs of each step, and
  existing processes with which each step must interact.
- Illustrations and diagrams:
  Mock-up reports to show which elements are included; grouping, and sort order of critical elements. Do not be too restrictive; stick to the essential elements.
  Basic process flow diagrams: Even though this is fairly consistent from one product to another, diagram the process to include the existing internal processes in order to verify the ability to integrate tools and procedures.
- General design: This diagram will show how and where components are expected or permitted to be placed. This will prevent the creation and adoption of a system that will not conform to policy.

Many of the requirements will come from the details of the technology selection process. See Chapter 5 on selecting technology prior to generating your requirements.

8.5 Security Architecture Proposal

Although we have discussed technology and VM architecture, there are some key components that must be included in a security architecture proposal to get the interest and acceptance of various key groups. The groups most important to include in any proposal are Network Operations, Network Engineering, Security, Compliance, Systems Administration, and Systems Engineering. Each of these groups will be affected by a security architecture in different ways.

The timing of the security architecture proposal in the overall project plan should be after a survey of available technologies and after the creation of a short list of vendors from whom you plan to request proposals. From a basic question-and-answer session with each vendor, you should already have discovered the following:

type of vulnerability system (active, passive, agent, or combination);
network requirements;
host scanning requirements (if applicable);
host compatibility (operating systems [OSs] supported);
negative interactions (host or network);

requirements for authentication in active scanning system, installation of agents, special network settings; and

methods of deployment (especially with agents: how are they installed, distributed, and configured?).

After getting a good idea of the type of system(s) you will deploy, it is important to also know your basic architectural requirements. These requirements will help toward making a lot of decisions about how the VM system will integrate with the existing components. Later, additional requirements will be revealed once other groups vet the proposed architecture. For example, after careful review, the systems group may determine that the best way to deploy agents is through the patch management system and not using Windows Server® Update Services (WSUS). If that is the case, a new requirement is created that the vendors will have to meet.

To summarize, following is the basic process for an architecture proposal:

1. Identify the requirements of security, basic networking, and compliance.
2. Review and select a short list of suppliers.
3. Create an architecture proposal with all necessary diagrams. (Technical people generally prefer diagrams.)
4. Review with all key technology and business groups.
5. Gather feedback for new requirements.
6. Refine the architecture until all relevant groups approve.

8.6 RFP

As a part of the technology selection process, product requirements will have to be created. These requirements should be articulated at a high level in a request for proposal (RFP). At a minimum, the type of system (active, passive, agent, or combination thereof) should be decided in advance. The RFP should contain the following sections:

objectives,
operating environment,
existing systems and processes,
locations and sizes,
network types and bandwidth,
user groups and roles (describe the role of and data needed by each of these groups; specific use cases are essential to having the vendor understand the applicability of their functionality to each role):
  – senior manager—process performance;
  – security engineer—vulnerability analysis;
  – systems engineer—remediation;

— risk manager—overall risk by location, network, organization;
— bid submission process and rules; and
— communication (principal contacts and method of contact).

8.7 Implementation Plan

Once the product has been selected and the processes defined, an implementation plan is necessary to ensure delivery on time and according to specification. This plan is important because of the relatively intrusive nature of many vulnerability assessment technologies in a network. If active scanning appliances are used, for example, then many of the previously discussed technological considerations must be accommodated. If agents are selected, then testing of the agents with various baseline desktop images will be necessary. Following is a list of some of the more important elements of the implementation plan:

■ Site preparation checklist: A list of all of the basic requirements necessary for a site to implement the technology, some of which can be discovered through testing. Included on this list of items are the following:
  rack space (units of rack space required);
  power supply (120 V/240V, 50Hz/60Hz, connector type);
  network connection(s) (bandwidth, physical connection type, addressing);
  security (firewalls or access control list settings, intrusion prevention system [IPS] exceptions, target host security settings);
  network equipment (specify which network equipment models do not qualify for introduction of active scanning equipment; this might be any firmware or hardware that the manufacturer specifies as having reported adverse reactions to audits);
  minimum skill set of personnel on site; and
  single point of contact for implementation and escalation for each site.
■ Implementation schedule: For each site, the following information should be recorded as part of the schedule:
  proposed date for implementation;
  time estimated for installation;
  single point of contact, phone, and e-mail address;
  special, named resources required; and
  date goal of the first audit.
■ Installation procedures: Detailed procedures with images showing exactly what actions to perform to install the device. Never make an assumption about the knowledge or skill of the installer since it is likely to vary from one location to another. These procedures should include what needs to be communicated to the business and the VM system manager at appropriate points during installation.

- Program implementation presentation: This is necessary to explain the details of the program to participants in affected locations. This presentation is essential because it is likely that most of those who will be implementing and using the technology both directly and indirectly will know little about it. The presentation should explain how the technology works, the impact on workflow, what is expected from each participating role, and the time line for a given site. It should also address potential questions about the security of the data collected and the privacy of employees. Groups that may be affected include the following:
  network engineers,
  local and global help desks,
  system owners and administrators,
  other systems support personnel,
  IT security personnel, and
  local IT managers.

8.8 Operations Process Document

Once there is a defined process for VM activities, it must be documented in a manner that can be understood at two levels. Process managers will need to understand each step and how it relates to other processes with which their groups interface. This means that the VM process documentation needs to show escalation paths, process inputs, and outputs.

The second format of this document resembles an operation run book. It explains in checklist fashion each step that can be followed in the various use cases encountered by the role. If existing procedures are already in use, then either the new procedures should use the same format or the existing procedures should be updated to include the new steps.

An example procedure for a use case of defining a new network might look like this:

Vulnerability System New Network Procedure
  – Use Case: New Network
  – Description: A new network has been implemented in the organization to accommodate a new user segment.
  – Required data: Internet protocol (IP) address range or classless interdomain routing (CIDR) block, risk level of targets on network, agreed-upon audit window (frequency, start time, and duration), permitted bandwidth consumption, excluded target IPs
  – Actions:
      Define network specification in VM system.
      Define excluded IP addresses.
      Define audit parameters (schedule, bandwidth).

Create security change request for firewall and intrusion prevention system (IPS) exclusions.

When preceding change is complete, run test audit.

Evaluate results of test audit and adjust parameters as necessary.

Communicate any audit parameters changes to security and target owners.

– Activate regular audit procedure.

End of Procedure

Not all procedures are so simple and some will require modifications to existing processes. Following are some factors that can contribute to these changes:

■ Communications required between new processes and existing ones will no doubt be necessary for escalation and discussion of change management issues.

■ Added responsibilities for current staff. Any new system will most certainly introduce more responsibilities for some staff but should eventually result in better service and long-term lower personnel cost through avoided reactions to security breaches.

■ Introduction of new VM data into current system may require different handling procedures. For example, if no automatic interface between incident management and VM systems is built, then incidents may need to be created manually.

■ Incompatibilities of new VM system with existing systems may force manual steps to be added or altered.

8.9 Asset Valuation Guide

Anyone responsible for evaluating and assigning risk parameters to assets in the organization will require a standard guide so that assessments are consistent. Some organizations choose to use a spreadsheet with formulas and rules to minimize the complexity of making the assessment. Such a spreadsheet amounts to a series of questions requiring narrowly defined responses, such as yes/no, or a level from 1 to 5.

In cases where simplicity is desired and there are a few closely interacting risk managers who understand the assessment methodology, the assessment is faster and simpler. Each asset may be assigned a risk impact level with little significant analysis. It may be sufficient to assign a high level to any system that is handling customer information, financial data, or intellectual property, and a low level to anything else. Following are examples of some of the questions that may be included in an asset valuation form:

■ Does the asset transport, store, or process personally identifiable information (PII)?

■ If the asset were to fail to operate or experience an outage in violation of its service level agreement (SLA), would the cost to the enterprise be low, medium, or high?

■ If the data stored or processed by the asset were to be corrupted, would the damage to the business be low, medium, or high? (*Note:* The following amounts depend on the organization size and risk tolerance.)
  - Low = less than $10,000.
  - Medium = $10,001 to $100,000.
  - High = $100,001 and higher.

The approach depends on how security controls are implemented and the variability in cost and complexity of those controls. For example, some companies will implement the same rigid security controls for all systems and add one additional control for critical systems.

This approach is not always practical in a large organization where the cost of security can be very high and time frames for implementation are very long.

8.10 VM Policies

Before any systems or processes are developed and deployed, careful consideration must be given to developing policy. This policy should be based on a relative asset value and risk analysis of the current business operations environment. The amount of effort and priority assigned to remediation, for example, will be determined by the business value of the asset. The policies should address this and other critical issues at a high level. Then, standards will follow to provide more specific detail. Following is a list of some items to be included in the VM policy:

■ Require that all assets be classified or valued. A broad statement of the general levels of classification should be made. The mechanism for classification is left to supporting standards.
■ Assign individual roles responsible for asset classification. These roles may be termed "asset owner" or "primary stakeholder," or maybe even "system manager."
■ Mandate a process for remediation. A clear process for prioritizing and budgeting remediation efforts must be in place and the responsibility for that will lie with the previously mentioned asset owners or equivalent.
■ Define a primary resource for resolution of disputes and questions regarding remediation or classification activities. This will likely be a top-level risk manager or security manager who is knowledgeable about the needs of the business, policies, and systems in question.

Reserve issues about remediation time and frequency of audits for inclusion in the standards. These items may be too dynamic to assign this type of detail at a high level. To guide such standards decisions, a general statement of intent to identify and remediate vulnerabilities according to the risk presented is necessary.

8.11 Deployment Strategies

The deployment of a VM system is only moderately complex and is mostly an exercise in logistics. However, some challenges vary by organization.

8.11.1 Basic Strategy

The basic approach to rolling out a VM system and indeed any global system is to start in small, controllable rings and increase the radius over time. As the confidence and knowledge in deployment and support staff grow, larger user populations can be accommodated. More complex sites at the outset will tend to overwhelm and discourage deployment, whereas rapid gains can be seen from cookie-cutter networks. Some tips on strategy:

Start small. Perhaps deploying to a few hundred users in the local office will deliver immediate benefit.

Test first on each network and then deploy full scale. There is no way to predict the impact to the network devices and hosts without some degree of testing. No two sites are identical, but sometimes they can be sufficiently similar to minimize required testing.

Monitor progress based on targets covered in each deployment cycle and number of unresolved issues. If more or the same issues show up in later deployments, it is important to be prepared to address them before moving any further.

Assign specific resources to handle server and DMZ (De-militarized zone) deployments. These systems are generally more critical, and appropriate resources for testing and monitoring should be available to avoid disruptions of service.

Large organizations should avoid linear deployment as it may lead to very slow adoption. This can be kept to a minimum by carefully planning and having top-level IT management mandate adoption by a certain date.

8.11.2 Risk-Based Strategy

A slightly more difficult but perhaps more palatable approach is the risk-based strategy. The idea is simple. Take the most critical networks in the organization and establish the VM process there first. The number of hosts will be limited and the rate of growth in audit scope will rapidly diminish. Following is a list of typical candidates for the initial rollout using this strategy:

Public-facing DMZs are generally important because they are the electronic face of the organization's brand. Ensuring that vulnerabilities are kept to a minimum at the outset can have a beneficial effect on the brand goodwill.

Mission-critical systems are well understood and easily identified in any company. Any system without which the company would be unable to generate revenue, collect receivables, pay employees, and conduct essential operations is mission-critical. Lowering the risk to these systems is an early win in any VM deployment.

Back-end database systems usually are holding all the data needed by many other upstream systems. Keeping their vulnerabilities to a minimum is obviously a priority since they concentrate value.

Similar to mission-critical systems, communications systems are the heart and arteries of business operations. The accounts payable system can afford to be unavailable for a day or two but, if you cannot e-mail, make phone calls, or send instant messages, then operations can quickly grind to a halt. This is especially true of any company that has more than one geographical location. That usually means every company that is not a small business.

When starting out, it is best to perform the initial installation of equipment and VM services in the largest, most critical data center. The engineering staff, systems administrators, and supporting services are colocated with numerous critical systems. This makes deployment, monitoring, and response to any problems more efficient. It is also likely that the majority of issues will be identified more rapidly. Future deployments in other data centers and offices will go more smoothly with fewer surprises.

When deploying active network scanning on a collection of servers, start with a single server that provides some redundancy, then assess the results. A good starting place is a domain controller in an Active Directory® environment. By initially performing the audit against a single domain controller and assessing the results, it is possible to identify any adverse effects. Then, the deployment can continue outward to larger groups of domain controllers. Once enough confidence has been gained in the directory administrators, you will have momentum to deploy to other infrastructure systems.

With the infrastructure team now on your side after several weeks, moving to other essential business systems will be easier since the VM technology will be considered a part of the infrastructure. Business stakeholders are more likely to accept the advice of their trusted infrastructure partners than a single security or audit group with a brand new system and no track record.

Finally, we get to the important but less significant systems. Desktop computers and laptops are to VM what individual customers (versus commercial customers) are to telephone companies. Single workstations and their users and user groups are high maintenance and lower risk. Workstations require the same amount of technical effort to audit as do critical servers but typically have less direct risk. This is not to suggest that desktop computers go unaudited. The one computer that is left with a critical vulnerability will be used to leapfrog into other more critical systems.

Nevertheless, by using the momentum of your success in auditing critical systems, it should be much easier to get a positive reception from desktop administrators. Also, if the workstations are being scanned without an agent, then there is less fear of a disruption or additional help desk cycles to support installed software. Following is a list of some important points to emphasize to desktop systems managers:

It will require no installation of software on the targets.

There is minimal impact to operations as evidenced by your experience with more critical systems.

All that is required is the creating of auditing credentials provided through the authentication systems administrators. These are the same administrators who have already started using the VM system.

You can quickly demonstrate the audit process on a few example systems and then deploy one VLAN (Virtual Local Area Network) at a time. The support personnel can assess the impact at that time.

The VM technology has been around for some time and its stability and reliability are well known.

8.11.3 Revised Schedule

Any deployment strategy must be flexible enough to respond to changes experienced during previous stages. Although there may be an initial, agreed-upon schedule, it is not uncommon to discover problems that have not been considered.

Example: An initial deployment may use credentials created on an Active Directory system, which then replicates to all of the domain controllers worldwide. However, after beginning this rollout, you discover that other companies that were acquired over the last two years have maintained their own directory services and associated authentication systems. Those administrators were never part of the project plan. Complicating matters is the fact that the acquired companies and the primary corporate entity are sharing the same physical infrastructure in several offices. The program manager will now have to go through much of the same process of planning deployment for the separate entity. It may be determined that the systems of an acquired company should be considered in reports separately from the primary company so that remediation can be managed by different administrators. Since the program manager and the VM development team have not considered this possibility, the VM system and all related processes may have to be reevaluated to develop a solution to these challenges.

8.12 Deployment Metrics and Progress Reports

Since those funding the program would like to know what they are paying for, the success and progress of deployment will have to be monitored and communicated. This is true for any project and certainly for any kind of operation. It starts by defining the criteria for success. These criteria should be tied back to the program charter:

Percentage of systems audited on a regular basis: Creating this metric relies on being able to provide a total count of systems or estimated number of systems in the organization.

Estimated percentage of targets not audited per network: This metric is a little more technical and involved to obtain. It can be either the percentage of targets on which complete/authenticated audits are not performed or the number of audited systems in the network divided by the total number of targets known. This metric will help a risk manager determine how much risk he does not know about. This is equivalent to a margin of error in statistics. It helps to determine the reliability of overall organizational risk assessment. The metric also helps gauge the overall project progress since a certain amount of audit coverage is expected, as stated in program goals.

Estimated time to meet chartered number of systems: This is a project administration activity based on an estimate agreed upon by the network administrator and the vulnerability manager.

Number of newly audited systems per week since initial deployment: A simple measurement taken each week from the vulnerability system to show a progress trend. The metric will help identify whether the project progress is stalling.

List of issues encountered and resolutions during each week: Another important project management activity to enhance status communication and facilitate resolution.

Percentage of systems regularly audited that have begun remediation activity: This figure is the number of change management system entries divided by incidents created by the vulnerability system.

Percentage of all systems engaged in VM-related remediation activity: Similar to the previous metric, this figure shows the number of change management entries related to VM divided by total estimated systems in the organization.

8.13 Summary

The benefits of planning are indisputable. The important aspect of planning a VM project is to follow the same structured process that is accepted in your organization. Since this activity is a combination risk management and infrastructure project, it is important to provide solid communication using the tools discussed in this chapter. The early steps of developing a business case and requirements not only communicate the objectives at each phase, they also have the broader benefit of fostering inclusiveness of the variety of parties required for success. Inclusiveness breaks down barriers; auditing systems and processes have the effect of creating barriers between people. The idea of an audit or monitoring tool can be intimidating and should therefore demand a large degree of openness instead of the image of judgment from a high ground.

In the later phases of implementation, metrics are very reensuring because they make the included parties feel not only that the project is making progress but also that their contributions are not wasted. Then, the project manager has turned a program that would otherwise have met with a lot of resistance into one that the participants support. VM is unique in this strong need to build support, so process and communication are the overarching goals that will guide the whole program plan.

End Note

1. McGraw-Hill, 1979.

Chapter 9

Strategic Vulnerabilities

9.1 Introduction

Now that the reader has gained a comprehensive understanding of what vulnerability management (VM) means from a technical, procedural, and management level, we will explore how vulnerabilities show up on a larger, strategic scale and how they can be remediated. No technology or special process will identify these things. It requires experience and a particularly pragmatic mindset. The manager must understand their enemy not only by their methods but also by their motivations and goals. The specific targets and attacks are less significant when analyzing strategic weakness. This chapter explores VM at a very high level in the organization where business strategy and technology strategy are considered in more abstract terms.

To put strategic vulnerability into perspective, it is important to remember the basic relationship of VM to other key IT and business functions. Figure 9.1 shows these relationships and the type of information conveyed to each from VM. Risk management and business strategy reside in the tier of strategic alignment whereas change, incident, and configuration management are operational processes in information technology. At a discreet technology level, VM is a supplier to other processes, including risk management. However, VM is also an integral part of the risk management process and not a separate entity. This fact gives it a dual operational-strategic position leading to the tight process coupling, which will be discussed later in this chapter.

Vulnerabilities are found in strategy and require a less technical approach to assessment. But VM can also be applied as a strategic decision support tool that influences the decision-making process. Strategic vulnerabilities should be assessed prior to committing the resources of the organization; therefore, they facilitate risk management in the business planning process. Unless this approach is taken,

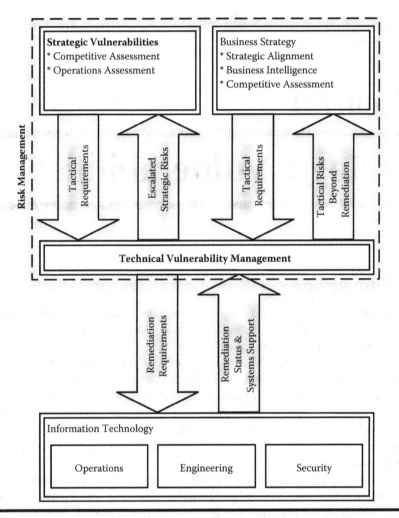

Figure 9.1 Strategic vulnerabilities interacting with technology sphere.

considerable additional cost can be incurred through tactical remediation activities. Although on rare occasions organizations find a simple tactical means to recover from potential disasters, many situations require the extensive deployment of operational resources.

In many cases, strategic blunders result in a blame-finding scenario where disasters occur that force strategic VM to be applied to faults in the risk management process itself. For example, access to the anthrax spores in 2001 was possible because the strategic focus of security was only on the risk of intelligence data leaking to enemies. It did not take into consideration that a dangerous material was being handled that could be used with lethal intent. This failure, in my opinion, was the result of a failure to include assessment of motivational factors in identifying potential perpetrators. One might say that this falls into the realm of threat assessment of which vulnerability assessment is a part.

To further clarify the definition of a strategic vulnerability, let's consider the military view: "The susceptibility of vital instruments of national power to being seriously decreased or adversely changed by the application of actions within the capability of another nation to impose. Strategic vulnerability may pertain to political, geographic, economic, informational, scientific, sociological, or military factors.[1]" So now we can modify this definition to address more directly the private sector. We can replace the words "national power" with "business" and "another nation" with "competitors, detractors, or social actors." Then the definition takes a much more relevant shape: "The susceptibility of vital instruments of business to being seriously decreased or adversely changed by the application of actions within the capability of competitors, detractors, or social actors to impose. Strategic vulnerability may pertain to political, geographic, economic, informational, scientific, or sociological factors.

A very effective way to identify vulnerabilities is to examine the sources of threats and the targets, as shown in Table 9.1.

What can be distinguished from this list is that targets can be categorized by general attack area:

■ Strategy—These are targets that, if successfully attacked, will suffer diminished capacity to carry out the mission of the organization. The ability to adapt and contingency plans can significantly mitigate such attacks.

Table 9.1 Vulnerability Types

Source	Target
External Threat	**Strategy**
• Natural Disaster	Financial
• Terrorist Attack	• Cash Flow
• Hacker-Activists	• Stock Price
People	• Proprietary Information
• Employees	**Sustaining Resources**
• Customers	Infrastructure and Information
• Terrorists	• Computer Systems
Supply Chain	• Networks
• Vendors	• Suppliers
• Raw-Material Suppliers	**Leadership**
• Manufacturers	Publicity
	• Good Will
	• Reputation
	• Stock Price

■ Sustaining Resources—If attacked, the organization experiences a significant impact on the ability to continue operations. In some cases, this can be mitigated by disaster recovery procedures and technologies. In others, prevention is the only solution.

■ Leadership—Attacks of this kind undermine the credibility and effectiveness of leaders in carrying out their vision. Some types of mitigation are public relations initiatives and an adaptive strategy.

The three key topics that should be used to address strategic vulnerabilities are:

1. Constantly reevaluate the operating environment for vulnerabilities involving the previously mentioned targets and sources. For example, if an online lumber-trading business decides to specialize in a type of wood found only in ecologically sensitive areas, they may well draw the ire of environmental activists with strong computer networking skills. Sufficiently motivated, they will seek to target the infrastructure as the weakest point of the business. General George S. Patton put this principle very well, "To win battles you do not beat weapons—you beat the soul of man, of the enemy man. Decide what will hurt the enemy most within the limits of your capabilities to harm him and then do it.[2]" This is precisely how the adversaries of a business will naturally think, and this is also how the vulnerability or risk manager must think. The advantage the vulnerability manager has is greater knowledge about the enterprise and its operations; therefore, he can fashion a durable defense.

2. Manage external factors with various internal and external strategies. Too often, business strategy is developed without consideration of the vulnerabilities created to make that strategy work. Alternative approaches must be considered to minimize possible external threats. This chapter will discuss aspects of the environment external to an organization, how to analyze them, and how to mitigate them.

3. Internal vulnerabilities must also be controlled and represent a challenge to any organization regardless of its charter. Commonly experienced internal factors include employee fraud, flawed business processes, and industrial espionage. These factors often target the fundamental product or service of the organization and can threaten its very existence.

In the sections that follow, we will discuss various examples of how strategic vulnerabilities arise, are identified, and mitigated. While reading these examples, consider how strategic VM can operate as a pervasive participant in all business activities and as an integral part of an overall risk management team.

This chapter describes VM as it guides business and technology strategy. We will also discuss how VM, in the risk mitigation role, finds emerging vulnerabilities in existing strategies.

9.2 Operating Environment

The conditions in the IT operating environment are a critical factor in the structure and conduct of the VM process. So, let's take a second to clarify what is meant by IT environment and how the characteristics of the environment will affect process vulnerabilities.

There are two components to the IT environment, the internal area and the external one. The internal area includes all aspects of the business and related technology operations. Items to be considered in the internal area are:

- Personnel skills and turnover
- Computer systems and related configurations
- New business processes and related system changes
- Business acquisition rates, target sizes, and business models
- Types of applications and rate of critical vulnerability discovery
- Pervasiveness of a particular technology platform

These elements are closest to the IT operations and are, to some extent, controllable or manageable through direct action. For example, if there is a critical skill set in IT that experiences a lot of turnover, then that turnover can be analyzed and reduced. If a particular standard systems configuration is problematic, plans can be made to correct that configuration on a global scale.

The external business area presents factors outside of the business IT activities that affect operations and security posture. Items in the external area are:

- Regulation of the industry
- Standards to which the industry is held, e.g. payment card industry (PCI) standards
- Reliability of vendors whose software your company widely employs
- General visibility and public opinion of an industry or your company
- Amount of public-facing business conducted

These factors are distinguishable by the fact that they are very difficult if not impossible to control. Some minor influence may be possible under the right circumstances but generally changing these factors has a low cost-benefit ratio. The last two items directly affect the risk profile of a company and can make a particular vulnerability all the more important to remediate. In context, external factors such as reliability of a vendor, public opinion of the industry, and public customer exposure can combine to make the vulnerabilities of a particular target more significant than in other businesses. For example, a tobacco manufacturer with a large Internet presence would be more concerned about a flaw in Web server software than would an accounting firm with only corporate clients.

Industry regulation is certainly well known for its influence on IT operations. Legislation such as Sarbanes–Oxley has created onerous burdens on security and compliance personnel and very expensive audit and assessment requirements. Although industries in general try to influence such legislation, the complex relationships between business and government always create a bureaucracy that applies regulation to industry with little regard to the impact. The point at which industry and government negotiate is a political one and therefore avoids specificity, commitment, and accountability for the policies created. The best that the manager of strategic vulnerabilities can hope to achieve is to apply efficiencies as much and as quickly as possible in anticipation of the impact of impending regulation.

Standards creation is similar to regulation when it is used in audit results to continue licensing of a product. PCI is a good example of this. When these standards are changed, the impact on technology architecture can be significant as can be the cost. A strong understanding of these standards will help identify likely areas for future changes that may impact the organization. Then, planning can be done for such potential changes leaving flexibility to adapt.

9.3 Managing External Factors

When considering external factors, the idea of adaptability becomes a recurring theme. This is because those external factors are more difficult to mitigate than to accept and prepare for which is usually more difficult for the risk manager to embrace. Two powerful organizational concepts that have been around for many years in information technology can help in many reaction scenarios:

- Modularization—IT components and processes can be encapsulated into modules of functionality with specific inputs and outputs. This will allow them to be moved, manipulated, and modified with less impact on the organization as a whole.
- Coupling—This programming concept is applicable in many areas of process, system, and organization design. When processes are more tightly coupled, they become more dependent on the functionality of other processes rather than the simple inputs and outputs. Loose coupling supports modularization in that a loosely coupled process need not concern itself with how an input is created but only that it is present when needed.

With modularization and loose coupling, there can be more flexibility and adaptability of operations to a changing threat environment. When newly competitive business models emerge, the organization can be prepared to rapidly change course to meet that competition. An excellent example of an organizational strategy that provides adaptability in the face of changing strategic challenges is the Kyocera

Corporation. The founder, Kazuo Inamori, created a culture that adapts to change while maintaining excellence. The structure employed is known as the "amoeba management system."

When a business purpose arises such as new product development, an amoeba is formed to create the product and is then disbanded. Those resources, human, equipment, financial, or other are then selected for use in an existing or new forming amoeba. In this way, resources are efficiently reused or eliminated when no longer needed. This is a highly adaptable and low-risk approach to structure. If a particular business function is under strategic threat, it can adapt because it is small. If it cannot adapt, then it can be eliminated with relatively low cost to the overall organization because it has little systemic linkage to other areas of the company. This keeps the risk of a company low while strengthening the response to adverse events.

Another attribute is the potential for design with minimal reliance on common infrastructure and services. These basic capabilities can be supplied in any needed form from a central organization but only the essentials where economies of scale can have a significant impact. It is not necessary for one amoeba to extensively form ties with another. Ubiquitous network and system designs are not necessary, and therefore widespread risk of vulnerability swarms can be kept to a minimum. Common, shared services such as payroll and benefits are few and less likely to be targets of attacks.

Amoebas can be used at many levels to manage risk. Reducing commitment to a particular strategy when it is uncertain will provide another possible benefit. For example, if a firm in the 1970s were committed to making Betamax® (Betamax is a registered trademark of the Sony Corporation and/or its affiliates) tape when VHS was a strategic threat, then dedicating an amoeba to each technology would have helped reduce exposure to the vulnerability typical in high technology competition—in this case, recording time. When VHS became the preferred format, the Betamax amoeba could have been disbanded and the resources shifted to supporting the more successful technology. There was certainly overlap in expertise.

Instead of embracing an adaptive strategy for competitive pressures in a technology industry, Sony created a vulnerability by committing itself to a single path and betting heavily. They went further by attempting to mitigate that risk by trying to control an unwieldy external factor, the consumer. A more efficient and adaptive approach would have been more successful.

9.4 Controlling Internal Vulnerabilities

Strategic vulnerabilities can be found nearly anywhere in an organization. This is because, as in the systems development life cycle, risks are only considered in the context of the current environment. Strategy development typically does not take into account that the environment is dynamic and the world may react to competitive changes in malicious ways. This is the typically unforeseen threat that emerges because the basis for the original assumptions has changed. Whatever the circumstances, the overarching characteristic of a strategic vulnerability is that it represents a threat to the health of the entire organization. Strategic vulnerabilities are bound to the goals of the business or government itself.

9.4.1 Business Model

The basic business strategy is often developed with an optimistic eye and lacks sufficient review of the underlying assumptions. What is true today for a new business may no longer be true in the future when the environment changes. Just as it is for vulnerabilities in software so too is it for a new product or service. America Online (AOL) has experienced the same problem. Prior to the popularity of the Internet, AOL recognized the need of people with computers and modern communications equipment to form online communities and share information. The business model was quite successful for many years until and cheaper, more open, and widespread alternatives arrived.

In the 1980s, a small company called Quantum Link provided the ability to share online information through a basic bulletin board system (BBS). It adapted strategy to meet the communication needs of a variety of emerging computing platforms. Online games were the big attraction in the early stages but evolved to provide innovative communication tools that were easy to use. Beginning in 2001, subscribership began to decline since barriers to global communication came down with the availability of the Internet to the general public. Many existing and potential customers recognized that the closed community of AOL offered a relatively high-priced and low-valued service.

As a survival strategy, AOL merged with Time Warner, which could supply exclusive content. This kind of reaction seems appropriate in retrospect. The business model had to change drastically given the threat from changing technology. But the change was not that rapid and perhaps foreseeable. As early as 1996, the promise of this technology should have come to the attention of strategic vulnerability managers. Earlier adoption of the new technology could have lessened the impact from the change. This is what distinguishes a market leader from a decliner. The cost of developing and then scrapping various possible business models is often less than the cost of watching the core business decline without a leading approach to alternatives.

From this example, the definition of a strategic vulnerability should become clearer. A strategic vulnerability is one that is broadly reaching in depth or breadth and that requires similar adjustment for remediation or mitigation. Vulnerability management is more than auditing internal business technologies and looking for vulnerabilities. The external environment and competitive marketplace offer strategic threats to vulnerabilities in the business strategy itself.

9.4.2 Business Process

Processes are prone to manipulation by clients and employees alike. It is a common avenue for fraud and legitimate gaming of the system. When an inconsequential process for a small business function is exploited, there is loss—but not so great as to threaten the viability of the entire enterprise. It is a matter of size of impact that can make the vulnerability strategic. For example, if a company is in the lottery business and someone discovers a pattern of how to pick the winning number every time, then this small flaw can become a large strategic vulnerability resulting in huge losses.

9.4.3 Complexity

A popular observation made by security leader Bruce Schneier is that complexity is the enemy of security. Although he was referring at the time to encryption algorithms, it is no less applicable to security strategy. Complexity can obfuscate vulnerabilities and is often unrecognized when an operations strategy is developed.

9.4.3.1 Vulnerability Scenario

The complexity of a supply chain is a good example of how small details can have a far-reaching impact. If many unrelated organizations are involved in various phases of the development of a key component, then the manipulation of even the smallest supplier can have broad-ranging consequences for an industry or a single company. For example, an LCD TV manufacturer, company A, may purchase LCD displays from company B to incorporate into their product. The LCD display maker uses the liquid in liquid crystals supplied by company C. Company C purchases a key raw material, indium, from company D. Company D is based in Canada, which produces most of the world's supply of the crucial element. If the supplies in Canada are disrupted, then prices will rise rapidly throughout the supply chain. Yet company A may not be monitoring this situation and taking strategic steps to minimize their dependence on one source or one product.

9.4.3.2 Mitigation Strategy

The supply chain is often a long and complex series of parties working together, yet loosely, to meet the needs of customers. In recent years, supply chains have grown shorter due to disintermediation efforts driven by Web technology. However, this evolution in supplier relationships has had the adverse effect of insulating the business from upstream supplier relationships that carry more information about supplier operations.

For example, knowing that your supplier relies on a key raw material from only a single source might suggest to a vulnerability manager that additional, contingency suppliers should be sought who rely on alternative raw material sources. It is the equivalent of creating redundancy in the supply chain where the weak links exist. In the case of our LCD manufacturer example, it would be well advised to seek an alternative supplier of LCD panels whose indium source is different from the primary vendor.

This scenario illustrates an internal vulnerability because the primary cause is an internal strategic decision that is controllable through assessment and mitigation rather than planning for a response.

9.4.4 Response Scenario

Some internal strategic vulnerabilities cannot be proactively remediated, and yet the prospect of accepting the risk is unacceptable given the potential rewards. In this situation, the understanding of the behavior of threats to vulnerabilities is essential. A strategic vulnerability that presents itself to a malicious actor is tempting to the point where he forms a tunnel vision of the desired outcome and the tactical details. This singular focus will enable the vulnerable target time to respond with a contingent strategy.

For example, a company may develop more than one method of delivering goods and services to the customer. If the vulnerability in the business model is the method of delivery, alternative strategies can be made if an attack occurs upon the primary delivery method. The following is an example of how such a scenario may present itself.

9.4.4.1 Vulnerability Scenario

Spam Free Corporation has developed a proprietary method for filtering unwanted e-mail for large corporations. Using the Software as a Service model, their customers route e-mail messages through their gateway to be processed and then forwarded on to the customer mail servers. The arrangement works well for customers and requires no additional hardware or software. The programming for the Spam Filtering system is small and efficient for one or two customers but requires dedicated servers when handling the e-mail traffic of many customers. The Spam filtering software learns from the experience of handling e-mail for many customers thus improving the overall reliability.

There is little new to this approach except that Spam Free is using an especially efficient filtering algorithm and aggregates the spam experience of many customers.

9.4.4.2 Mitigation Strategy

Recognizing that other companies can enter this market by overcoming only small barriers, Spam Free has created an alternate model of Spam filtering. This model requires customers to install the Spam filtering module on their e-mail gateway.

The software will communicate back to the central server occasionally to contribute heuristic data and receive updates. E-mail moves faster because it does not have to be routed through Spam Free's gateways but instead goes directly to the customer. The disadvantage is that software must be installed on the customer site.

After 6 months in business and over 125 customers, a competitor enters the market with a similar service at a lower price. Spam Free is finding that they now have to compete head to head on price, which is eroding revenue. As a differentiator, Spam Free begins to offer the new service as an option at a lower price while extolling the virtues of the strategy for the customer. More customers like the option and elect this over the competitor's offering.

A mitigation plan has been turned into a competitive advantage. It was not deployed until there was a competitive threat because the support costs were higher and profit margins lower. During the development of new business strategies, many alternatives can come up, many of which are not used for profitability reasons. However, they can always be perfected over time with few resources to be prepared for a changing competitive environment.

9.4.5 Vulnerability Methodology and Change

Business technology assets are deployed for maximum effectiveness, or at least they should be. Although the position of a server, network, or even an entire business function may seem optimal, it can create vulnerabilities over time that ultimately will lead to greater risk. Figure 9.2 illustrates how the threat level increases as a vulnerability goes unobserved over time. Since the vulnerability is present for a long time, there is more risk in potential threats emerging. This is caused by the changing threat landscape resulting from changing target asset values relative to the business function as well as maturing exploitation capabilities.

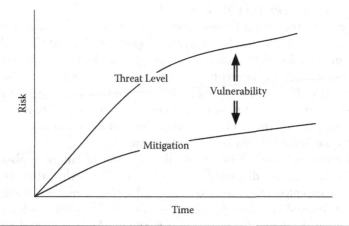

Figure 9.2   Threat level versus mitigation.

For example, a particular supply chain for a product may change over time to become more dependent on critical resources. Alternatively, new technologies may emerge that render the current ones upon which an enterprise is dependent less effective in a competitive market, as we saw in the AOL example. What is more striking is the second line on the chart in Figure 9.2 showing how remediation focus is not aligned with this threat landscape change. There is a gap, which represents an enhanced vulnerability. The most common reason for this is a failure to develop a VM strategy that reassesses the value of assets over time.

The issue is the lack of mitigation resources to meet the threat. As previously demonstrated for AOL, spawning additional exploratory businesses to find mitigating solutions can be cheaper than the realized threat. In this case, one could just as easily substitute "Internet" for "Threat Level" and "Exploratory Business Models" for "Mitigation".

Another real-world example of the latter is perhaps Microsoft's reaction to open source software. The CEO of Microsoft has made it quite clear in the past that the open source Linux operating system is a threat. The most significant defense might be to make cost-effective management tools that are easy to implement and operate.

There are also examples of a changing environment that can be very destructive to a company when they fail to adapt quickly. A good example is the use of the IPX protocol, which was so popular in the 1980s and early 1990s. With Novell maintaining a tight lock on the use of this protocol, customers sought more competitive resources. The lack of IPX entrenchment in a rapidly evolving technology landscape led to adoption of an open standard alternative, transmission control protocol/ Internet protocol (TCP/IP).

Novell had two choices: Adapt by using TCP/IP while moving customers away from IPX or struggle for entrenchment in the market to ward off the threat. Novell was slow to adapt and Microsoft was able to integrate TCP/IP into an increasingly ubiquitous operating system (OS) very rapidly.

Furthermore, the market for networked computers grew far faster than Novell was able to respond. The burden of legacy support for IPX and the challenge of moving a product line to IP proved to be too much for Novell. Though they are a growing and successful company today, they are a far smaller player in the market.

In fairness to Novell's management, it is often difficult to recognize a vulnerability in an underlying technology when confused with the ubiquity of the platform that supports it. This is obvious today now that Microsoft has emerged as a major presence in the majority of the world's computers.

The increase in vulnerability is usually the result of failure to allocate sufficient resources toward discovery and mitigation. To do this, there must be a vision of the complete chain of risks combined with constant awareness of that which is at risk and its value. As we can see from the examples, what is at risk and the associated chain of threats is ever-changing. Any model of determining the risk should support some probability function or otherwise assume the worst case. Some key points to remember in achieving the appropriate level of strategic vulnerability control are:

- Maintain an understanding of what is of greatest value to the business.
- Form a collaborative group to own the vulnerability. This may include representatives from Legal, Incident Management, HR, IT, operations, etc.
- Keep investment and budget for a solution aligned with the potential impact.
- Continually assess the vulnerability from the point of view of a stakeholder.

9.4.6 Complexity

It is more difficult to discover vulnerabilities in a complex environment since they hide in the details along with the bad guys. By reducing this complexity the task of identifying and remediating vulnerabilities becomes easier, but security is then more of a challenge to implement without creating critical paths. For example, a simple network architecture with two tiers of security will no doubt be simple to monitor for vulnerabilities and to implement security.

In a simple network design, there may be two basic levels of security; an Internet DMZ (demilitarized zone) and an internal network. Surely this is a simple matter to protect with security components at the edge, core, and on individual hosts. This architecture is clearly simple to manage but is unrealistic in a complex world with complex business requirements.

If so, an extremely complex architecture is more difficult to manage and conceptualize in an attack. The source of vulnerabilities becomes more difficult to identify and remediate. This is especially true while a critical incident is unfolding. Depending on the technology environment, there are some useful methods of addressing this.

9.4.6.1 Centralization and Regionalization

Globally diverse networks with adapted and evolved designs based on local business models require some amount of consolidation for economies of scale and more focused administration and monitoring. A company with hundreds of sales offices with unique sales applications, some accessible via the Internet and others only available to internal corporate users is a prime candidate for consolidation.

This and other scenarios have the characteristic of a uniform business or application access model. The types of access are essentially the same throughout except that the functionality of each application is targeted toward a particular user group's requirements. However, since they are globally distributed, checking for vulnerabilities and monitoring incidents is more difficult.

A more salient strategy would be to consolidate application servers in either a single location or region. This will enable more consistent management monitoring and vulnerability assessment of the targets. It would also be possible to gain the economies of scale associated with centralized purchases and more efficient use of network resources. The most significant security benefit is that many vulnerabilities that may otherwise go undetected or unremediated by local IT personnel can be more closely handled by a smaller, highly trained staff. This approach also permits the organization to derive more benefit from the network traffic analysis-based vulnerability assessment.

9.4.6.2 Standardization

When for political or technical reasons a regional or central approach is not desirable, standardization and audit are an alternative. Although these activities are required regardless of the strategy employed, it is significantly more important that these activities take place with a decentralized approach.

Standards must be created in multiple languages and support a variety of environments. The most challenging aspect of standardization is getting all IT locations operating at a good baseline. The critical items that must be standardized are:

■ Method and frequency of vulnerability assessments
■ Remediation procedures—that is, ticketing, verification, and closure
■ Change management process to support remediation
■ Active scan parameters
■ Service levels for VM based upon host score

Regular audits are necessary to verify compliance with standards and policy. The audits can be conducted through inspection of automated reports. It is rare that a visit to the remote site is necessary unless obfuscation is suspected.

9.5 Principles of Mitigation

Although this sounds like it is purely the purview of network and system architects, the threats to architecture are seldom fully considered. This is because the architect is more concerned with operational success rather than defense. Best practices guide the architect in his task, but a security architect has the more pragmatic or even cynical eye of the attacker.

Where a network architect sees an efficient method for routing traffic, the attacker sees a new target to disrupt by poisoning routes and address resolution protocol (ARP) tables. For the sake of judicious use of equipment, network architects will multi-home servers with one leg on an internal backup network and the other on a DMZ. The attacker sees an opening through a firewall to a set of vulnerabilities as exploitable by backup protocols.

Vulnerabilities in architecture are not always so obvious. Although the position and function of each component is clearly stated, engineers probably will have considered other use cases for which the architecture can be adapted in order to maintain flexibility for changing business requirements. This can ultimately compromise the original security intent of the design. The following principles will help ensure a more secure technical architecture:

1. Controlled path to each planned destination—This principle means that too much flexibility built into any design leaves room for vulnerabilities. The design should allow for only the specific paths necessary to perform the required function. The definition of path is less rigid, however. The intent is not to suggest, for example, that network routes cannot change and be updated using routing protocols, but it does require that those routes be confined to a certain acceptable range. This leads us to the next principle.

2. Positive control of all activity in a technology system—Again, this is not intended to remove flexibility but only to confine that activity to a specific set of operational parameters. Just as firewalls are used in various strategic points in a network to confine the source, destination, and protocols used, so too should every component of a computer system apply similar constraints. This principle should be applied to the access controls at the field validation level of an application on a network storage system.

3. Redundancy is not repetition—When creating redundancy in a system, it does not necessarily mean that duplicate systems are required. If one system's vulnerability can be compromised, then the duplicate system only doubles the exposure. Many products are built and recommended by manufacturers to be implemented as exact duplicates with some arbitration between them. This is a good example of how only a single use case has been envisioned.

   Typically, the manufacturer has decided that the duplication is for high-availability through redundancy. However, the designers have not considered a more robust security objective. Although it is impractical to code an application two different ways and expect consistent performance, it is practical to consider implementing more than one configuration that achieves the same purpose. Although in many cases this is not an easily managed solution, it can reduce exposure to product-specific or version-specific vulnerabilities.

4. Build-in speed of response to all critical enterprise activities—One important attribute of a strategic vulnerability is that time can amplify the impact of exploitation. The ability to respond to an incident quickly can partially address this phenomenon. Contingency planning and disaster recovery (DR) procedures are the appropriate tool to achieve this. However, those plans must be continuously revised to address changes in the threat landscape and then tested for effectiveness.

5. Vulnerabilities inevitably will be discovered—Constant vigilance is required in identifying vulnerabilities. If they are not discovered by the owners of the assets, then they may be by the attacker. The asset owner has the key advantage of unfettered access to assessment and knowledge of the asset value. The only attacker type that could possibly match this advantage is the insider.

6. Vulnerabilities are not always inanimate—People can be a significant source of vulnerability. Any security strategy must include remediation of vulnerabilities in people. This means implementing a continuous and evolving security awareness program. Why is it that so many organizations are happy to spend large amounts of money identifying and remediating technology vulnerabilities when it is even more cost effective to do the same for employees? Very little specialized technology or process is required.

7. Process, not technology drives a business—Although this book has focused primarily on the technological aspects of VM, this chapter should make it abundantly clear that vulnerabilities do not only exist in technology. It is the processes that define how business objectives are achieved. Vulnerabilities are found there, too. Ignoring them is the equivalent of simply not patching a publicly facing Web server.

9.6 Understanding the Enemy

Any military strategist will tell you that an understanding of the enemy will guide your defenses. In the context of VM, defenses are simply another asset to be attacked, and those defenses are often inflexible and do not match the more nimble enemy. The corollary is that every asset is another defense to be fortified and tuned so as to remain unexploitable. Imagine the devastation to a military force whose own gun emplacements have been captured and turned inward. The asset has then become the liability, doubling the damage. This is what the enemy is seeking: an easy advantage upon an apparently stronger enemy.

The following are some important principles to guide your understanding of the enemy and how your prioritization of vulnerabilities and remediation methods are affected.

9.6.1 Weakness and Strength

Do not assume that the enemy is weak because they are few. Modern technology has changed this idea since the weaker assets of the Internet have been seized by the enemy and turned against you. Worse still, the technology has been designed with flaws that allow what was once a single shot pistol to become a distributed mass of cannons. One only need have some experience with a distributed denial of service attack to validate this idea. Some strategies to help:

■ Separate the system architecture into zones of protection. This is very effective at providing more time to remediate critical vulnerabilities where the remediation may disrupt service without extensive testing. The capabilities of each zone should be well understood when making priority decisions.

■ A denial of service attack can be perpetrated by anyone with minimal hacking capabilities. Any targets located in a zone close to such attackers should have any denial of service (DoS) vulnerabilities remediated quickly. These kinds of attacks can change over time where a blocking strategy works today will fail the next day. Domain system attacks are a good example. Maintaining an authoritative server puts the defender in a position of protecting one of the most valuable assets supporting an organization's visibility to the world. A denial of service directed at DNS and Web-facing servers and network devices is common.

■ The closer the security zone is to the Internet, the more vital it is to remediate any vulnerability. Consider doubling the threat level of any vulnerability in this zone versus in other. Although the assets themselves may not have as much value, the damage to the company's reputation and public image can be difficult to repair.

■ Keep the aperture of attack small on targets handling critical data. Database servers are a good example. They contain information critical to the organization and therefore should be kept in their own defensive zone. This zone should restrict traffic to the bare minimum required. Additional security devices can keep the systems and data safe while the remedies to zero day attacks surface.

■ Use mutually supporting defenses. Similar to the establishment of zones, the security features of a particular zone can be used to contribute to the overall security of other zones. Similar benefit comes from centralized correlation of events from all the zones in a manner that identifies vectors quickly. Mutually supporting defenses work because attacks often must traverse multiple zones to reach the final target thereby being subjected to the security measures of each zone. In terms of vulnerabilities, this has two benefits. First, it enhances the ability to stop an attack for which vulnerabilities may not yet have been detected or remediated. Second, vulnerability data have the opportunity to participate in the defenses by informing correlation services of the threat level at the target.

9.6.2 Real-World Events

Real-world events both present and past, though seemingly unrelated, provide a valuable lesson to the vulnerability strategist. The motives are often the same—only the methods may vary. Terrorism, sense of justice, glory, revenge, delusions of protecting others, or saving the world are common themes that have misguided others into the betrayal, viciousness, and justification for harm to others. So it has been for centuries. Some key items to pay attention to:

■ The most sensitive areas of an enterprise are typically the ones with the most employee stress. Since some employees simply must have access to key systems, managers can address vulnerabilities in process by managing stress. It is often a small cost compared to the potential impact of exploits from an internal, authorized user.

■ Identify and eliminate the incentive to perform bad acts. If your organization has information assets such as credit card numbers that can generate cash on the street, then those who have appropriate access should be sufficiently compensated. Furthermore, make sure the security controls are clearly palpable to the employees but not intrusive. Organize employees so that there is division between those who must conspire to succeed in a theft or destruction of data. And, as is usually overlooked by many IT organizations, employ the principal of least privilege where employees will have to make an extraordinary effort to elevate their access privileges beyond the minimum necessary to perform their jobs.

9.6.3 Goals versus Objectives

The attacker is focused on his goals though his objectives may seem unpredictable. He is not completely irrational or lacking in intelligence. The attack vectors that the enemy uses are not necessarily directly related to the goal but will be equally effective in achieving it.

If the most likely attacker to an oil company were someone concerned with environmental issues or safety, then the vector may not be to directly release oil into the environment but rather to disrupt the systems supporting the supply chain. This would cause disruptions resulting in longer lines and higher prices at the gas pump. The long-term impact on public perception would be to characterize the oil companies as evil. The oil company is bound to the asset of oil and the supply chain in which it participates. The nature of the business requires large, concentrated facilities and transport. These are all targets subject to attack. Some methods for addressing the goals of the attacker require a focus on possible objectives:

■ Alter the nature of the asset to diffuse the vulnerability. A simple example is to distribute data to other areas of the business with different security levels. It is the basic process of classifying data and placing them in appropriate secure locations based upon the threat. This strategy can go a little further by making it more difficult for an attacker to obtain the fully useful data set (objective). This will decrease the probability that a single individual will gain access through unauthorized means. It will also decrease the value of any one data source without the others. Every data source would require an entirely different approach to compromise, thus raising the bar of compromise. An oil company may not be able to achieve this cost effectively, but information assets certainly can since they can be less physically concentrated.
■ Minimize logical concentration points of data to the minimum user group necessary. This is a follow-up remediation strategy to the previous ensuring that when data are collected from different sources, only the needed data elements are transmitted and used in processing. Temporary storage points and unsecure output are minimized. When the information from two or more

sources is required to be damaging to the enterprise, it should be provided—but only in a restricted use case commensurate with the value of the concentrated form.

■ Consider the impact of any data breach or system disruption in terms of how it might be used by competitors, adversaries, or disgruntled employees to harm the company as a whole. A publicly disclosed data breach naturally undermines the good will and credibility of a company. Also, a failure to deliver services can directly impact customers or disrupt a critical revenue stream that will benefit a competitor. Part of the data and system classification process should involve the value of that asset to a competitor or attacker and not just the direct benefit to the organization.

■ Find ways that a competitor might discover that your processes or methods in the sales process are somehow flawed or inferior. This is especially useful in the IT industry where the nuances of technology can be used to cast a negative light on competition. You can prioritize your remediation efforts by how a successful attack on an asset might benefit the competition's public relations efforts. Anyone who has been approached by a technology salesperson will understand this. The attack strategy becomes apparent when a salesperson asks, "What other products are you considering?"

9.6.4 Time Amplifies Impact

One of the most overlooked impacts of vulnerability exploitation is the impact of time. For example, damage to the reputation of a company or even an industry will occur as the result of long-term, highly publicized attacks on the underlying security of information. The retail and payment card industries are good examples. When a major retailer is attacked once, the damage is temporary but takes time to dissipate. When the same or similar retailer is attacked again, there is damage to the original target retailer and similar businesses through confusion of association in the mind of the public. People will think twice about doing business with a firm that has had customer data exposed or even potentially exposed. Over time, the credibility of the retailer and the industry becomes irreparably damaged.

An even wider impact is felt on the payment card industry. Since credit card numbers and consumer information is the critical asset of the industry, the protection of that information is a priority. The more data breaches involving this asset, though not directly under the control of the credit card company, will gradually diminish the business growth potential over time. How many people do you suppose have concerns about the number or credit cards they possess and the use of those credit cards in making purchases?

The response of the payment card industry has been the PCI standards. While well intentioned to improve security, the industry unfortunately has directed attention to compliance with the standard and not to better security. But the industry does what it can.

So how is one to address potential vulnerabilities that are harmful over time? Some methods are:

■ Have plans to clean up potential negative publicity quickly and quietly. If your firm is at fault either from direct failure to secure the asset or indirect failure to oversee external factors, admit it quickly and present an action plan. A template for this process is helpful.
■ Make sure data expire after they are no longer useful. Some companies keep information on customers far past its useful life, which constitutes a vulnerability. This interminable retention is either because there was never a plan for what was to be done with the information or no one considered that the liability of retention is far greater than the benefit of potential use in yet unforeseen business models.
■ Coordinate security efforts with companies in the industry through security associations. All companies in an industry have a mutual interest in staying secure. It would not be giving away any trade secrets to share practices in security and shore up the credibility of the industry as a whole.

9.6.5 *Political Environment Enhances Attacks*

Legislators unwittingly amplify data theft attacks by demonizing the companies for the content of the data itself or the failure to protect. It is a lose-lose situation that makes the information all the more valuable. This phenomenon presents another opportunity for attackers of "big oil" to discover and expose information about profits or supplies to the public. Little public sympathy would go to the oil company that was the victim of data theft and more outrage would be directed at the content of the data. The Saudi government recognizes the importance of oil supply data in public relations and the security of the Saudi Royal family. This is evidenced by the fact that oil production data are classified as a state secrets, affording this data the highest level of protection.

Another example is the loss of consumer data by a credit-reporting agency. These companies are the custodians of individual property or personal information that is deemed inadequately protected. Politicians are anxious to rush to the rescue of fearful consumers by casting a credit agency in a bad light and calling for more regulation. It certainly is a vulnerability of the company and possibly the industry as a whole to be in this business, much less without very strict controls on vulnerabilities.

Another good example of a criminal act that is amplified by the political environment is the disclosure of investment information that shows the avoidance of taxes by wealthy individuals. The German intelligence service paid an informant for stolen data from a bank in Lichtenstein, which were used to attempt prosecution of tax evaders. This was an ugly mess to be sure because some politicians themselves may have had their illicit deeds revealed. Foreign governments attempting to identify and prosecute offenders used the theft and disclosure of this data. Germany wisely has tried to get as much publicity for the issue as possible to intimidate its own citizens into avoiding potential tax havens such as Lichtenstein.

As objectionable as a government benefiting from or even encouraging illegal methods may seem to one's sense of justice, the reputations of the parties involved are still severely damaged by a failure to manage key vulnerabilities in process and systems. The enemy was possibly an employee who had access. By extension, the attacker is any government that might be willing to attempt to purchase illegally obtained information, thereby encouraging the behavior.

9.7 Summary

Strategy is how a business or government decides to fulfill its goals. Those goals can change over time as can the environment in which those goals are pursued. Strategic VM is a way of managing the risk created by those changes. Much as software installed on a computer system does not operate in a static environment and has undiscovered flaws that result from use cases that were unanticipated by the original designers, the same may be true for strategies.

The key factors that lead to the success of identifying and remediating strategic vulnerabilities are:

1. Stay closely linked to business strategy development through relationships and process.
2. Maintain the point of view of competitors and other potential enemies.
3. Look for impacts to existing strategies from the changing environment.
4. Find new ways to innovate opportunity as a means of mitigating vulnerabilities in new strategies.
5. Maintain knowledge of what is most valuable to the business.
6. Establish collaborative teams with members from key departments to own the problem.
7. Align investment with the potential impact.

These methods require leadership, creativity, communication, persistence, and openness to change. Although this is not the rigid, scientific process typically found in VM for technology, it is nonetheless necessary to maximize the effectiveness of the enterprise. For strategic VM to be accepted by executive management, the contribution to the financial health of an organization cannot be understated.

End Notes

1. *Dictionary of Military and Associated Terms*, U.S. Department of Defense, 2005.
2. Patton quotation citation.

Chapter 10

Managing Vulnerabilities in the Cloud

10.1 Vulnerability Management in the Cloud

This chapter provides insight into vulnerability management where cloud computing resources are concerned. It is intended to supplement the lessons of previous chapters by addressing the issues of identifying and managing vulnerabilities in a cloud world. The basic principles of vulnerability management are unchanged by cloud services. What will change is how the principles are applied.

Until now, I have described vulnerability management from technical and process points of view. These dimensions remain consistent and relevant for those who own or control infrastructure and software. In the cloud computing world, however, ownership and control can become more complicated. Ownership is easily established since contracts of sale stipulate the ownership and scope control of what was purchased. One may purchase software but not control the underlying code components. This is an important point for vulnerability management since the software may need a patch that is controlled and issued by the seller. I have addressed that issue throughout this book mostly with attention to vulnerabilities in a restricted physical environment. With cloud, the customer becomes a renter of various resources. The relevance of this and how vulnerabilities are managed will become clear later. First, it is important to understand the reasons for cloud, which will help the reader understand why vulnerabilities must be managed differently.

Consumers of IT services today have sought to decrease capital expenditures and reduce the potential waste and burden of underutilized assets. In other words, they wish to obtain the required resources on demand and adapt quickly to changes in the enterprise. The traditional in-house IT model requires one to maintain control of excess IT capacity in anticipation of unpredictable workloads. These IT systems require maintenance and become obsolete over time. So, when the organization requires a new technology that is not supported by the current, underutilized installation, there is potential waste.

Alternatively, there are considerable benefits to an agile technology environment that can respond to business needs in days, hours, and even minutes rather than weeks and months. These capabilities can yield competitive and cost advantages.

To achieve these benefits, cloud service providers now manage computing resources for numerous customers at lower cost and with faster provisioning. When the IT manager needs to deploy a new finance application requiring compute and storage, a corporate credit card and 10 minutes online will have the infrastructure ready. In other cases, the software itself will be available in a production-ready environment immediately and only requires a subscription and the upload of any data and configuration information. Note that there is far less control of the operating environment.

Layers of abstraction are an important effect in the effort to maximize the utilization of resources and lower costs. This has resulted in development of software tools such as "OpenStack" to manage and monitor services sold to customers rather than selling hardware and software. Flexibility and speed have dramatically changed the course of how IT is designed, built, and maintained. Necessarily, the ability to manage vulnerabilities has become more important and more challenging to a larger audience.

When considering vulnerabilities in a virtual world, the previously mentioned "abstraction" can be a pervasive factor in the risk environment. Abstracting technologies can reduce risk and keep costs low, or they can conceal risks since they are no longer visible. Consider the technologies that are virtualized versions of what were once considered to be an immovable foundation. The Host Computer has become a virtual machine. The physical switching and routing in a data center are now a virtual network. Traditional VPNs (virtual private networks) are ubiquitously integrated into the former. Even wide area network (WAN) switching and routing has evolved into software-defined networks.

In computing, most IT professionals have become accustomed to virtual machines where one does not necessarily know what physical CPUs, memories, or disks are in use for a given system, application, or network component. Virtualization has been further diversified by containerization of specific tasks rather than committing even one virtual machine to a single function. Multiple instances of a container can exist in multiple cloud locations, and load balancers distribute or load-balance application requests among these containers. In either case, the results are returned to the requesting application component. Understanding the state of these containers sometimes sounds like trying to determine which birds in a flock are male or female as they fly around.

Additional blurring of lines occurs when a combination of virtual machines, containers, and software defined networks (local and wide-area) are combined across multiple data centers in diverse and changing geographies. To further understand the challenge of identifying, prioritizing, and remediating vulnerabilities, not even the application itself is all that clear. Many applications share some of the same microservices spread across myriad systems and communicate through a changing, adaptive network. Visibility into this jumbled, shifting virtual world can seem impossible.

So, one does not control most of the resources in use and cannot even consider scanning and patching. Some things can be patched and others cannot. There are two key activities to successfully manage vulnerabilities in this world. First, clearly define the dimensions that are your responsibility and what part belongs to the cloud service provider. Then, implement the appropriate controls for both. *Never lose sight of the fact that you are managing risk more broadly and not just software vulnerabilities.*

So, what exactly is a vulnerability that is specific to the cloud? The "cloud" quickly becomes less mysterious when one realizes that it is just infrastructure, software, and services of varying types that you might find in a traditional, in-house IT environment. But, there is a difference. In order for cloud services to be scalable to many tenants, there has to be orchestration software, shared equipment, virtualized networks, and some specialty software to make it unique and competitive. It is these latter components that become intrinsic to cloud vulnerabilities. To step beyond the straightforward view of scanning and remediating in a traditional IT environment, look for the vulnerabilities that are unique to the definition of cloud. From NIST SP800-145[1], the characteristics of cloud are broadly defined. Here is the short list with some clarification:

NIST Description	Elaboration
On-demand self-service	Order through a web page or in-house specialized software.
Broad network access	Internet and/or internal virtual network.
Resource pooling	Share hardware, software, and network platform with other buyers of the services.
Rapid elasticity	Add and remove any resources or technologies you wish.
Measured service	Pay by the year, month, day, hour, or even minute.

10.2 Dimensions and Challenges of Cloud Service Vulnerabilities

In previous chapters, I have described the process of identifying, assessing, prioritizing, and remediating vulnerabilities. If one recognizes that at some point in the dissection of the virtual world there still are hardware, software, and people, then the general process has not changed. Only the participants, their roles, and methods have changed. There may be an operating system patch management role, but it is not in your organization. The firewall engineers responsible for protecting an application may work for an outside service provider. Physical facilities are protected and monitored by several other parties spread around the world and governed in different jurisdictions by different sets of standards and regulations. The techniques for remediating vulnerabilities will vary.

This model is not new. The world has depended for millennia on a complex supply chain and numerous providers of materials and services combined by multiple layers of third parties resulting in an end product that is sold by yet another party. The reader can refresh their perspective by watching the economics lesson in the 6.5-minute video "I Pencil"[2] that can be found with a simple web search. However, there are specific aspects of how cloud operates at a high level that bear elucidation (see Figure 10.1).

Note that there are many parties working in concert, but only one party is held directly accountable for security, the Application (Software) as a Service Provider. The physical data center servers and network are all managed by another party. Yet, the contract between the application provider and the customer at the top of this chain can only hold one party directly accountable for security. Networks, physical security, audits, and so on are two levels removed. This loss of governance and control makes it necessary to break this supply chain down into smaller parts to examine some of the options for identifying vulnerabilities or holding other parties accountable, albeit indirectly.

Generally following the Open Systems Interconnection (OSI) model, a cloud service is provided at one or more of these levels: Physical, Data Link, Network, Transport, Session, Presentation, and Application. However, they are not necessarily wrapped up in a complete package. There are myriad relationships and intervening parties who directly or indirectly provide these layers. All of them can introduce vulnerabilities, and one or more of them have responsibility for detection and remediation.

Naturally, this state of affairs has created some misgivings about cloud services since visibility is limited. And while it is important to manage risk, it is equally important to seize the opportunity found in the competitive advantages of cloud where productive results are obtained faster and more cost-effectively. In fact, the economies of scale are immense. Businesses can adapt more quickly to changes in customer and regulatory demands because there are other experts at work in the supply chain.

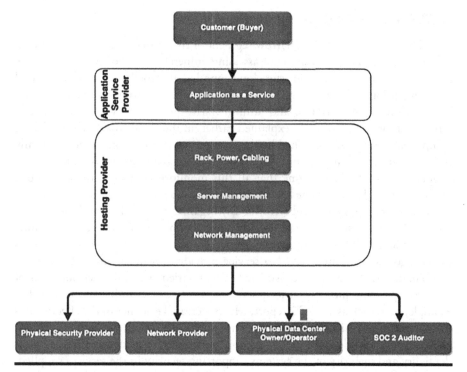

Figure 10.1 Service provider tree.

Furthermore, the buyers of cloud services only need spend as much as is necessary to perform the task at the moment. In the traditional do-it-yourself model, there is a costly amount of planning and build-out of resources in anticipation of a project. This sometimes results in the IT manager over-purchasing to be prepared to rapidly respond to unplanned business demands. The cloud model anticipates this across numerous customers and lessens the "slack" in budgets or plans.

Cloud services are also, in some respects, an equalizer between David and Goliath. The same, cost-efficient services are available to parties small and large. At a very large scale, it may be possible to negotiate some marginal advantage, but only to the extent that it does not become cheaper for Goliath to build his own data center, networks, applications, and software licenses.

All such cloud services can be grouped into the categories: Data Center, Infrastructure as a Service (IaaS), Platform as a Service (PaaS), and Software as a Service (SaaS). Each of these has their own risk and vulnerability management challenges that require unique approaches. In the next few sections, we will discuss the broad methodology and some specifics about how to manage risk in each of these areas. With myriad options available, it would be wise to determine the strategic direction of IT and develop a consistent set of processes across all services in order to provide a global governance view.

10.2.1 Risk Management Methodology

Thus far, I have focused on a narrow segment of risk management that deals with technical and procedural aspects of assessing vulnerabilities. For the vulnerability management journey through the cloud, one has to broaden their view beyond scanning, prioritizing, and remediating. Before cloud, operating system, infrastructure, software configuration, and administrative procedures were enforced and monitored for compliance. As explained earlier, in the cloud world, many of these components previously governed by the consuming organization are now partially or fully invisible usually because third parties have taken this responsibility. Early adopters of cloud often assume that all this monitoring and governance is done properly and feel it is just one less thing to worry about.

The latter case is a tactical error for any organization. Lack of visibility creates increased risk exposure or, at the very least, provides no assurance. We will examine these challenges in the various cloud service models and then identify some ways to manage the associated risk. No service provider, organization, or IT strategy combination is the same. The risk needs are as varied as infinite permutations of business operating models. I will describe a variety of tactics in this section. For example, tools such as a SOC 2 report, which is created evidence of the effectiveness of controls in a service organization, can be obtained from any supplier who has chosen to use outside auditors. This report provides some assurances of the confidentiality and integrity of the systems supporting security in the services supplied. But a few tactics are not a panacea for a comprehensive risk management program.

A very useful approach to planning the risk management program for both internal and cloud provider services is to create a matrix of provider security control types and determine the appropriate method of validation based on the risk level. If consistency and balanced decision-making are to be observed, internal activities of your own organization should be no exception and also should be considered service providers.

Begin with a matrix of control types and risk categories for a particular provider. Figure 10.2 shows one possible matrix.

The simple idea is to determine the types of security controls desired from a cloud service where your own administrative security controls can be used for validation. Those controls may vary by:

- the type or classification of data being processed or stored
- business criticality of service provided
- financial impact of a loss event
- legal or regulatory requirements

It would not be unusual to have a different version of this matrix for each category of business data or function. Looking back at Figure 10.1, it is evident that an application (software) as a service, or SaaS, is purchased directly by the customer. However, there are several underlying elements of the service to take into consideration with

Service Control Requirement	Control Validation Type				
	External Audit	Direct Audit	Certification	Contractual	Technical
Identity and Access Mgmt	N	O	N	N	R
Regulatory Compliance	R	O	R	O	N
Data Provenance	O	R	N	R	N
Data Segregation	N	N	N	R	R
Data Recovery	R	O	N	R	R
Monitoring and Reporting	N	N	N	R	R
Business Continuity	O	O	N	R	R
Patch Management	N	O	S	O	N
Security Monitoring	Y	N	R	O	S

R-Required: A control is required for this type of provider.
O-Optional: If required controls are met, this optional control can be used in selecting the provider.
N-No required control.
S-Specific control type is required: A control such as certification or accreditation from an external authority (e.g., Microsoft's "MCSD: Azure Solutions Architect" or Cisco's "CCIE Data Center"). Other certifications such as PCI DSS (Payment Card Industry Data Security Standard) or HIPAA (Health Insurance Portability and Accountability Act) may be applicable depending on the application.

Figure 10.2   Control-type requirements matrix.

the understanding that these too can introduce critical vulnerabilities. For example, the application provider gets network services from an outside provider, yet that network may be the primary transport mechanism for your critical data.

Due to the variety of layers in this stack of services, there are a variety of approaches to managing risk. If the application in question handles confidential data, then it would be prudent to have a matrix governing the secure access to any systems holding or transporting the data. In this case, vulnerabilities may be identified through audits or reviews of security controls prior to contracting. Risks identified can then be addressed through remedial activities such as:

■ Encryption of the data at rest and in transit
■ Contractual obligations for the service provider to prevent, detect, and report vulnerabilities or incidents
■ A contractual right of the buyer to (one or more of):
   – audit the security procedures provided or governed by the contracting service provider
   – receive a security report of controls quarterly or annually
   – confirm the security or technology certification of the provider and their staff

Note that subsequent checks should be performed regularly to ensure continued compliance with stipulated risk controls. One might consider this the administrative equivalent to updating vulnerability scan checks and performing another scan.

But these are contractual and technical controls. There is also the option of using administrative controls such as contracts, direct audits, or verification of annual certifications. Referring back to our grid in Figure 10.2, if we are expecting the provider to have an identity and access management service support of the application, then we could use technical controls such as logging or LDAP (Lightweight Directory Access Protocol) integration to assess some of our own overarching control of that service element. Conversely, where there is a requirement for patch management service, one can apply a specific control related to the service used such as certification in the software or patch management practices. It may also be a simple matter to use the administrative control of having the supplier provide a quarterly report of patching activity or a notification of scheduled patches.

The European Network and Information Security Agency (ENISA) issued a paper in 2009 called "Benefits, risks and recommendations for information security." This paper provides an excellent list of security vulnerabilities to be found in cloud services. In general, the list holds true for cloud and on-premises technology services alike. The report relies heavily on Gartner™ reporting, a Cloud Security Alliance report, and the opinions of several contributors. The overall assumptions are that cloud service providers have common, observable vulnerabilities. Note that these observations are subject to change and variation across a now massive marketplace for cloud services. So, the report is clear in that it provides some broad advice: "The scenario was NOT intended to be completely realistic for any single cloud client or provider but all elements of the scenario are likely to occur in many organisations in the near future.[3]"

One very important finding is the potential and possibly stealthy risk of loss of governance. The loss of visibility and control at each layer of the OSI model can governance and oversight. As a result, it becomes essential to understand the vulnerabilities associated with that loss and formulate an appropriate management plan. As the reader will see in the sections that follow, there are some common mitigating controls intended to address the risk of the "unseen" in so far as there is sufficient assurance of a secure computing environment.

10.2.2 The Data Center

Physical data centers are the lowest level of service that has major capital and operational challenges in the hierarchy of services. The data center provider typically has physical facilities, multiple circuit ingress points (often referred to as DMARCs or demarcation points), video surveillance, guards at a desk to escort visitors, cages for each customer, backup power systems, and sometimes racks in shared areas.

When assessing risk for a data center provider, there are several tools available depending on the services and flexibility of the provider. One way to identify the right service provider is to decide what significant physical risks there may be with any provider and what will be the cost-effective approach to mitigate them. For example, if the data in a company's application are subject to a standard concerning the protection of cardholder data (i.e., in-scope for payment card industry [PCI] compliance), then before making a contract with the service provider, determine if PCI requirements can be met. Can the data center manager supply access logs, video camera footage, and any other PCI requirements relevant to a physical data center holding cardholder data?

If the answer is no, either you will have to find another, more suitable provider or create a control (or mitigating control) to remain compliant. For example, one could place surveillance cameras in the rented cage in the data center and maintain an access log. Alternatively, it may be more practical to use strong data encryption of data in transit and in storage. It would become increasingly difficult for an auditor to argue that there is a physical risk to cardholder data.

If none of these options are available, another approach may be to negotiate a contractual agreement to supply the required services at a reasonable cost or demonstrate through independent audits and certifications (e.g., SOC 2) that the provider is sufficiently secure. Naturally, it also will be necessary to regularly perform an audit of the data center for compliance or obtain evidence of their current certification. Typically, this is not wanted by many data center providers since it carries an additional operating expense, but doing so could be a competitive advantage. The opportunity to obtain this information is greatest at the time of contracting since there is pressure to close a sale.

With physical facilities, one typically manages risk through contracts, certification, or mitigating controls. The occasional visit to the data center to perform a vulnerability assessment sometimes is necessary for due diligence. Before doing so, it is advisable to have a checklist of items to verify and a scheduled appointment; otherwise, the visit is going to consume a lot of time and be less productive. While the checks shown in Figure 10.3 are common for traditional data centers, just because infrastructure is provided as a service does not eliminate the need to validate them.

10.2.3 Infrastructure—Bare Metal

Inside a data center, one or more other service providers may offer bare metal services. These typically are rack mounted servers of varying sizes along with network switching and available routing. This approach to IT services removes the requirement for significant capital expenditure and tax chores such as depreciation schedules. With bare metal, the risk analyst is challenged with not only the physical data center security controls but also those of the systems and processes that enable installation and maintenance. Often forgotten are the risks associated with firmware updates, which could have an impact on operating systems and

Area to Check	Potential Vulnerabilities
Presence of video cameras at ingress and egress points (This should also include any loading docks.)	The ability to retrieve and examine video will help identify exploited weaknesses in the process, training, or technology of the physical security systems.
Secure doors requiring authentication for access	Some doors may have week, disabled or easily exploited controls. For example, a door propped open will allow unauthorized people to enter the facility. This can be mitigated with audible alarms when the door is open for too long.
Personnel on-site to confirm deliveries and visitors	Lack of oversight can lead to unauthorized visitor access to secure areas.
Escorted access to authorized areas	Unescorted visitors and delivery personnel can steal or damage infrastructure without accountability or control.
Register of visitors with arrival and departure times	This basic logging is fundamental in root cause analysis for security incidents.
Clear identification procedures for visitors—photo ID on official document	Failure to confirm identity of a visitor is a weakness that can allow abuse of identity and privileges at the responsibility of the impersonated individual.
Physical security controls on tenant cages	Large data centers have frequent visitors to the same floor to nearby cages. The potential for accidental or intentional access to the wrong cage can result in significant damage.
Power and network ingress to facility from diverse demarcation points	Destruction of power and network resources through accident can result. Redundant sources make it less likely to impact critical systems. Also, cameras in these locations can help detect or discover perpetrators.
Background check procedures for personnel	This basic control reduces the risk of hiring individuals with ulterior motives or who are more likely to succumb to temptation of former criminal associates.

Figure 10.3 Physical security vulnerability controls.

hypervisors. Government agencies have been known to tamper with the firmware installed in numerous systems. Furthermore, it is common that personnel are on staff who will provide "remote hands" assistance in installing and maintaining system components.

When employing Infrastructure as a Service (IaaS), patching of the operating system remains quite important and is often the purchaser's responsibility. Some IaaS providers supply low-level compute resources such as bare metal and a network with remote console access to the customer. The orchestration software then is used to automatically deploy the operating system of choice.

In other cases, the customer provides a copy of the operating system or purchases it through the provider and has it installed with the aforementioned remote hands service or uses custom software supported by an orchestration tool such as OpenStack. Once installed, scanning and patching of the OS are the customer's responsibility.

Consistent with our methodology, there are security questions concerning the implementation and maintenance of infrastructure services provided. A limited list of these should include:

1. Certification of the physical facilities—mentioned in the last section.
2. Background checks of personnel providing remote hands services.
3. Certification of the service provider and the scope of the services for which they are certified. Since there are network components, how are these governed and protected?
4. Licensing of any software provided to the customer should be confirmed. If this is not practical, the contractual control becomes more important in order to assign liability.
5. A process of verifying that the installed software version and patches provided are current or at the desired functional level for the planned application.
6. Service level agreements for patching of firmware should be an amendment to any contract with some penalties for failure.

As described earlier, there are many dimensions to infrastructure and one cannot be certain of how these dimensions are built. For example, with a bare metal server, it is well understood that there are physical connections to a "top of rack" or "end of row" switch. At a minimum, these connections carry the physical and data link layers in the OSI model. In scenarios where the service provider has many bare metal servers and electronically sets up one for your use, it is possible that the server is provided through a blade in a chassis of many bare metal servers. The top-of-rack switch may very well be integrated into the blade chassis.

At this point, the cloud consumer will have to rely on the practices and standards of the service provider. The assumption then is that connections to other servers of other customers in the same data center, rack, or chassis are kept segmented.

It is not always necessary to simply trust the service provider at this level. There are simple technical checks that can be performed in the link state of server connections. The MAC address list on the server and logs associated with locally established connections can be used to detect improper configuration. Furthermore, if privacy is a concern, and since it may be possible in a shared physical infrastructure to copy traffic from an interface, encryption can be used as a mitigating control. There are additional options in a bare metal setup related to virtualization. In fact, it is quite likely that the bare metal leased from a cloud service provider will have additional layers of virtualization in order to facilitate segmentation scalability across a global infrastructure. For example, it is entirely possible for two bare metal servers on the same virtual local area network (VLAN) to reside in two different physical data centers. This will become more apparent in the next section.

10.2.4 Infrastructure—Virtualization

Other flavors of infrastructure services include virtualization and migration, which enable deployment of the OS on various types of hypervisors using orchestration tools such as OpenStack supplemented by custom software. Similar problems arise except that now, more software components are introduced by the provider. These components generally are invisible to the consumer of virtualization services except as they are presented in custom software from the provider. Some of the provisioning services often provided are:

- Self-service on-demand computing (bare metal and hypervisors)
- Bare metal (configure BIOS and operating system installation)
- Network (create VLANs, virtual private networks [VPNs], virtual switching)
- Storage (build volumes, install databases, cryptographic services)

As will become apparent later, layers of virtualization often are used to aggregate the layer-2 or data-link layer to reduce the cabling and overlapping VLAN IDs that become exhausted at a certain volume of connections. For example, two different tenants in a single physical data center may have the same MAC address that, if part of the same VLAN, would cause a conflict. Furthermore, there may be the same VLAN number used by each of the different tenants. To allow massive scalability and distribution, the provider is able to form each of these VLANs into a virtualized VLAN transported over layer-3 (network layer). As a result, traffic out of the single chassis for multiple tenants is transported and aggregated over the same cable yet remains invisible to others. The mitigating controls for risk remain the same. At higher layers in this stack of connections, encryption can ensure confidentiality and integrity of the connections.

Once virtualization is provided, all of the underlying infrastructure is in place and the consumer of resources takes responsibility for the virtual machine where the operating system is installed. This necessarily leads to configuration of virtual network elements including virtual routing and switching as well as optional virtual firewalls. The customer has considerable control without having to be concerned with the hypervisor and the underlying bare metal.

However, it is natural for service providers to offer services with high capacity components to add other services such as network firewalls, VPNs and storage. These add-ons spare the customer the responsibility for mundane administrative tasks and costly licenses that instead can be spread across many tenants.

With this level of resources provided, the security analyst should consider how each component will be validated for its security and compliance attributes. A firewall or VPN can be quickly validated if the administrative interface is available for inspection or configuration by the tenant. In other cases, look for the ordering process to define the characteristics of the service. For example, storage can be selected and should indicate clearly that encryption is used and specify the strength of the encryption as well as the permitted key sizes, types, and how keys are conveyed and/or stored for the customer.

10.2.5 Infrastructure (Limited Platform) — Containers

Open-source software is pervasive and quickly adopted, especially in the container realm. Many of the services obtained today are provided through containers and the microservices architecture they support. "Containerization" supports software delivery cycles that are very short, which is consistent with the Continuous Integration/Continuous Delivery (CICD) model in DevOps. There is a huge benefit in a fast-moving business world where new features and enhancements can be deployed very quickly.

Scanning and patching *application code* in a production container environment is not very practical. Containers are deployed as Docker™ images from a repository. Deployment is commonly orchestrated using Kubernetes, an open-source system for container management. Since each image that is deployed is a set of code components to perform a function, it is important to understand fully what is inside that container and any vulnerabilities that should be resolved before deploying as an executable.

Once in production, it is helpful to keep track of the last security state of the container. To do this, consider taking advantage of labels. These labels, which are structured as name:value pairs, can be used to readily identify the attributes of the particular pod release. Assuming that the reader has some familiarity with the Kubernetes architecture, an example of labels might be: "version=1.1." There are many strategies to using labels. For example, if a historical library of the releases is retained, it would be easy to determine that "version:1.1" is not current and 1.3 is the latest. With an accompanying record of vulnerability patches between those releases and the dependencies on other pods, a DevOps team can determine the risk in that particular module. Another effective approach is to note the ID of the last scan (e.g., "scanID:0123456"). By comparing this with the latest scan ID in your scanning software, it will be easy to identify the deltas.

There are commercial tools available to manage code releases and perform vulnerability assessments of images in container environments. It is even possible to perform more container-centric scans with such tools. Patch management may involve wholesale replacement of the system or virtual machine upon which the container environment is built. This has become a common practice since the deployed image is considered a stable, tested release and is not always patched in place. The principles of operation in the world of containers notwithstanding, process and policy are instrumental in successful patch and vulnerability management.

This section has discussed container services as a limited platform. The reason for this is that the service provides a choice in technologies that contribute to the overall ecosystem. Tools to manage and monitor containers are sometimes included along with add-on features such as firewalls and software development or deployment tools.

10.2.6 Platform as a Service (PaaS)

Platform as a Service (PaaS) is a category of combined services for a complete development, deployment, and operational solution. It includes all of the underlying infrastructure, although the details are not always clear to the customer. When a customer wishes to be very specific about the underlying IaaS components, the price likely will rise. But what the customer is often seeking is simplicity in a solution that does not involve maintenance of licenses, resolution of interoperability issues, and underlying capital costs. PaaS is well suited for the IT department that cannot afford the considerable dedicated expertise or is not prepared to make a long-term commitment to a specific technology.

Development platforms, on the other hand, provide additional services that will require close attention with the understanding that there is underlying risk that cannot as easily be identified in the software development lifecycle. The stack of services will raise more questions concerning how security is provided in each of the services:

- Are the code modules and development tools patched and at what frequency?
- Are there service level agreements (SLAs) associated with patching?
- Do the build and test tools include some means to test for code weaknesses?
- Does the solution include tools to track development progress and code submission?
- Does a test environment accurately reflect the state of the production environment?
- Are there sufficient tools to help meet industry-specific security requirements (e.g., encryption of data at rest and transaction logging)?

- Are data centers available in the required jurisdictions?
- Can secure, alternate channel connections be established for development apart from the production and testing environments?

Managing vulnerabilities in this model is, in some instances, a shared responsibility with the service provider. Application development, network controls, and directory infrastructure may be provided, but the purchaser of the service is responsible for configuration and monitoring. The buyer's responsibility not only involves discovery of vulnerabilities in the platform and development components but enforcing service level agreements for remediation of findings.

It is this last point that is important with PaaS. The service provider has complete responsibility for the operating system, physical host, and physical network. The contracts and service levels related to securing these components should be carefully considered.

One very popular hosting platform, Docker,™ provides an environment for storing, deploying, and operating cloud applications or components typically designed as microservices. For those unfamiliar with microservices, these small programs are intended to be small, quickly replaceable, and function as a part of one or more applications. One might think of them as the tradition subroutine that can operate independently. This application design enables rapid upgrades and replacements of these parts without affecting the entire application. Naturally, the operating flexibility facilitates the "DevOps" continuous improvement/continuous delivery (CICD) model.

Herein lies a specific challenge with vulnerability management principles. A container could have server components, including some commercial or open-source libraries. Each of the components of the container requires checks for vulnerabilities, remediation, and potential regression testing of the application prior to production deployment. The applications to be deployed in a container typically are kept in the previously discussed "trusted repository," which has restricted access and modification controls.

Once deemed ready for production, the code from these repositories can be deployed to the available and appropriate compute resources such as a pod on a Kubernetes cluster on a host. But, where and when are the vulnerability scans performed? Note: Even the Kubernetes people will tell you that it is not a full PaaS solution. However, it can be considered an integral part of a platform; therefore, I liberally cite it as an example.

Some service providers provide the ability to scan for vulnerabilities and deliver a report when the code is in the repository. It is also possible to perform the scan in the container that gets deployed, although that may be a bit late for remediation. This might be considered regression testing in a nonproduction instance. But both approaches serve different purposes. Scanning of code in the repository provides

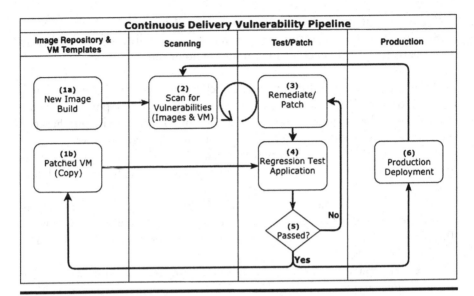

Figure 10.4 Continuous vulnerability management pipeline.

the current state of code that ready for deployment. Remediation activities can be performed in place and prior to production.

Scanning production containers has the benefit of providing a current running state. Some production containers have a low attack surface and can endure without vulnerabilities requiring immediate remediation. On the other hand, repositories can age or the code may change with new libraries required. The latter libraries may contain vulnerabilities requiring checks prior to production release.

These possibilities make it important to formulate a consistent process for scanning and remediation aligned with the development-deployment cycle. Figure 10.4 shows an example of a continuous scan, patch, and delivery cycle that accommodates a container environment hosted on a virtual machine. Both the VM and the containers are scanned for vulnerabilities and regression tested. Note that on the left side of the process, there is a container image repository and a "garage" of virtual machine templates. These contain the latest, patched and production-ready instances of a given solution. They can be deployed to the appropriate pod and cluster when needed.

With each release of the application, this process must be followed left to right:

1. Update or build:
   a. the code in the container
   b. an instance of the virtual machine
2. Scan vulnerabilities in the VM
3. Repeatedly submit containers into a repository until automatic scans are clean.

4. Once steps 2 and 3 are successful, perform a regression test of the application. Many development teams seem in such a hurry that they skip this important step.
5. After step 4 is complete, a copy of the VM should be retained in the aforementioned "stable" prior to being sent to production, step 6.

10.2.6.1 Other PaaS Risk Concerns

The development and delivery of applications is not the only function of a PaaS solution. There are important services typically available from a menu that can be added to any solution: Storage, Networks, Databases, Network and Host Security, domain name system (DNS) services, Load Balancing, and any number of other components that an organization might find useful. The simple idea is to get the customer interested in one thing and use that as a means of selling them additional add-ons that will entrench them with the provider.

This is not a bad state of affairs and, in some cases, is essential for a growing or even sprawling enterprise. However, there are strategic vulnerabilities involved with these choices. One might consider any systemic components that might present an unforeseen attack surface. For example, if a single vendor is responsible for all of the components to be used, there may be specific code libraries or architectural attributes with weaknesses yet unknown across the entire solution stack.

One way to mitigate this risk is to choose a provider, architecture, or solution set that has vendor diversity built in.

There are service providers who provide a low price and offer most of the services as a homegrown solution. This will create a greater requirement that the provider have strong development and risk management practices. Indeed, the homegrown solution may offer features and functionality most suitable to the consumer of services. Furthermore, the price can be compelling and the risk low.

Other providers have a well-curated collection of integrated tools to help manage risk for customers of their platform. For example, once you lease computing resources, there are add-on controls for network security, vulnerability scanning, container management, secure storage, x.509 certificate management, log collection and monitoring, and firewall and intrusion prevention. These services can quickly help manage vulnerabilities and compliance requirements. Specifically, IPS services function as virtual patch mechanisms to mitigate vulnerabilities in your solution for a period of time during which you can scan for the vulnerabilities and remediate them.

As for compliance with the reporting requirements, there are services to help directly. The European General Data Protection Regulations (GDPR) are partially met through encrypted database services, and some PCI requirements are met through firewalls, certificates services, and security monitoring solutions.

All of these services should be monitored and reevaluated for quality and relevance to your needs over time. It is not uncommon for a consumer of services to operate on autopilot and spend on services that are no longer needed. Additionally, both security needs and service capabilities change. These need to be periodically realigned to avoid stealth gaps that can raise risk.

10.2.7 Software as a Service (SaaS)

From the point of view of the service consumer (customer), SaaS is a very simple approach for providing application services. None of the elements of the platform are exposed to the user. Instead, only the user interface of the applications is presented, which provides administrative simplicity. This also means that the hardware, software, network, storage, power, and data center are invisible. The provider does not wish to expose any of these details because lower cost, speed, and simplicity are the objectives.

To achieve these objectives, the service provider has to aggregate some of the resources—notably software licenses, hardware, storage, and network components such as routers, switches, and firewalls. This allows for economies of scale and better profit margins and/or reduced prices. None of these facts establishes any judgment of the security or compliance of the solution offered. A partial list of the areas of security not revealed to the customer directly include:

- Software development methodology
- Release schedule (sprint frequency)
- Model, version, and patch level of software, including:
  - Database engine
  - Operating system
  - Programming language
- Host monitoring
- Network resilience and load balancing methods/performance
- Firewalls, IPS, and Web application firewalls
- Virtualization tools
- Vulnerability scanners (infrastructure and application)

A typical agreement made with a provider is that they will provide these components and manage them appropriately according to best practices and that the customer need not be concerned. While this may be adequate for an inventory management system at a mid-size manufacturer, it certainly will not suffice for highly regulated industries such as banking and commercial finance. Taking the full range of customers and the potential purchase sizes of their services into consideration, there are several questions to consider:

- Is the provider financially accountable for their actions or inactions related to security?
- Are there service level agreements for performance and availability?
- How frequently are application vulnerabilities patched (read release cycle)?
- Are the developers trained in secure coding practices?
- Can application logs be provided in a continuous stream?

- Is there any security standard followed for which they will be audited?
- Can the application integrate with an identity management solution?
- Will you receive a copy of the audit report?
- What is the frequency of the audit?
- Will any findings of the audit be remediated according to a published plan?
- If there is a security breach, how soon will the provider notify you?
- How much information will be provided about the root cause and scope of the breach?
- Are there monetary consequences for the provider's failure to patch, detect, report, contain, or remediate?

For SaaS customers who spend considerable amounts of money for a custom SaaS offering, it is sometimes possible to negotiate more visibility and control the operating environment. While it is still unlikely that the provider will allow the customer to perform their own scanning and patching of the solution, it is practical to ask that certain scan and remediation service level agreements be established. It is also possible to expect that the state of some security controls be present. These are typical for a solution that is customized for the buyer's operational and regulatory needs. A simple example is the integration of authentication into the application through the corporate directory.

So, why not ask that critical vulnerabilities in the software stack be remediated within a certain time frame and that issues and outages that may impact the customer be reported in a timely fashion? Furthermore, as the buyer, you are entitled to know when there are events that may affect the service and what measures will be taken to remediate these. This is especially important when it comes to patch management. Even the most basic of web applications that are broadly used by the public will inform users when the service will be offline for maintenance or improvements.

Additionally, the DevOps operating model today can allow for frequent and rapid changes to the environment with very little loss of service. It is not uncommon for features, enhancements, and fixes to be deployed every 2 or 3 weeks. That in itself is a double-edged sword. Some of these rapid releases can introduce new vulnerabilities that end up getting fixed in the next CICD cycle.

10.2.8 Blurring the Lines—SDWAN

Software-defined networking is another cloud technology that blurs the line between a conventional network and a virtual one. This innovation allows the customer to implement their own WAN and integrate with their LAN without purchasing dedicated circuits or expensive services like MPLS (Multiprotocol Label Switching). Instead, the customer defines the behavior and features of their WAN through software. The network transport is conventional Internet access with connections among sites protected through a variety of options in VPN services. Decisions about performance, content caching, routing, and prioritization of traffic are configurable by the customer.

Another line that is blurred is between infrastructure and software (IaaS and SaaS). Although there commonly is a piece of hardware installed at the perimeter of the network at a given location, there is also software at play. This software is produced and maintained by an SDWAN (Software Defined Wide Area Network) manufacturer and sometimes installed or patched by a service provider (e.g., telecommunications company). So, vulnerability management decisions will have to be made just as they would when an SaaS provider is engaged.

The configurations and performance-tuning options are managed using one or more servers with specialized software. This software can be hosted and managed by a telecommunications carrier with expertise and technical resources, or it can be directly managed by an organization of sufficient size and resources. The logical extension of this technology is to further integrate the routing (control plane) and application (data plane) into a virtual or cloud software infrastructure. So now, the infrastructure that we customarily use for our applications and data can also support network routing and performance management.

However, similar to Software as a Service, this solution uses software and related configuration items to manage traffic flow. In many cases, the same questions concerning software solutions apply to SDWAN. The software must be built securely and the implementation and management should be properly governed. Assuming that an external service provider is responsible for management of your SDWAN implementation, Figure 10.5 shows some critical security questions to ask.

Technical Monitoring	Inspection	Contract	Risk/Vulnerability Topic
N	Y	Y	Are the personnel properly trained and their backgrounds checked?
N	Y	Y	Are the hosting facilities securely managed for all the physical controls discussed in the data center and infrastructure topics?
Y	Y	Y	What is the patch status and service level for the software?
N	Y	Y	Does patching follow a prioritized approach and have service levels?
N	N	Y	Will the provider inform customers when patches are being applied and if any operational impacts should be expected?
Y	N	Y	Are WAN connections encrypted and with what levels of encryption?
N	N	Y	Do the administrators have access to traffic flows through the network?
N	Y	Y	What are the controls on monitoring administrative activity consistent with other laws?
Y	Y	Y	Are there additional infrastructure or application services added on to the service?
N	Y	Y	What are the controls around the added services?
N	Y	Y	Are annual audits conducted on the operating controls?

Figure 10.5 SDWAN security questions.

10.3 Scanning and Remediation in Cloud

Up to this point, the discussion has been concerned with establishing the mindset of cloud and the vulnerabilities or broader risks therein. Now, if we consider cloud as a means of replacing infrastructure and platform but not full control of the application or environment, the need for vulnerability scans remains essential. We have touched upon, in part, the idea of checking for vulnerabilities in a dev-ops environment. This requires further elucidation.

There are two scenarios for vulnerability scanning that are most relevant in the present technology environment: virtual machines (VMs) running on a hosted physical infrastructure and containers running in VMs or a a service-provider container cluster (e.g., Docker™).

10.3.1 Scanning Virtual Machines

When a VM is hosted in a public cloud, you have little to no control of either the hardware or hypervisor. The network is invisible to you, and there is no clarity in the patch state of the underlying software. However, if you consider your hosted VM as your domain, it must be protected, updated, monitored, and governed. The vulnerability scan is a critical component of this and can be implemented in one of two ways: network scan and host agent scan.

10.3.1.1 Network Scanning a Virtual Machine

When scanning a VM over a network, it is important to take into consideration the real position of the scanner versus the target VM. Network scanning can take a heavy toll over the network components given that they are likely a combination of physical and virtual networks. The scanning of 65,000 transmission control protocol (TCP) ports (rarely needed) in a discovery phase will consume considerable resources and may not be permitted by a service provider.

However, it is possible that there is dedicated or at least sufficient physical infrastructure and a minimally shared hypervisor that may be able to accommodate such a scan without causing a denial of service. In all cases, however, it is advisable to minimize the impact of the scan by reducing the number of ports and IP addresses in a given period and to decrease the frequency of scans to a tolerable level. This is most feasible in server environments because there is more control over the services that are installed and the changes made to configurations.

One might also say that if two VMs are on the same subnet, they will not have a problem with the heavier network load. While this may seem logical in a physical environment, it is not at all so in the virtual world. In a cloud service provider, it is very common for a VM deployed on one host in a/24 subnet to be on a different host and possibly a different data center from another VM in the same subnet. There may indeed be 5 to 10 physical and virtual network devices touched by a scan of the same subnet.

An alternative approach, which has gained rapidly in popularity, is to install an agent on the hosts. This solution is more elegant and has adapted and grown to be very stable since its introduction many years ago. Agents need not perform port scans and have a very low impact on compute resources. Furthermore, remote command and control of system resources can be gained through the agent and vulnerability information securely retrieved.

Local scanning agents have also become increasingly integrated with patch management. So, through a single agent, the security administrator can now monitor the patch status of the VM and initiate patches to system components manually or automatically. Detailed templates, rules, and policy enforcement of configuration items, patches, and event software installations are available.

Having discussed agents versus network scanning, I would like to call attention to a potential discrepancy with agents, the PCI standard, and your auditor. As of this writing, the PCI Data Security Standards call for a network scan of all 65,000+ ports of a host. That is a very big hurdle for a network-based scan, and yet an agent need not perform this action. The agent can determine immediately if the host has any of these ports open. In fact, some agents are able to monitor these ports from inside the host and prevent unauthorized ports from being opened. Furthermore, in a complex network environment, there are some devices such as small-network DSL modems that respond to a TCP port that has nothing to do with the server or application behind it. So, an external network scan may reveal open ports where in fact there are none on the PCI-scoped system.

If you choose to use an agent and have PCI-scoped systems, consult your auditor to reach an understanding of security versus blind compliance with a standard. The goal of PCI standards is to secure cardholder data, and there are many solutions. The goal of vulnerability scanning through agents is to secure the endpoint of any kind in furtherance of securing the overall cloud ecosystem.

10.3.1.2 Scanning Containers

As mentioned in the last section, containerization provides speed and short delivery cycles for new features. But, speed is a double-edged sword when it comes to risk. Although this is a benefit when remediating vulnerabilities, the patch windows are also shortened. One must take advantage of this situation and prioritize remediation of vulnerabilities in code equally with new feature development. There is a tendency to asymmetrically deploy features and related vulnerability patches. This can occur when a new feature uses a service that has a vulnerability not yet reported. Then, shortly after deploying the new feature, a critical vulnerability is discovered in one or more of the system components that are dependencies for the feature (e.g., operating system libraries or add-on libraries for databases, encryption, or monitoring infrastructure).

While this is sometimes avoidable, the reporting of vulnerabilities, patch availability, and software deployments can create a situation where a minimum of 3 weeks, and possibly 6 to 9 weeks, may pass before sufficient regression testing can be performed. So, in the Scum methodology, the product owner will have to take responsibility for prioritizing the vulnerability into the backlog. Prior to this, it is very important that the vulnerability analyst or risk manager communicate the severity and impact potential of the vulnerability as early as possible.

Another concern is the vulnerabilities discovered through network scanning. The container space commonly is implemented in VMs that are rendered almost immutable so that the operations team knows the operating state of the environment. Do not be deceived by the term "immutable." Turning off the remote shell or removing the command shell altogether does not truly render a host immutable. There are other ways to attack a system.

Furthermore, traditional scans are not practical for a production container environment because the operating environment often has numerous containers with private, internal IP addresses. The container platform typically provides firewall rules to control access among the containers using numerous criteria. Privileges are assigned allowing certain containers to communicate with other containers using only specific protocols. Checking the vulnerability state of a VM over a physical network layer and trying to reach subnets internal to a specific host is not going to work well. Orchestration of a network scan from an outside scanner can become very complex. In all likelihood, the internal IP addresses of a container cluster have no external routes advertised to make them reachable.

Vulnerabilities must be detected in the build phase (pre-production) where a replacement virtual machine or system configuration is prepared. The goal is to have a continuous integration and delivery process that includes detection and remediation of code vulnerabilities as well as testing prior to submission into a trusted container registry. Figure 10.4 illustrates an example of such a process.

Fortunately, the market place has solutions for scanning a production container environment, and additional investment may be required. Any organization operating containers on a large scale should consider the advantage of a scanning agent installed on the host. Also, there are some scanners built into the container management environment that can analyze the binary of the installed components and report any significant vulnerabilities. A valuable selling factor to the development team is that the known state of the production environment can be better described with a scanning agent that can report all vulnerabilities on demand.

Equally useful is the ability to automatically perform scans anytime a new image is pushed into a repository. That approach works very well with a CICD (Continuous Improvement, Continuous Deployment) operation saving time and reducing the time gap between a change and vulnerability discovery. There will be more discussion on the process related to scanning containers later in the Platform as a Service section.

10.4 Cloud Risk Management Strategies

Since cloud services are by definition delivered by an external organization, the control of vulnerabilities and the ability to identify them is often limited. This happens for many reasons that the service provider does not always consider when originating their solutions. At first, the provider sees the natural monetary benefits to their customers but does not fully share the same risk-management vision. This is not an attempt to deceive but rather the natural evolution of the market.

As a result, it is important that the consumer of these services take measures to mitigate the risks inherent in a rapidly evolving technology ecosystem. The consumer is king when two service providers must bid for services, and the one meeting the most security requirements will gain an advantage. Some very useful instruments for managing service provider risk are: contractual agreements, implementation of mitigating controls, a vendor-risk assessment program, and a competitive bidding process in a diverse market.

10.4.1 Service Diversity

When feasible, consider the option of building diversity in the choice of service providers. The simple example is where there are multiple applications to host that require no direct communications. These can be spread appropriately across providers or data centers within a single provider. The fact that multiple suitable service providers are available can be used as a means of lowering the costs of services while tactically obtaining the mix of security controls desired.

Another scenario is to identify for each application what controls are essential and which ones are optional and at what addition cost. Using this information, one can select the optimal service providers having an acceptable balance of performance, capabilities, risk and cost. Since wide area networks can be virtualized at higher layers of the OSI (Open System Interconnect) model, one need not be bound to a single provider.

10.4.2 Contractual Agreement

Contracts are the legal tools that are the risk managers' friends because they outline a general framework or scope for security governance where the service provider is concerned. Some security managers consider contracts a complex and arduous process involving attorneys, conference calls, and the exchange of many document revisions. It behooves the risk manager to align the risk appetite with contracts and learn the art of mitigating controls. Armed with this information, work with your organization's attorneys to ensure that your risk concerns are addressed in the contract. Prior to contracting, however, establish and follow a vendor risk assessment program to identify the appropriate controls.

10.4.3 Vendor Risk Assessment Program

Vendor risk assessment is a common practice in any organization. For IT migration or ongoing operation in cloud, there is no special exception. The methods have to evolve but the general practices are the same:

- Define the business purpose and solution
- Build threat models where applicable
- Profile the technical environment
- Determine the risk
- Build governance requirements
- Establish controls and metrics

Some IT organizations are mistrustful and believe that only they can truly manage risk and give comfort to the organization. That approach is incredibly expensive and is not necessarily effective when trying to flexibly meet rapid changing business requirements. One approach to managing risk in the cloud is to determine the real risk to the organization and gain an understanding of the data, functions, and real exposure. Just because the application is moving a cloud model does not mean risk increases. It is only the insecurity experienced from a false perception of loss of control. To address this, consider the following guidance:

1. Become informed—Gather detailed information about the solution that meets the business requirements. Security details *are* business requirements. Virtualization of an entire application (lift and shift methodology) can provide easy assurance but is not always the best solution. Perhaps it is a stepping stone to containerization, which can increase resiliency and performance.
2. Establish external assessment program—Audits, attestations, penetration tests, and scans all have a place in vulnerability management for cloud. Know which combinations of these are truly necessary to identify well-defined risks. Simply demanding a control without purpose is often a waste of time and resources.
3. Build a cloud monitoring platform using controls that match the present and future. If the organization is accustomed to managing CPUs, memory, patch status, security events, and incidents, it should also be able to continue this with added controls. For example, rather than collecting simple syslog events from cloud (many cloud solutions no longer produce syslog), use tools such as

Prometheus. This is a an extremely versatile and efficient means of monitoring using time-series name/value pairs. It provides consistency and versatility to data collection more efficiently than trying to parse syslog events.

10.4.4 Compensating Controls

If the contractual process is not the right route and you do not control the risk environment, you will have to find compensating controls. Consider these worst-case circumstances:

■ A vulnerability goes unpatched in a vendor system.
■ The entire application (SaaS) has an operational vulnerability that is likely to remain present for several months.
■ One or more of these vulnerabilities are determined to be severe and unacceptable to the organization.

Under some combination of these circumstances, it will be necessary to find a compensating control. Scanning, patching, contracts, and moving your data to another provider are not practical. You can take other actions such as:

■ Implement a technical control to:
 – Hide the critical data from the application through encryption.
 – Restrict access to the cloud service by forcing users to pass through your security/content inspection infrastructure.
 – Use an external risk monitoring service that can support your particular web application.
■ Implement one or more administrative controls (in many cases, you should do this anyway):
 – Require users to reaffirm their access to the application more frequently.
 – Perform monthly or quarterly data quality, access, and usage reviews.
 – Restrict the user roles permitted in the application (reduce threat level).

10.5 Cloud Security Assessments

The industry working groups have established some tools to help with automation and consistency in security assessments. Center for Internet Security (CIS) Benchmarks are used to assess the configuration of cloud IaaS services using best practices established in coordination with the CIS and numerous security professionals (Figure 10.6). Some cloud service providers support automation through vulnerability scanning solutions to use application program interfaces (APIs) to access configuration data. This information can be used to assess a service's compliance with the benchmark. It does not, provide a complete picture of the vulnerability

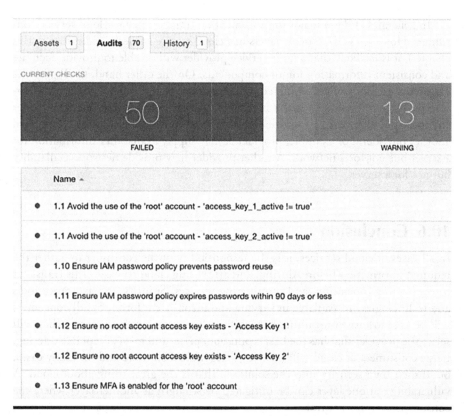

Figure 10.6 Cloud provider security compliance checks.

state of a cloud service. One simply gets assurance of the best-practices configuration consensus found in the benchmark.

Another useful tool could be the CloudTrust Protocol (CTP)[4]. This protocol calls for transparency to support "digital trust." The simple idea is to provide a certain level of transparency into the security state of the cloud service offering. The provider is not necessarily going to provide you with vulnerability scan results nor will they provide any configuration items. Instead, the CTP consumer of a cloud service gets high-level information about the compliance and security state of the service. A commonly cited example is up-time of the service, which is conveyed in an SLA-compliance formation composed of promised state versus observed state. For example, up-time over 10 days was at least 99.8% and the provider commitment is 99.7%; thus the consumer knows there was compliance. In order for this protocol to work properly, the service provider is obligated to establish service and asset classes. These are used to map specific attributes of a service or asset in order to accurately convey compliance.

In general, CTP is a major improvement on transparency to cloud service consumers. However, with so many layers in a cloud service (as described earlier in this chapter), it is unlikely that a large service provider will be able to provide accurate and consistent information for all components. On the other hand, CTP provides consistent methods of obtaining compliance and risk information should the service provider find ways to make it reliable. Naturally, in a multi-cloud provider environment, the metrics from one provider may not be the same as those from another provider. For example, provider A may supply availability information for a server but not for a network. Another provider may provide network availability but not for a server.

10.6 Conclusion

In all cases of cloud services, it is the responsibility of the consumer to gather the required information before, during, and after using cloud services. This translates to contracting, operating, and terminating services. Security and assurance tools and technologies are available in varying and inconsistent forms. Small consumers will be able to insist on minimal capabilities by "voting with the feet." They will select the provider that has the best reputation, price, and most acceptable offering. Large consumers of cloud will be able to negotiate a bit more and, in many cases, build their own security into the solution. That is the great thing about cloud. A vulnerability at one layer can be mitigated by strength at another layer where the consumer has more control.

End Notes

1. https://www.nist.gov/publications
2. Competitive Enterprise Institute, https://cei.org/i-pencil
3. European Union Agency for Network and Information Security (ENISA), 2009
4. Cloud Security Alliance, 2018 https://cloudsecurityalliance.org/working-groups/cloudtrust-protocol/#_overview

Chapter 11

Summary and the Future

11.1 Introduction

The process of vulnerability management (VM) can seem complex, but this is misleading when one looks at the technical details. There is little chance that vulnerabilities, misconfigurations, and urgency of patching will end anytime soon. Early in the formation of the vulnerability management industry, the process of scan, remediate, verify, repeat was viewed as proactive security. The simple idea was to identify the vulnerabilities before the enemy would and clean them up. This approach for years was accepted as common sense.

Since many vendors offer solutions, the competition has been to see who can identify and include the most vulnerability checks.

Like intrusion detection systems (IDSs), the problem of false positives became an issue. Sales materials from major vulnerability management vendors have shown us that in the fine print, it is really difficult to decide which product is most suitable. Corporate users would have to continue to perform trials and make comparisons to requirements. Then, the selected product would only be as good as the requirements. What has become apparent is that accuracy and comprehensiveness are not the most important measures for a vulnerability management system.

The next step in the industry has been to enhance vulnerability scanners or expand their functionality with user-definable vulnerability parameters. Protocols such as Open Vulnerability and Assessment Language (OVAL) and the Common Vulnerability Scoring System (CVSS) have provided a framework for achieving just this. But in the struggle to remain competitive and distinguish their products, developers have adhered to old ways in execution and kept their systems relatively closed. More and more vendors provide XML interfaces that accept the evolved industry standards for checks such as OVAL. One obvious reason is technical in that standards like OVAL help integration with other products not directly supplied by the same vendor. With an established standard for encoding all types of vulnerability checks, it is possible that separate subscription-based services will emerge to provide checks separately from the hardware and software that use them.

Of course, scanners need constant vulnerability check updates necessitating annual maintenance payments. And recurring revenue is essential to sustain a business with limited prospects for growth over the years. Given this latter point, it is likely that more features and integration will be offered both in cloud and on premises.

So, the next challenge has been to make the products more enterprise friendly. One would at minimum expect integration in the following ways:

- The return to offering scanning agents on hosts that work without initiation by the central command and control system
- Support for scanning container images in repositories and in the execution environment
- Directory services integration to authenticate users of the systems
- Optional Remote Access Dial-In User Service (RADIUS) authentication
- Structured query language (SQL) and NOSQL (Non-SQL Database) support for an open database outside of the appliance model
- Security data exchange with other network and security devices
- Support for more modern security data structures allowing service providers to share vulnerability data in detail or aggregate with service consumers

So where is the industry going from here? There are two high-level views of this future. The first view is an integration or collaboration across disciplines. This already takes place in some measure through process. The need is clearly recognized when the data collected by vulnerability management are often fed into other areas such as a configuration database and security event and incident manager (SEIM). But this can certainly stand improvement to provide more context and business relevance. Another view of the future is to more closely align technologies. Many technologies stand to gain considerable benefit from vulnerability management data, and the reciprocal is also present.

I think we will also see the emergence of sharing of vulnerability data from service providers to service consumers. This will be more important in highly regulated industries that demand strong security in the entire supply chain of technology services. Since a pay-as-you-go service model is rampant, customers will insist on some measure of compliance and security visibility.

11.2 Cross-Discipline Opportunities

The vulnerability management industry is struggling to find a niche. One does not acquire a vulnerability management system to eventually have it morph into an all-encompassing security management platform. Such a strategy would be difficult for customers to swallow. Other solutions considered have been extension to other related functionality such as compliance monitoring, risk assessment, and configuration management. These areas can make a lot of sense technically but are more challenging from a process point of view. Compliance management makes sense because the function is very close to vulnerability management. However, more complete and customizable compliance checks need to be created, and those checks have to be extensive enough to match many of the common compliance frameworks being authored today.

The technology has to be simplified for compliance management because compliance officers typically are not technologists. Some simple method for defining policy in a user interface must be made available without having to know the relevant features and functionality to be tested in the target system. Other vulnerability scanner configuration items such as scheduling, bandwidth, target system resources. and vulnerability check updates should also be simplified to remove operational challenges for non-IT personnel.

Risk management is obviously a function that the industry has done a lot to address but has further to go. As detailed in this book, vulnerability management is a key contributor to the risk management function, but the higher-level risk management functions have been left to other vendors or largely ignored. The problem for risk management products is that many companies will not formalize the function, which makes assigning ownership difficult. In other cases, risk management has been conducted in a rather abstract manner because analysts have not had access to accurate, detailed data. It would seem that the details could be provided by a vulnerability management system.

The barriers to success in a risk/vulnerability management product have been bidirectional. Risk management vendors do not have the resources or expertise to collect the necessary data and cannot compete against those who do. Vulnerability management vendors do not have incentive to enter a market of limited size and revenue. So solutions are cobbled together and customized.

Configuration management is one other obvious area where vulnerability management can make a significant contribution. Initial data collection for a configuration management database (CMDB) can be performed by a scanning system. Additionally, some vulnerability management products are ideally suited for monitoring several configuration items for change, which is similar to a compliance monitoring function. The primary barrier here has been the interdisciplinary expertise. The understanding of vulnerabilities and remediation is a very different thought process from the Information Technology Infrastructure Library (ITIL) discipline of developing and managing a CMDB.

11.3 Cross-Technology Opportunities

So there are other, more technical approaches to creating value for the enterprise. In the security realm, a great opportunity exists to inform intrusion prevention systems (IPSs) with vulnerability data. The examination of high-speed network traffic for attacks is a major resource challenge to the IPS. Since these devices are being called upon to examine the traffic for hundreds or thousands of possible attacks and then decide whether or not to block that traffic, performance is critical. While the technology has improved dramatically from the old IDS days, latency and throughput are still a concern especially when it comes to the cost of purchasing the next larger unit. An IPS must break apart packets by protocol at several layers or reassemble fragments to analyze the content for an attack. This is a very taxing activity especially if it must be done without introducing delay into the network.

Furthermore, the demands for better bandwidth capacity in order to simplify implementation have put pressure on IPS vendors. The enterprise wants to detect all attacks on a local network with the implementation of a single technology. This often involves placing a device on an access or core switch and pushing much of that traffic through the IPS. To enhance the performance of this design, vendors have tried to create clusters of devices, added load balancer, and put as much muscle into the individual units as they can.

With all the horsepower in place, the cost and complexity begin to rise again. So security analysts begin to sift through the risk assessment data to determine which attack signatures need to be monitored and which ones do not. Why bother monitoring for attacks for which the vulnerabilities do not exist? If all of your web servers are not vulnerable to a handful of specific attacks, then removing this unnecessary workload from the IPS often will decrease the latency on traffic passing through it. It would seem to be a relatively simple matter to send the relevant vulnerability data to the IPS.

But some barriers exist. Our earlier discussion about standardization is one such barrier. The solution has been in Common Vulnerabilities and Exposures (CVE), OVAL, and other standards. If an IPS signature and a vulnerability check can reference the same identifier, then periodic updates can be performed. Another logistical challenge is making sure that only the vulnerability data to the relevant network segment are transmitted. There can be hundreds of megabytes of vulnerability data of which only a few kilobytes might apply to the IPS function. Some standard method of communicating the range of IPS addresses or host types to which the vulnerabilities apply needs to be developed. It is likely to be a two-way handshake between the two technologies.

11.3.1 Agents

The use of agents in the VM industry once had less market interest due to the difficulty in installing and maintaining them. However, this has changed. Numerous vendors have perfected the agent to be very reliable and even enhance scanning with an ephemeral agent that exists only during the scan.

An emerging type of agent that participates in the endpoint security process becomes another opportunity to reduce risk. When a network access control (NAC) pre-admission process is performed, the controller can supply a small, temporary agent compatible with the system requesting access. This is known as an on-demand agent. It is loaded and executed during the NAC process to verify the compliance and the security state of the system requesting a connection.

The concept is simple but the NAC architecture strategy is more complex and widely varied. To confine the scope to vulnerability management, the following explanation should suffice:

1. The host connects to the network access switch, which then first allows communication only on a quarantine virtual local area network (VLAN).
2. An NAC controller on the quarantine VLAN scans the system for compliance either by active scanning with limited effect or with an on-demand agent for more in-depth analysis.
3. The security state of the host is communicated back to the controller, who verifies the results against policy.
4. If the host complies with security requirements, which include credentials, then it is admitted to the appropriate production VLAN. The agent then removes itself from memory on the host.
5. If the host is noncompliant, the agent notifies the user with a message stating what needs to be corrected. If patches or configuration items are required, the remediation could possibly be automated. Then, the process returns to step 2.

Agents have a great advantage over other technologies in that they can perform the vulnerability and compliance assessments of the host before they are connected to the network. This is done using the last known policy. If the policy is not changed upon connection, then access can be granted with no further effort. The methods may vary from the aforementioned example; however, conceptually, the process is the same.

11.3.2 Patch Management

A perfect opportunity for integration of VM technology is patch management. The two are ideally suited because a large percentage of the vulnerabilities in packaged software is corrected with patches. This could even be applied to custom, in-house software.

When one considers the complexity in process after identifying vulnerabilities—create a change ticket, perform the change manually (patch) and close the ticket—it would seem impractical to skip automation of patch management.

Of course, not all patches can be automatically applied. Some impacts to production systems must be considered. Therefore, the ability to patch should be confined by some rules from the administrator. Either by system or application type or both, the administrator should be able to specify what can be automated. Web browsers, for example, are generally low risk when applying patches. Java servers are more risky since existing applications can break if functionality is changed.

Overall, the opportunity to add value and save a lot of time is available in this type of technology integration.

11.3.3 Application Penetration Testing

Vulnerability scanning is commonly a precursor to a penetration test. The enumeration capabilities allow for more targeted exploitation of applications. Attacks are more frequently targeting applications themselves instead of the underlying infrastructure software. For example, once the enumeration process finds that a web server is answering on transmission control protocol (TCP) port 80, the checks for vulnerabilities in the web server software are interesting but not so valuable when you can go straight for the data.

The next step in penetration testing is to attempt a variety of application weakness attacks such as cross-site scripting (CSS or XSS) and SQL injections. Those who understand the most common application coding mistakes and the vulnerabilities they create will have quickly scripted the ability to recognize and exploit them.

Other easily exploited vulnerabilities are:

- Format String—When user input is unfiltered, this technique can be used to populate input fields on a web form with character sequences that can cause certain programming languages to perform other functions, revealing classified information.
- User Name Enumeration—This is a brute-force technique that can easily be evaluated by an automated tool. By entering a variety of user names and checking the variation in the error response, the attacker can determine what user names are valid. With this information, an attacker can then proceed to work on the password.
- SSL/TLS weaknesses or protocol negotiation flaws.

These exploits are easily corrected but must be tested in every instance of usage. So time consuming is the testing process, that it makes a vulnerability scanner the perfect tool for this type of automation.

11.4 Process Deficiencies

The standardization of the vulnerability management process has far to go before delivering sufficient consistency to relegate the tools and personnel to a more routine status. Every company must, of course, have unique steps to accommodate other intersecting, internal processes. However, the results of the vulnerability management process are far less predictable, and the expected outcomes not well established. The big questions that are often not being asked are:

1. How much more secure will the process make my organization?
2. How quickly should I expect a vulnerability to be remediated on critical systems?

3. What should my average cost per vulnerability be for remediation?
4. How do I know the process is doing all that it should according to best practices?
5. How does our company's vulnerability management performance compare to that of other companies in my industry?

These are tough questions. Many other technology disciplines know exactly what metrics make sense, and related organizations collect information to support best-in-class performance benchmarks. What does it take to be "best in class?" What exactly does this term mean? For this, we commonly have the CIS Benchmarks. According to the Center for Internet Security, this refers to "...140+ configuration guidelines for various technology groups to safeguard systems against today's evolving cyber threats."[1]

Having top proficiency at operating a process that delivers a positive result meeting the most important needs of stakeholders, managers, and business partners is also a good definition. It fits perfectly in the subject of performance management. This is where, in a *Harvard Business Review*[2] article, Robert S. Kaplan and David P. Norton have introduced the balanced scorecard.

The simple idea of a balanced scorecard is to tie the current actions of an organization (processes) to the long-term strategy. This can help us in vulnerability management by trying to tie processes of identifying and remediating vulnerabilities to the strategy and goals of the organization. In various situations, a different strategy is required. The risk management function should work with other senior managers at a high level to identify the appropriate strategies for security concerns and goals. These can then be reflected in a balanced scorecard.

Consider the first question of the previous five. How might a VM program answer this question for senior managers? It is a broad question that can have many answers. Those answers are presented through a strategy map. We begin with a map of the organization's strategic objectives by theme. Table 11.1 is a sample map.

This map shows the four primary themes of financial, customer, internal and learning. In the "customer" theme, for example, the strategic objective is to minimize risk to personal data of customers. This obviously will have a very large impact on customers and the company image. The measure used to address this in vulnerability management is the monitoring of the rapidity of remediation of critical vulnerabilities. The target value that represents successful achievement is an average remediation within one week. The initiative to achieve this is a prioritization process for handling such vulnerabilities.

Although many product vendors provide metrics, little is clearly defined industry-wide to tell us that the best organizations will provide metrics X, Y, and Z, which will definitively answer the previous five questions. In some cases, an organization may need other, custom metrics to answer questions more specific to their business model. For example, a company that handles medical records may want to have specific metrics on the security state of systems handling patient data

Table 11.1 Sample Strategy Map

Theme	Objectives	Measures	Targets	Initiatives
Financial	Profitability	Lower financial exposure in IT	25% fewer crucial vulnerabilities annually	Optimize detection Automate remediation
Customer	Minimize risk to personal data	Rapid remediation of critical vulnerabilities	Average remediation within one week	Priority handling of critical vulnerabilities
Internal	Minimize risk of employee theft of data	Restrict access to sensitive data to authorized employees	95% policy compliance	Detection and remediation of privilege escalation vulnerabilities
Learning	Strong support for security from employees	Comprehensive security awareness training	98% security awareness training completed	Computer-based training

versus systems handling payment information. Put in simple terms, entirely different internal organizations may have different scorecard requirements. At some point, an organization with security leadership such as SANS (SysAdmin, Audit, Network and Security) or National Institute of Standards and Technology (NIST) will develop some benchmarks or references that will help in gauging overall VM program performance. For now, these benchmarks will have to be developed to conform to the requirements of each unique situation.

Where a VM process fails is in not defining the desired outcomes of the system first. Subsequently, understanding how the process steps can be measured for effectiveness in achieving those outcomes will go far toward developing the appropriate mechanisms for data collection and reporting.

11.5 Changing Operating Environment

The technology environment in which vulnerability management takes place is changing rapidly. The trend toward power conservation, distributed computing, telecommuting, and server consolidation is throwing many challenges to system designers and product pricing models. It is also making the identification of vulnerabilities more complex.

11.5.1 Saving Time

Active scanning is a time-consuming process for large networks. A simple ICMP ECHO REQUEST is not trusted as a means to find a host. Therefore, other methods are used such as transmission control protocol-synchronization (TCP-SYN) packets on a variety of commonly used ports. These and other methods are used over possibly hundreds or even thousands of IP addresses without finding a single host. This usually is due to a lazy network-addressing scheme.

In the cloud world, active scanning over a network can be equally difficult. In some cases, the target host is behind a firewall that significantly restricts the network scanner's ability to gather useful information. Some vulnerabilities are just not safely detected through simulated exploitation. Agents then become a friend to the security team.

Technological methods of querying central administration systems for more accurate data need to be applied to accelerate the scanning process by targeting systems that are known to be present. In the Microsoft environment, Windows Management Instrumentation (WMI) can be used to identify Windows hosts, their IP addresses, and running services thus greatly accelerating the scanning process. However, at this time (2019), it seems to also have the potential of significant CPU consumption.

Combinations of other tools can also be used such as DHCP databases and configuration management systems. These information sources should not be seen as confining the scanning process to the extent that they would lower accuracy. However, they will quickly provide the means to rapidly find the targets and select the appropriate authentication mechanisms to successfully audit systems.

11.5.2 Power Conservation

As mentioned in Chapter 7, when performing vulnerabilities audits during non-business hours, many systems may not be available because they are either shut down or in power-saving mode. If an active audit is performed over a wide-area network (WAN) link, it is unlikely that those hosts will be awakened even with the Wake-On-LAN (WOL) function active. This is because WOL can only be activated by sending a specialized packet on the local segment directed at a particular MAC address. Remote TCP-IP connections cannot carry this information. This leaves us with four choices:

1. Install a local scanner that can be configured to send such packets 30 seconds prior to performing the audit of the target.
2. Run vulnerability management agents on the target hosts that can wake the host on schedule and perform the audit.
3. Perform the audits during the daytime with a slow, low-bandwidth scan consuming very little resources. This may require a server days to a week to complete.

4. Coordinate IT resources to have all target machines left on during a particular time window. This wastes the most energy but is certainly preferable to leaving all hosts on all the time.

A more effective solution is to install vulnerability scanning agents on each scan target. When the system is available, it will perform a local scan with almost no impact on the network. With network access established, the agent will report the findings to a central console for analysis. When systems are mobile, difficult to access from outside or have an unpredictable availability, the agent can provide enormous flexibility and reduce the duration of risks.

An alternative approach is for vendors to begin making virtual machine versions of their products to be installed on hosts meeting minimum hardware specifications. These virtual versions of the vulnerability scanner can be shipped electronically without the inefficiencies and interference of local governments. The vendor is still likely to charge for these installations to provide support and updates, but this should be considerably less than the depreciation and maintenance costs built in to hardware products.

11.5.3 Distributed Computing

Distributed computing and the cloud present us with challenges not well-supported by vendors of vulnerability management products. Virtual private network (VPN) connections, changing security zones, web services, and Software as a Service make vulnerability assessment difficult. Vendors, not surprisingly, have yet to adequately respond to these changes in the IT environment. It is a more challenging story when someone else is controlling the infrastructure or application.

VPN connections, while well-understood, create certain challenges to non-agent-based approaches to vulnerability assessment. Continuous scans of the VPN IP space are not practical since they create additional load on the infrastructure even when no tunnels are established. The complexity of corporate networks can also lead to a target having a tunnel established to a network segment whose scanner uses completely different parameters from the target's home network. This is a phenomenon of changing security zones. While in some cases, this may be desirable to conform to the local site's security policy, in other situations, it may not be appropriate because when the target returns to the home network, it will be out of compliance.

What is needed to resolve this situation is the ability to apply a security policy to a directory group or computer name pattern. For example: An accounting computer user who is placed in the accounting group in the directory will have a strict compliance policy and corresponding scanning parameters assigned. When that user travels to a remote location and connects to a VPN gateway in a nearby sales office, the group to which the computer belongs will trigger the application of accounting group policy parameters during a vulnerability scan.

Also, when a vulnerability assessment is performed on a pool of VPN IP addresses, the discovery process is executed. During this process, tunnels are set up and broken down continuously. Why perform the discovery process at all since we already know the connection status and identification of every machine connected to the VPN gateway? Some simple interoperability is needed here to allow the VPN gateway to inform the vulnerability management system of the connection of a target to the network. The vulnerability scanner will then determine if it is the appropriate time and place to perform an audit and execute accordingly.

Web services are also an area neglected by all vendors. A business application, or more abstractly, an automated business function, is no longer built on a single host. A variety of web services distributed around the world operating at different security levels coalesce in functionality to form the intended business service. While the risk of a particular host can be assessed technically, the risk to the business application cannot. Since the application is composed of services provided by disparate targets, there needs to be a way to define each target as some portion of the overall application. Then, the risk assessment should be reported in a way that takes into consideration the security posture of all these services.

Conversely, the vulnerabilities of a target providing web services are easily assessed. However, the risk to that target may not be so clear since there is no risk profiling performed on the target based on the classification level of the hosts using the target's services. For example, a host providing a web service responsible for compressing data will handle data from system A, which carries publicly available information, and system B, which carries critical business secrets. If the web service host has a vulnerability, what is the real risk to systems A and B? What is the risk of the web service being unavailable if the vulnerability is exploited causing a denial of service? Vulnerability management systems must be able to correlate these relationships and generate reports sufficient to feed the risk management and vulnerability management processes.

Grid computing is another facet of distributed computing that presents challenges to vulnerability management tools. Since processing is performed by many, unspecific machines that are members of a grid, the threats to a particular business function may not be well-known. The vulnerability management system needs to be grid-aware so that the total risk to a grid can be assessed. Also, it must provide reports showing the status of a grid as it is defined by application or classification level since, in principle, the computer is a loose conglomeration of grid members.

One other distributed computing challenge for the entire vulnerability management industry is the Software as a Service model. Currently, there is no effective way to perform vulnerability research or vulnerability assessments on software provided as a service. Doing so would constitute an attempt to breach the security of the service provider and would most certainly be a violation of the terms of service.

What is needed is a broadly accepted or standardized method of articulating vulnerability status to web services customers so they can assess risk to their classified data. Absent this ability, it is unlikely that many corporate customers will allow widespread use of these services. Imagine employees in a multinational bank using software provided by a vendor over the Internet. The risk of data leakage would be a complete unknown and there would be no vetted audit results to verify compliance.

In such a standard, the severity of the vulnerability should be communicated in the context of the type of access required for exploitation and the overall impact. This standard would be similar to CVSS except that the specific vulnerability would not be included as a part of the information. Instead, the scoring method would summarize the level of vulnerability by type of access. The result would resemble the following example:

Access Method	DoS	Control	Data Access	Information
Remote	5	3	4	2
Local	3	3	1	3

This example shows us in the first line that remotely accessed vulnerabilities create a high denial of service risk, a medium system control risk, medium-high data access risk, and medium-low information disclosure risk. The second line shows the same categories of risk associated with vulnerabilities that are locally accessed.

11.6 Reporting

The industry as a whole has failed to help companies with a mature vulnerability management practice to optimize their existing processes and more quickly identify broad trends and threats. This is certainly not for lack of information. As described earlier in this book, several reports are needed to achieve this. Yet, most of these reports are not available in any automated fashion from vendors. Obviously, selling new units to companies without vulnerability management requires some basic reporting.

Furthermore, it appears that there is not enough revenue in selling advanced reporting capabilities. These are enhancements that are only useful for long-term customer retention. I see this as an opportunity to distinguish one's self from the others. Beyond providing discovery and basic reporting, there is a great professional services opportunity to deliver process, deployment, and project management.

11.7 Service Level Agreements

With wider adoption of IT service management, vendors are still lacking useful underpinning contracts to customers. This is perhaps through lack of demand. However, due to the critical nature of some vulnerabilities and the need for faster response, vendors should try to compete more aggressively by committing to a service level in developing and releasing checks for new vulnerabilities. These service levels should at a minimum require reporting within 24 hours of disclosure that the vendor has begun work on a new vulnerability over a certain CVSS score. It should also report the status of the development work within one week of disclosure to indicate if the check will be released in the next seven days or later.

The value of this approach is that risk managers can determine if they need to take manual action to identify and remediate the vulnerabilities on critical hosts or whether should they wait for the automated system to perform the audit with the appropriate check. This is a gaping black hole of risk that is unaddressed by the industry.

One other, simpler underlying contract term that should be considered by vendors is the time to initial response metric for support calls (i.e., problem management). This is a basic capability that requires some attention. If a critical system that detects vulnerabilities cannot have some measure of reliability in recovery from problems, the key risk identification tools become less useful.

11.8 Conclusion

Vulnerability management is entering its age of maturity. While the initial focus has been on identifying and remediating vulnerabilities, process excellence has emerged as the next great challenge. That excellence can be realized in bread-and-butter vulnerability management and extended to integration into other risk management and IT management processes. To achieve this, vendors, standards bodies, and customers must work to identify the limits of vulnerability management and the opportunities for extension. Like any other discipline, vulnerability management must be integrated into and supportive of other organizational processes.

Vendors have done a good job of addressing the technical concerns of IT managers and risk analysts. The market for vulnerability tools is not near saturation, yet processes have matured in the installed environments. In many ways the potential of vulnerability management to contribute to the bottom line of business and the needs of government have not been realized because no vendor has led the way and no customer has insisted. The flexibility of products is woefully insufficient to meet future requirements. This requires vision and a commitment to successful integration of technology and process to its fullest potential. The lessons in the book are the starting point, but the real innovative challenge to the risk manager remains.

End Notes

1. https://www.cisecurity.org/cis-benchmarks, Center for Internet Security, 2019.
2. *Kaplan, Robert S; Norton, D. P. (1992). "The Balanced Scorecard – Measures That Drive Performance". Harvard Business Review (January–February): 71–79.*

Index

Printed in the United States
by Baker & Taylor Publisher Services